NEW STUDIES IN ARCHAEOLOGY

Artefacts as categories

NEW STUDIES IN ARCHAEOLOGY

Series editors

Colin Renfrew, *University of Cambridge*
Jeremy Sabloff, *University of New Mexico*

Other titles in the series
Ian Hodder and Clive Orton: *Spatial Analysis in Archaeology*
Kenneth Hudson: *World Industrial Archaeology*
Keith Muckelroy: *Maritime Archaeology*
Richard Gould: *Living Archaeology*
Graham Connah: *Three Thousand Years in Africa*
Richard E. Blanton, Stephen A. Kowalewski, Gary Feinman and
    Jill Appel: *Ancient Mesoamerica*
Stephen Plog: *Stylistic Variation in Prehistoric Ceramics*
Peter Wells: *Culture Contact and Culture Change*
Ian Hodder: *Symbols in Action*
Patrick Vinton Kirch: *Evolution of the Polynesian Chiefdoms*
Dean Arnold: *Ceramic Theory and Cultural Process*
Geoffrey W. Conrad and Arthur A. Demarest: *Religion and Empire:
    The Dynamics of Aztec and Inca Expansionism*
Graeme Barker: *Prehistoric Farming in Europe*

Artefacts as categories

A study of ceramic variability in Central India

DANIEL MILLER

Department of Anthropology,
University College London

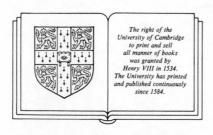

The right of the
University of Cambridge
to print and sell
all manner of books
was granted by
Henry VIII in 1534.
The University has printed
and published continuously
since 1584.

CAMBRIDGE UNIVERSITY PRESS

CAMBRIDGE

LONDON   NEW YORK   NEW ROCHELLE

MELBOURNE   SYDNEY

Published by the Press Syndicate of the University of Cambridge
The Pitt Building, Trumpington Street, Cambridge CB2 1RP
32 East 57th Street, New York, NY 10022, USA
10 Stamford Road, Oakleigh, Melbourne 3166, Australia

First published 1985

Printed in Great Britain at the University Press, Cambridge

British Library cataloguing in publication data
Miller, Daniel
Artefacts as categories: a study of ceramic
variability in Central India. – (New studies in
archaeology)
1. Pottery craft – India
I. Title II. Series
306'.47   TT919.7.15

Library of Congress cataloguing in publication data
Miller, Daniel, 1954–
Artefacts as categories.
(New studies in archaeology)
Bibliography: p.
Includes index
1. Pottery, Prehistoric – India. 2. Pottery – Analysis
3. India – Antiquities. I. Title. II. Series.
GN855.I4M55 1985   934   85-6699

ISBN 0 521 30522 5

TO RICKIE

CONTENTS

MAPS

PREFACE

My interest in the specific problems that form the core of this study stemmed from two main influences during my undergraduate and postgraduate studies at the University of Cambridge. My initial interest in the importance of artefactual variability for the interpretation of archaeological remains was inspired by the enthusiastic teaching of the late David Clarke, and to this was added the impact of structuralism, then the dominant influence in the Anthropology Department. Since then, I have been able to develop these interests at University College, London, where the Department of Anthropology has for many years taught courses under the title of Material Culture, within which prehistoric and contemporary materials are freely interchanged.

The research described in this volume derived from my experience as an archaeologist dealing with the minutiae of prehistoric pottery and my feeling that such studies could contribute towards more general anthropological goals, precisely because of this peculiar focus on the object world. I hoped that such studies might, therefore, contribute to both disciplines, but in particular to the increasing interest in material culture itself as a neglected source of evidence in the social sciences. As with so many people working in South Asia, I rapidly became an Indophile and this academic study forms part of a larger desire to understand that complex and fascinating society. An underlying reference has also been to the extreme diversity of the material culture of my own society, and to the nature of objectification and alienation this engenders.

The claim has often been made that the goal of archaeology is to use the often boring and curious collections of objects it uncovers in an attempt to understand past societies. It is my belief that archaeologists have on occasion fulfilled this pledge with extraordinary ability, and my hope that material culture studies might assist in this highly problematic task of translating objects into peoples, by acknowledging, but also where possible by overcoming, the difficulties encountered.

The fieldwork which forms the basis for this volume was carried out during a three-year studentship from the Department of Education and Science. I should like to express my gratitude to Vishnu Wakankar of Ujjain University for his support throughout, and to my two research assistants, Kailash and Rajveer. During my stay in India I also received support from members of the Department of Archaeology, Deccan College, Pune. In particular, I wish to thank the six pottery-producing households who daily bore the brunt of endless and apparently absurd enquiries, though my gratitude extends to every household in the village, none of whom entirely escaped having to provide time and attention to an outsider who could offer little in the way of recompense. I apologise to them for any misrepresentation they may feel has occurred.

This volume is a revised version of my doctoral dissertation. An article similar to Chapter 7 has appeared in a monograph edited by J. Picton on potteries from Asia and Africa, published by the Percival David Foundation for Chinese Art and Archaeology. Raymond Allchin, my thesis supervisor, has provided continual encouragement and support. During the course of the research I have received vital advice, criticism and general encouragement from a large number of people, in particular Barbara Bender, Roger Blench, Mary Braithwaite, Fred Brett, Phil Burnham, Mary Searle-Chatterjee, Linda Donley, Ian Hodder, Adrian Mayer, Ann Maclarnon, Jonathan Parry, Mike Rowlands, Colin Shell, Debbie Swallow and Chris Tilley. My greatest debt for sustained critical comment and support is, however, to Rickie Burman.

D.M.

REFERENCE LIST OF POTTERY AND COMMON METAL VESSELS

Key

Name of vessel
Usual form of decoration / Type of metal
Most common use
Scale 1:12.5

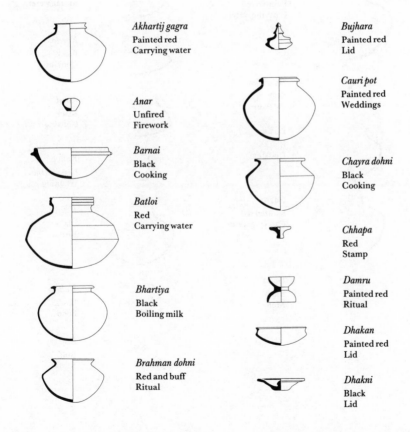

Akhartij gagra
Painted red
Carrying water

Anar
Unfired
Firework

Barnai
Black
Cooking

Batloi
Red
Carrying water

Bhartiya
Black
Boiling milk

Brahman dohni
Red and buff
Ritual

Bujhara
Painted red
Lid

Cauri pot
Painted red
Weddings

Chayra dohni
Black
Cooking

Chhapa
Red
Stamp

Damru
Painted red
Ritual

Dhakan
Painted red
Lid

Dhakni
Black
Lid

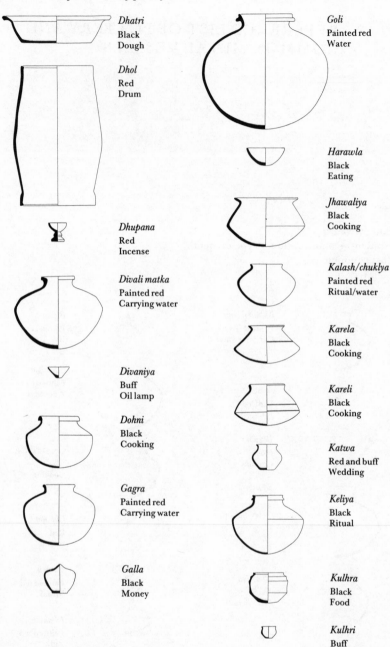

Dhatri
Black
Dough

Dhol
Red
Drum

Dhupana
Red
Incense

Divali matka
Painted red
Carrying water

Divaniya
Buff
Oil lamp

Dohni
Black
Cooking

Gagra
Painted red
Carrying water

Galla
Black
Money

Goli
Painted red
Water

Harawla
Black
Eating

Jhawaliya
Black
Cooking

Kalash/chuklya
Painted red
Ritual/water

Karela
Black
Cooking

Kareli
Black
Cooking

Katwa
Red and buff
Wedding

Keliya
Black
Ritual

Kulhra
Black
Food

Kulhri
Buff
Ritual

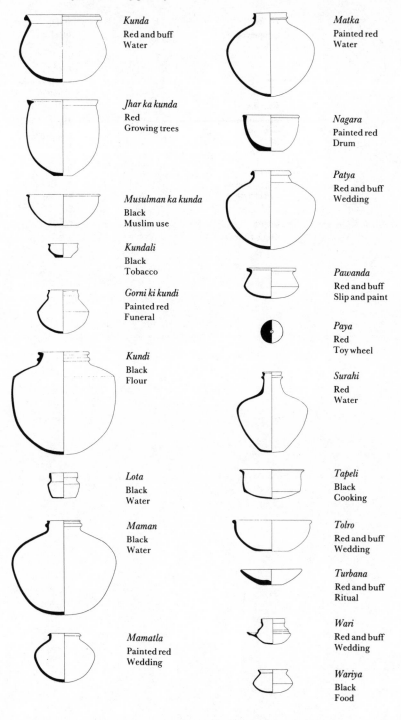

Kunda
Red and buff
Water

Jhar ka kunda
Red
Growing trees

Musulman ka kunda
Black
Muslim use

Kundali
Black
Tobacco

Gorni ki kundi
Painted red
Funeral

Kundi
Black
Flour

Lota
Black
Water

Maman
Black
Water

Mamatla
Painted red
Wedding

Matka
Painted red
Water

Nagara
Painted red
Drum

Patya
Red and buff
Wedding

Pawanda
Red and buff
Slip and paint

Paya
Red
Toy wheel

Surahi
Red
Water

Tapeli
Black
Cooking

Tolro
Red and buff
Wedding

Turbana
Red and buff
Ritual

Wari
Red and buff
Wedding

Wariya
Black
Food

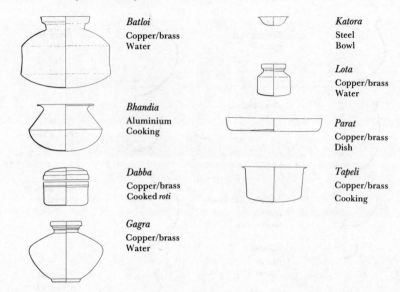

Batloi
Copper/brass
Water

Bhandia
Aluminium
Cooking

Dabba
Copper/brass
Cooked *roti*

Gagra
Copper/brass
Water

Katora
Steel
Bowl

Lota
Copper/brass
Water

Parat
Copper/brass
Dish

Tapeli
Copper/brass
Cooking

1
Introduction

The central aim of this study is to explore the factors underlying variability in artefacts. The major proposition that it employs is that artefacts, as objects created and interpreted by people, embody the organisational principles of human categorisation processes. Through the intensive study of a specific corpus of contemporary artefacts – the earthenware pottery in an Indian village – it is intended to investigate the manner in which these organisational principles generate variability in material forms. The variability of objects is significant as a major source of evidence for the study of society, the artefactual environment being one of the main products of social action. It is anticipated, therefore, that an understanding of the forces which create artefactual variability can also contribute towards an understanding of the social.

Its focus on the relationship between objects and society situates this volume within the area of material culture studies. The study of material culture cuts across disciplinary boundaries, but one of its original foundations lies in the discipline of archaeology for which the material world provides a prime source of evidence for social relations. The intention of this introduction is to focus upon some limitations in the manner in which archaeology at present posits the relationship between the material and social worlds.

This study takes the form of a micro-analysis of the pottery found in a single village, including the details of rim form, body angularity and decorative technique which are the familiar domain of a vast number of archaeological analyses. The carrying out of this exercise in the unusual domain of a modern ethnographic setting is not intended as a 'cautionary tale', pointing out the contextual information which does not survive for the archaeologist. On the contrary, the intention is to reveal the richness of information about social relations which these typically archaeological procedures are capable of revealing when applied to contemporary as well as ancient artefacts, compared to the more conventional subjects and methods of ethnographic enquiry.

An understanding of the variability of material objects, which is the

immediate problem often faced in archaeological analyses, is insepar-
able from an understanding of those forces which create social variability. The processes of categorisation may be used as a primary link
between these two. A brief survey is given here of the traditions in all
three areas by which variability has been analysed: archaeology, social
anthropology and cognitive studies.

Archaeology and the problem of artefactual variability

From its inception, the prime goal of archaeology has been the reconstruction and understanding of past societies. One of the major sources
(though by no means the sole source) of evidence for this task is represented by the humanly altered physical remains of these past societies.
Archaeologists have therefore invested considerable effort in the investigation of the variability of artefacts, which they have seen as reflective of
the variability of society. This has resulted in a prodigious quantity of
classificatory studies in which artefacts are attributed to 'cultures' and
'styles'. Under the influence of the natural sciences, the search for regularity in the behaviour of artefacts has become increasingly formalised,
developing into an 'analytical archaeology' (Clarke 1968) to complement
the techniques of excavation.

Today this interest in variability has extended into a number of broad
fields, including the techniques of quantitative manipulation (Doran
and Hodson 1975), individual stylistic variation (Hill and Gunn Eds.
1977), variability as either spatial distribution (Hodder and Orton 1976)
or temporal distribution (Marquardt 1978), or both (Dethlefsen and
Deetz 1966). To propose therefore that the investigation of artefactual
variability has major consequences for archaeological theory is to state
that which has always been evident to archaeologists.

Less obvious and more problematic is the suggestion that this very
focus in archaeology has led to peculiarities and bias in archaeological
investigations, often with consequences detrimental to its major aims in
respect of knowledge about past societies. If the approach to these
societies is always mediated through the study of their artefactual
remains, there will always be a tendency to 'fetishise', i.e. to substitute
material relations for social relations. Archaeology cannot ignore its own
symbolic processes. In theory the material form, such as a stone or metal
implement, is supposed to stand as signifier for the Celtic or ancient
Indian society under study. In practice, however, a symbolic inversion
may occur in such a way that the name of the society comes to act merely
as a label for the actual subject of the study, which remains at the level
of objects. Thus 'cultures', as movements of styles, were assumed to represent directly movements of peoples, and entities such as 'culture' and

'style' rather than society itself became the goal to which archaeological resources were primarily directed. Society then becomes an abstracted legitimation, a promise which is never realised. With the rise of the New Archaeology in the 1960s the model of past societies and human agency tended to become that which it was necessary to postulate in order to assume regularity in artefactual patterning.

In the New Archaeology, under the legitimatory principles of hypothetico-deductivism, human behaviour tended to be relegated to predictable reactions to stimuli, mainly the environmental and ecological background to past human behaviour. Culture was defined, following White (1959), as the 'extra-somatic means of adaptation' (Binford 1962), so that the social was tied to the natural. Schiffer developed a 'behavioural' archaeology in which the notion of cultural transformations was modelled directly on natural transforms (Schiffer 1976). The parallel notions of systems and adaptation linked these principles with disparate elements of human social behaviour through the observed variability of artefacts. Explanations based on these ideas ranged from Gunn's assertion that 50% of cultural change at Hogup Cave could be ascribed to (i.e. statistically associated with) the impact of the environment (Gunn 1975) to Terrell's use of human biogeography to explain the cultural variability of the Solomon Islands (Terrell 1977, Miller 1980a), or even to why the Tasmanians stopped eating fish (Jones 1978).

The resultant model of human society accords closely with the behaviourist view of human beings as passive reactors to external stimuli (Skinner 1972), with a functionalist view of society, couched in the language of systems theory and a determinist view of material culture, which seeks to explain variability almost entirely by reference to assumed functional attributes, although these may be distinguished as primary or secondary (Binford 1962). These are implicit assumptions, expressed and legitimised mainly at the level of arguments over appropriate modes of explanation in archaeology. This has tended to disguise what has, in effect, been the development of a particular model of society, shaped by its compatibility with the new methodologies (Miller 1982a).

In recent years these assumptions have been the subject of many critiques, from the standpoints of relativism (Hodder Ed. 1978), evolutionary theory (Dunnell 1980), critical theory (Miller 1980b), structuralism (Hodder Ed. 1982) and structural Marxism (Rowlands and Gledhill 1977). Some of these critiques have queried the search for 'explanation', as found in the natural sciences, and have preferred a notion of 'understanding', on analogy with the social sciences, as a more appropriate goal for archaeology. Except in the case of evolutionary theory, these critiques have assumed that archaeological theory should first develop as a more satisfactory social theory, which might then have

to be modified at a secondary level to accommodate the specific problems of archaeological methodology.

   The concern to develop a model of human agency and social institutions compatible with the necessary emphasis on artefactual variability has led to an increasing interest in studies of present-day
artefacts. These have tended in two directions, the first of these being
'ethno-archaeology'. A large number of recent studies (e.g. Gould Ed.
1978, Kramer Ed. 1979) have investigated problems of archaeological
interest, such as site formation and ceramic variability, in contemporary
settings. In general, this has involved the archaeologist in the fictive
stance of an 'as if it were a site' argument, attempting to interpret
materials without the additional contextual information provided by
informants (e.g. David 1971, Bonnichsen 1973). A second major thrust
has been the emphasis suggested by the theoretical basis of the New
Archaeology, which attempts to focus on behaviour assumed to be relatively free of cultural considerations and therefore amenable to an
analysis based on intrinsic functional relations, which could be projected
back into the archaeological record, whatever the cultural context of that
past. This is an explicit goal of Binford's recent work on Inuit use of bone
(1978). The emphasis on areas with extreme environments, such as the
Kalahari desert (Yellen 1977), the Australian desert (Gould 1980) and
the frozen tundra has tended to make the determinist assumptions of the
ethno-archaeologist appear more plausible.

   The disingenuousness of such an approach prevents it from contributing towards the goal of a more satisfactory model of the social. Since
most ethno-archaeological work concerned with society continues to
apply notions of 'culture', 'adaptation' and 'style', derived from the
nineteenth century, to its observations of contemporary societies, it is
unable to use the contemporary to challenge its own assumptions. Variability in artefacts becomes reduced to two areas. In the positivist tradition it is used to correlate with some absolute measure of human
'behaviour' outside history, or as style it either 'functions' e.g. to com-
municate information (Wobst 1977) or is seen as directly reflective of
social forms. In the present study, by contrast, the relationship to
archaeology is conceived of as mediated by material culture studies and
not by ethno-archaeology. Material culture studies are concerned with
all aspects of the relationship between the material and the social, and
are not determined by the logistical constraints of any particular discipline. The aim is to achieve a model capable of representing the complex
nature of the interaction between social strategy and artefactual variability and change. It is inevitable that some of this sophistication should
be lost with the formation of the archaeological record, but this loss
should be regarded as such, rather than minimised by starting with a
limited social theory more compatible with the paucity of evidence. It is

in this concern to explore the nature and interaction between society and artefactual variability that the roots and legitimation of the current work lie. As research in material culture studies, however, the work employs ideas from, and attempts to construct arguments relative to, the whole spectrum of the social sciences, including linguistics, social anthropology and cognitive psychology, as well as archaeology.

Variability in society

Archaeology is not the only discipline to have perceived the variability of its object of study as the prime source of evidence for the understanding of human society. The origins of anthropology also lie in questions posed by the variability of human social practices, revealed by the opening up of the world in trade and colonialism, alongside the emergence of physical anthropology as the study of the variability of the human species. The major drive in much of nineteenth-century anthropology was towards a search for the origins of human diversity projected backwards in time through the various evolutionary models, which were later assigned an additional spatial reference in diffusionist and folk-movement models. These models were all predicated on the synchronic differentiation of extant societies, seen as relics of the temporal process under study.

The search for an understanding of variability in social practices continued in the attempts to uncover pattern and process in culture by Kroeber and his followers (e.g. Kroeber 1948) and also underlies studies of the adaptation of societies to their particular environments (e.g. Forde 1934). The work of Lévi-Strauss demonstrates an extreme reduction of the very concepts of social structure and cultural forms, such as myths, to the play of categorisation as transformations creating diversity over space and time (e.g. 1970).

More closely related to the type of investigation being proposed here are approaches to the understanding of the mechanisms which generate internal variability in society. The emphasis on the division of labour and the linkages between the divided segments of a population are key motifs in Durkheimian and later functionalist analysis. Lévi-Strauss's work on internal classificatory systems employed a very different approach to the question of social divisions, which more than ever before were closely integrated with speculation on the nature of categorisation processes. South Asian society has often been cited as an example of highly-developed internal differentiation, in particular in Dumont's work on the caste system (1972; see also Lévi-Strauss 1977: 327). The question of internal differentiation is particularly crucial in any attempt to understand the nature of 'modernity', the experience of living in current industrial societies, with their extremes of social and material diversity (e.g. Simmel 1968).

The artefactual variability studied by archaeologists differs in its material physicality and its peculiar selection through differential preservation, but otherwise is generated by the same processes which social anthropologists attempt to understand. On occasion similar materials are addressed (e.g. Sahlins 1976: chapter four). The research presented here is based upon the selection of one particular approach to the nature of internal social variability as discoverable from material objects, that of categorisation.

Approaches to categorisation

Most approaches to categorisation stem from the ideas first systematically developed by Kant, who was concerned to formulate a theory postulating the innate structures which human beings must possess, in order to be able to experience the world (Kant 1934, 1935). Once the relationship between people and their environment was seen to be, of necessity, mediated by these structures, an alternative developed to the naïve empiricism which had preceded Kant's work. Kant's formulations were transcendent not only in his own sense of being prior to experience, but also in that he was not primarily concerned with the context in which categorisation operated, and it is this which has led towards a formalism in much of the work influenced by him. Kant's work may, however, lead towards a more 'constructivist' model of people in which the environment is not given, but constituted in this process of interaction (e.g. Furth 1969, Piaget 1972, Turner 1973).

Approaches to material forms based on categorisation processes have almost always been mediated by linguistics and the influence of linguistics on anthropology through Lévi-Strauss's structuralism. The basic divisions of Saussurian analysis have been widely applied to the material world (Saussure 1959). A number of analyses of pottery use approaches which parallel the syntagmatic and paradigmatic levels of articulation proposed for language (e.g. Clarke 1970, Friedrich 1970). Deetz (1967) attempted to appropriate these ideas as a more general approach to artefacts but the critique by Hymes (1970) should be noted. These methods have been used to analyse a variety of objects ranging from Mongolian spirit figures (Humphrey 1971) to Walbiri iconography (Munn 1973), and are implicit in Boas's (1955) earlier work on American North-West coastal art.

Other approaches used in both linguistic and material studies include componential analysis (Kimball and D'Andrade Eds. 1964, Hammel Ed. 1965, and Tyler Ed. 1969), which established the principles of 'hierarchy', 'contrast' and 'field' as major features in categorisation processes. Applications include archaeological studies of classification (Dunnell 1972), burials (Saxe 1973, Chapman *et al.* Eds. 1981) and

ceramics (DeBoer and Lathrap 1979). Chomsky's (1957) 'transformational grammar' which indicated the infinite generative power of
language has in turn been applied to shell gorgets (Muller 1977),
pottery design and production (Hodder 1982a: 174–71, Krause 1978,
Mead *et al.* 1973), and body designs (Faris 1972).

The extensive use of all these approaches since the 1960s has made
apparent several severe problems with their application. As Keesing
suggests (1972) of the employment of componential analysis, the
approach relates to an ideal logical language, in which something either
is, or is not, a member of a category. It ignores the nature of category
variability found in the real world, becoming an overused mould into
which things are fitted, rather than adapting to meet the challenge of
variability. Like the notion of 'mental template' in archaeology it thereby
becomes a normative approach, subsuming rather than explaining variability. Nor does it fit the evidence of psychologists regarding the nature
of categories (see below).

The more direct borrowings from structuralism have been attacked for
a similar formalism. Despite Lévi-Strauss's own attempt to distinguish
the two in his essay on Propp (1977), most critics see little evidence of
these ideals in Lévi-Strauss's own work (Sperber 1974). The lack of a
temporal context, implied in the fourth of Saussure's dichotomies, has
been criticised, and structural Marxists such as Friedman and Rowlands
have attempted to develop the dynamic implications of structural transformation in the analysis of societal development, using archaeological
and historical data (1977). Recent advances in structuralist-inspired
work on material culture has shown how some structural processes
generate related patterns in a variety of media (e.g. Adams 1973, Glassie
1975). Generally, 'social context' in material culture studies within
anthropology has denoted coherence with social categories in the
Durkheimian tradition (e.g. Douglas and Isherwood 1980), although
some recent work has been concerned with the social manipulation of
meaning (e.g. Barthes 1973, Baudrillard 1981, Hodder 1982a). A criticism of formalism has recently been made by Tyler (1978) who attacks
the assumption that relations of meaning can be studied without reference to a consideration of pragmatics, arguing from the conventional
basis of signification.

Further critiques of structuralism have come from post-structuralist
analysis, which has suggested that the relationship between signifier and
signified is not as straightforward as suggested in, for example, Barthes's
early work (Coward and Ellis 1977: chapter three) and has raised the
issues of power and ideology which were rarely discussed in the period of
high structuralism (Miller and Tilley 1984). The actual symbolic
mechanisms postulated by structuralism have also been attacked, and
Sperber's (1974) critique of semiological assumptions as to the 'mean-

ing' of symbols, proposing rather different cognitive mechanisms and a more flexible process of evocation, has been particularly influential.

Alternative approaches to categorisation

An alternative approach to human categorisation is best exemplified in the work of another philosopher who dealt extensively with the notion of category. Wittgenstein, in his *Philosophical Investigations* (1958), concentrated on the everyday use of language and showed how it diverged from abstracted, idealised forms. He emphasised the polythetic qualities of semantic and perceptual categories, and contextual factors in the determination of their meaning. These two areas of indeterminacy and context are precisely the factors which more formalist modes of analysis tend to ignore.

Indeterminacy in categories can be defined according to 'fuzzy set theory', originally a set of mathematical principles (Zadeh 1965), which is concerned with the nature of a logic whereby objects are not, as in conventional logic, either members or non-members of a given set, but rather are considered as better or worse representatives of that set. This may be paralleled by Lakoff's discussion of linguistic hedges which are expressions of indeterminacy such as 'A is a sort of B' (Lakoff 1973). The linguist Labov has employed pottery profiles to investigate the relationship between contextual knowledge and indeterminacy. Labov produced a series of such profiles with measured variance, such as a gradual increase in width in relation to height (Labov 1973). From this it could be graphically demonstrated how the shift occurs from the linguistic category 'cup' to that of 'bowl', by asking informants to draw a line in this series indicating the boundary between those profiles which they would call a cup and those which they would call a bowl. Labov shows that this depends not only on the increasing width–height ratio, but also on contextual knowledge, such as the number of handles, and whether the contents are, for example, coffee or mashed potato. Labov comments that, 'In the world of experience all boundaries show some degree of vagueness, and any formal system which is useful for semantic description must allow us to record, or even measure, this property' (p. 352). It is this fuzziness which is encountered whenever we try to apply categorisational ideas in a social context. It has been demonstrated also in our concept of 'function' (Miller G. 1978), in general discussions of ethnoclassification (Ellen and Reason Eds. 1979) and, as the ethnomethodologists would point out, is true of the process of analysis itself (Garfinkle 1967).

These ideas have been developed further by the psychologist Rosch in her work amongst the Dani of New Guinea and in America (Heider 1972, Rosch 1978, Mervis and Rosch 1981) and by the anthropologist Kempton in his work in Mexico (Kempton 1978, 1981). According to Mervis and Rosch, 'A category exists whenever two or more distinguishable objects or events are treated equivalently' (1981: 89). Equivalence for them is a matter of degree. Rosch shows that some members of a category are closer to its core 'prototype' while others are on the more indeterminate periphery. Kempton's work demonstrated how the category itself shifts in relation to the heterogeneity of the society in which it is constructed. Simply to map variability is, however, insufficient. Analysis has to proceed beyond 'social context', taken as an unproblematic base-line, and examine in detail the relationship between the various ways in which society constitutes itself in a series of representations manifested in both practical action and conceptual models.

These developments in the study of categorisation will be employed here to analyse the variability in ceramic forms. While the more conventional symbolic analysis may be employed to analyse the normative formal order, this must always be seen in relation to the variable 'informal' aspects which cannot be reduced to neat patterns of symbolic homologies. Two terms are crucial to the analysis of this informal variability, and both are used to relate material categories to their social context. The term 'pragmatics', derived from the study of the effect of context on meaning in linguistics (Levinson 1983), will be employed to examine the processes of differentiation which create the multivalency evident when consideration is given to where and when evocation takes place and to the nature of variability in the social context itself. The effect of pragmatics in creating an apparently highly diffused and variable relationship between an object and the pattern of its evocative potential is in part countered by the use of approaches which come under the term 'framing'. These are concerned with the processes by which contextual cues are used to decide which of the various possible interpretations should be given to the object on any specific occasion. Pottery will be found to work both *as* frames (Chapter 7) and *within* frames (Chapter 9).

These approaches to categorisation are concerned mainly with methodological and synchronic issues. In Chapter 10 an attempt will be made to examine the relationship between forms and their social context in more dynamic terms by examining the dialectic between changes in material forms and changes in social groups, with their differential ability to objectify their interests in the construction of the material environment. This demands a consideration of issues such as ideology and naturalisation as they bear on the material world and this will be discussed in the next section.

Material culture as evidence

The major source of evidence used in this study is the material world. The emphasis on variability and categorisation is derived from the need to work with objects rather than more conventional forms of anthropological evidence. For the present ethnographic study, as in an archaeological investigation, the significant dimensions of variability cannot be elicited by direct enquiry. The members of the society which produces and uses the objects may have very little to say about them; articulation at the level of language may be a poor reflection of the complex expression evidenced in the actual range of products and interaction with them.

This is an important factor in distinguishing between the way in which the terms 'categorisation' and 'classification' are used in this study. The primary subject of analysis is material categories. These represent an order that is imposed upon the world through the creation of material objects. As such they are a part of the overall creation of cultural order, and may be used for the study of the social and material relations of which they are a product. These categories may be the subject of a large variety of different classifications, both by their producers and by the analyst. Classifications by the producers include linguistic terms, which, as this study will illustrate, may vary depending upon who is classifying, when and why. In the present study such classifications are treated as only a secondary level of evidence. The methodology which has to be employed in describing these material categories at a primary level is therefore not substantially different from that used by archaeologists in analysing prehistoric material. There is therefore no *a priori* reason for archaeologists to equate evidence which is contemporary with the primacy of the 'emic' (Pike 1967).

There has been considerable discussion in archaeology over the status of classifications employed in analysis. In the 1950s this was centred primarily on the notion of attributes, types and morphological entities (e.g. Ford 1954, Rouse 1960, Spaulding 1953; see also Clarke 1968). Recent work on style, with its concern for the identification of the correct level of design or element, is, however, parallel (e.g. Hole 1984, Plog 1983, Washburn Ed. 1983). As classifications, these should be judged heuristically for their ability to reorganise the material under study in a convenient form for further analysis. What seems spurious to the debate is the question of the 'reality' of types or designs assumed to operate on a privileged level, universal to ceramic analysis and observable in the ethnographic record.

In practice, the dimensions and aspects used to create significant difference are varied, and their significance is best postulated on the basis of the contexts in which they are produced, distributed and used.

Ceramic variability may be described statistically, may evoke differentially for different people and is not reducible to simple empiricist accounts of denotative 'meaning'. There is no 'true' typology or taxonomy but, equally, the producers cannot be disestablished as the creators of the order under study and such order cannot be reduced merely to the hypotheses of the analyst (as in Hill and Evans 1972). A classification, whether constructed by the producer or the analyst, captures only a part of the order embedded in material categories and is always from a particular perspective. However, as will be shown, this is just as significant for the society which produces and uses the ceramics as for the external analyst.

The present study starts with very different assumptions about the nature of the relationship between objects and words. Far from assuming that the important dimensions of variability are those which are also found at an 'emic' level, it holds that order which is neither expressed nor acknowledged at the level of language may have a particular importance in the study of social reproduction, precisely because it acts to constitute social relations at a level which appears mundane, natural and therefore less open to explicit refutation or confrontation.

The manner in which material forms embody categorisation processes has rarely been used for the study of categorisation itself. The psychologists discussed above always study their subjects' classification of objects, and at no time acknowledge that the objects as cultural materials may already embody this same order. Structuralist and post-structuralist approaches vie with each other in their stress on language, and studies of the semiology of objects are always seen as a secondary source of evidence. The manner in which the material world is used to objectify conceptualisation, to naturalise social relations and to mark social categories has spawned a sparse literature, mainly concerned with consumption (e.g. Barthes 1973, Baudrillard 1981, Douglas and Isherwood 1980, Veblen 1970). This suggests a particular importance for archaeology, which, through a quirk of academic logistics, has alone maintained a consistent interest in the problems of interpreting artefacts.

The social theory which has proved particularly influential in recent archaeological approaches to material culture is that of Bourdieu (1977), as is evident in the contributions to two recent works (Hodder Ed. 1982, and Miller and Tilley Eds. 1984). Bourdieu's emphasis on the manner in which 'practical taxonomies' work as objectively orchestrated practices in the reproduction of the social world (1977: 163) constitutes a major contribution to the study of the naturalisation of cultural practices in the order of the everyday, as well as to the actual process of socialisation by which these are assimilated in the construction of social beings. His analysis of the homologies between structures to be found in diverse realms contributes to our understanding of the construction of subjectivity without falling into the trap of extreme objectivism found in all post-structuralist analysis (e.g. Lacan 1979, Foucault 1972). These processes of naturalisation are crucial in understanding how those objects found to be of major significance in contributing to the reproduction and transformation of social relations are nevertheless regarded as of a trivial nature and are often interpreted entirely in instrumental terms through concepts such as function.

The physicality of objects is most significant when they transcend the individual life to provide the material environment for the reproduction of society. This physicality does not imply an indifference to change. In this study great flexibility in human and material relationships will be demonstrated, indicating how the meaning of an object may change through alterations in the mechanisms of evocation, for example the relevant 'framing' devices. Nevertheless, there may come a point at which significant social change manifests itself in changes in the material world, which itself serves as a prime source for the objectification of social relations and conceptions as to the nature of society.

Bourdieu's work provides a powerful lead in the integration of material culture into studies of society. Although this is not attempted in the present study, a full understanding of the nature of social beings will transcend the apparent dichotomies of subject and object, and view the analysis of the interiorisation of objective structures as merely the necessary methodological stage towards a more profound dialectic, within which culture and being exist only as an ineliminable relationship.

The study trajectory

This study is centred on two pivotal, if limited, questions: firstly, how to come to an understanding of the very specific variability represented by a corpus of objects in terms of the social relations which constitute their context, and, secondly, how to approach this question through examining the nature of objects as categories. Artefactual variability is not usually studied as a process of categorisation. Most academic and 'everyday' assumptions about object variability are dominated by references to technological and functional factors. These are discussed and their limitations exposed in Chapters 3 and 4. It is found that, although they provide for wide parameters, they cannot tackle the specificity of the variability represented. An attempt is also made to 'recentre' these perspectives, that is, to analyse production as part of a study of categorisation, and to indicate the implications for terms such as 'style'. The preceding Chapter 2 provides a concise description of the village and its heterogeneity with respect to selected dimensions such as caste, family size and wealth. This is complemented by the first part of Chapter 5, which provides a more detailed account of the social and economic conditions of the pottery-producing households. The two are brought together in the second half of Chapter 5, where the mechanisms of pottery distribution, by which the products of these households are disseminated to the whole village, are described. Chapter 6 gives more detailed consideration to the variability represented by one aspect of pottery decoration, the paintings, using several approaches also applied to shape elsewhere in the study.

Through these descriptions certain basic configurations of the corpus emerge and are reinforced in Chapter 7, which describes the use of pottery in life-cycle and annual ceremonies. This evidence for patterning is synthesised in Chapter 8, in a general symbolic analysis of the corpus, which abstracts evidence for the internal organisation of the pots as a series, and indicates how they relate systematically to dominant principles of social organisation, such as caste.

Chapters 2 to 8 may be considered as detailed presentations of the material from a variety of particular perspectives. In Chapter 9, ideas on categorisation processes introduced in this introduction are employed in the analysis of the corpus as a set of categories. Chapter 9 is more abstracted and analytical; rather than presenting the material from a particular perspective, it draws on all the preceding chapters to tackle certain theoretical issues. Finally, in Chapter 10 an attempt is made to ground the model of artefacts as categories within a more diachronic characterisation of social context, illustrating how social strategies act in a dynamic fashion with respect to a changing and variable set of categories.

Pots are not 'facts' with unproblematic, measurable variability explicable in terms of general laws. Pottery is a 'construct'; a part of the creation of a cultural environment in which to live out practical pursuits and interests, which is at the same time a way of interpreting the world by representing the world. Manufacture creates a 'text', which is subject to reinterpretation according to the differences in perspectives of individuals and groups in the society, and the different contexts in which interpretation occurs. The analysis of pottery is not of a different order from this interpretation. The analysis is also a construct, creating dimensions against which variability is characterised. It is through the development of such constructs, and the ascription of interest to human agency, that the variability is not only 'measured' but appropriated; and through this process of appropriation is created the meaning that is ascribed to the pottery and thereby its interpretation. These principles, complex though they are, have become the foundation for the concept of social reproduction, the 'praxis' which understands human action as both an intervention, which continually reconstructs the real environment within which societies exist, and also a form of representation and interpretation. The aim of this study is to express this complex inter-action, not as a general principle of explanation, but in the 'archaeology' of the minutiae of the mundane.

2
The context of fieldwork

The choice of earthenware pottery and an Indian village as the context for this study followed from the aims of the project. In this chapter the reasons for their selection and the social and economic conditions of the village are presented. The choice of earthenware derived initially from its importance in archaeological research, which has arisen not only from the capacity of pottery to survive in the ground, but also from the variability of earthenware in many societies past and present, compared to other artefactual remains. This variability suggests that the malleability of clay may have made pottery particularly sensitive to the symbolic component of human creative activities. If so, then pottery is especially appropriate for the present study, which focuses on cultural factors in the creation, in material form, of category variability.

The method of research was to seek to understand the variability represented by this pottery by relating it to its social context. For this purpose, an Indian village presented several advantages. The intention was to undertake a focused piece of research, rather than a general ethnography, which meant that additional background information would be required. In India, a study of material categorisation has the advantage of a developed, literate, classical tradition, with detailed commentaries on the organisation and interpretation of many of the ideals relating to social organisation and ritual (e.g. Kane 1930–62). There has been a considerable amount of ethnographic study in South Asia, resulting in several synthetic surveys, such as those by Kolenda (1978), Tyler (1973) and, in particular, the work of Dumont (1972), who contributed an analysis of caste as a system of categories. These general anthropological works provided a comparative context for the specific forms of social practices observed in the village.

Fieldwork in a village in the Malwa area maximised these advantages, since this had been the context for a comprehensive study of caste and kinship in village practice (Mayer 1960) as well as an ethnography of religion in the region (Mathur 1964), a topic which is comparatively peripheral to Mayer's work. There are also abundant archaeological and historical data relating to the classical period in the Ujjain district (e.g. Jain 1972). The work by Mayer, in particular, obviates the need for any detailed presentation here of village social structure, although any discrepancies between that account and the observations made during fieldwork will be presented, where relevant. Ethnographies of the region vary in their approach, some, such as Mathur, stressing the ideals and models of the classical tradition, and others, such as Mayer, concentrating on daily practice as the evidence for any analytical classes. This account will follow more recent work (e.g. McGilvray Ed. 1982) in understanding observed practice as the detailed 'realisation' in village life of more general 'structural' ideals by which it is influenced but not determined. It will also, following Gilsenan (1983), construe these ideals as themselves constituted by their variable and specific interpretations.

Of equal value to this study is the abundance of descriptions of pottery manufacture. There are at least fifty accounts of pottery production in India, and although none of these utilises the particular perspective adopted here, they cover a range of alternative concerns. There are basic descriptions of technology by colonial officers (e.g. Holder 1897, Gait 1897) and more detailed modern ethnographies of potter communities, the most comprehensive of the latter being Behura's study of potters in the state of Orissa (1978). The anthropological survey of India published a monograph summarising a study of the entire country (Saraswati and Behura 1966), and there has been a further attempt to locate general clusters of associated cultural attributes (Saraswati 1979). There have also been a number of monographs published as part of the 1961 Census of India. Rye and Evans (1976) have produced a useful comparison between ethnographic observation of manufacture and the laboratory analysis of clays in Pakistan, and there are a number of studies investigating the archaeological implications of contemporary potting (e.g. Allchin 1959, 1978, Birmingham 1975). A useful comparative study to that presented here is based on a village in the neighbouring state of Gujerat, and provides detailed accounts of the manufacture and the secular and ceremonial use of pottery (Fischer and Shah 1970: 116–66).

The particular concern of the present study with the detailed variability of pottery form and decoration necessitated fieldwork based in a single village, with only short visits to other villages in the area and to the local town. The complexity of relevant factors revealed during research was felt to justify this narrow focus. This study can be complemented by area surveys, such as that of Behura in Orissa (1978), and that presently being carried out by Kramer in Rajasthan (pers. comm.). This does not mean that the 'village' as an analytical unit of study is accepted uncritically, and in this chapter an attempt will be made to consider its implications. Although any notion of 'typicality' remains impressionistic, in order to reduce the likelihood of obvious bias and to aid the possibility of generalisation, the particular village was selected for reasons other than those relevant to this study. The only clear requirement was the presence of active potters, which would be met by most villages in the region. Dangwara village was selected on the basis of an introduction secured through the local university. This more than offset the disadvantage of working in a village with a population of some 1,537 (1971 Census of India), which was larger than the average for the region.

The fieldwork methodology employed techniques from a number of disciplines. Two censuses were carried out, the second a selection based upon the first. Interviews were conducted with members of the households, and certain 'experiments' carried out on, for example, colour and shape identification. The basic recording of the pottery consisted of some 7,000 measurements, 400 drawings, 1,000 photographs and a catalogue of paintings from 400 of the pots. The study of manufacture was based on direct observation of the six pottery-making households, and most days were spent making 'rounds' of the six houses, observing and measuring. The local dialect is a mixture of Malwi and Hindi, and the tape-recordings of villagers were not comprehensible to urban Hindi speakers. My own linguistic competence was sufficient for conversations about pottery and for following the gist of other conversations. Hindi/ Malwi terms are given according to the orthography of McGregor (1972), though without subscripts. This means that words, such as Dangwara, which contain a flap, may be given by others as Dangwada (e.g. Wakankar 1982). The two periods of fieldwork carried out in 1979–80 and 1981 covered most of the yearly cycle, apart from the monsoon and the preceding high summer, when activities such as potting are comparatively restricted.

Dangwara village

Dangwara village lies in the fertile plateau of the Malwa region of central India (Fig. 1). It spans both yellow alluvium and extensive rich black soil, derived from the underlying Deccan trap rock. Wakankar has found mounds adjacent to the river, dating from the Kayatha period *c.* 2000 B.C. (Ansari and Dhavalikar 1975, Wakankar 1982: 225–7). The main ancient mound of Dangwara contains Ahar-associated ceramics in its basal layer, dated to *c.* 1800 B.C. (Sankalia *et al.* 1969); this is followed by a series of strata from prehistoric and historic periods, ending with remains associated with the Paramaras, a medieval local dynasty dated to the tenth and eleventh centuries A.D. The only significant break occurs before the Mauryan layer of *c.* 300 B.C. Details for the prehistoric levels are summarised in Wakankar (1982: 225–37). Research conducted into the origins of the present village and population, and the sequence in which various parts of the village were settled, suggested that the present site was inhabited with the abandoning of the archaeological mound, the major temple of the modern village being located at the base of the latter. The modern village represents a relocation of over one kilometre from the bank of the river Chambal, which is presently eroding the ancient deposits.

The materials found in Wakankar's excavation, including a quantity of coinage, suggest that the village formed part of the Classical settlement of the area from the time of the emergence of the kingdom of Avanti (Ujjain), one of the earliest kingdoms of India. The historical records for this period are supplemented by archaeological evidence, for example the massive fortifications uncovered in excavations at Ujjain, with remains dating from at least the sixth century B.C. (*Indian Archaeological Review* 1956–7: 20, 1957–8: 32, Jain 1972). This would suggest that the development of many of the facets of Classical Hindu-dominated society, which arrived relatively late in some other parts of South Asia, would have arisen in this area at a very early date. Ujjain has been an important centre at different times for a variety of religions, including Hinduism, Buddhism and Jainism, whose founder, Mahavira, visited the

Fig. 1. The Malwa area

city. Historical sources indicate that, even at the time of the Buddha, certain elements of the 'structure' of Hindu society had already existed for some time, including extreme 'untouchability' – that is, the assignment of certain groups of people to a position so low within the social hierarchy as to be physically excluded by most of the population. Such principles developed over two millennia with many additional influences, in particular from Islam, to produce the particular and highly complex series of ideals and conventions, whose interpretation in the local context will be discussed here in relation to pottery production.

In appearance, the area is a flat, intensively cultivated plateau, the sparse vegetation being dominated by acacia and the date palm. The 1971 census gives the area owned by Dangwara as 4,342 acres. My own census indicated the total area under cultivation as 3,801 acres of which 13% was irrigated, yielding two crops per year. The dominant crop is sorghum, followed by wheat and maize. These cereals are supplemented by a variety of pulses and legumes, including lentils and chick-pea. There are also groves of mango and tamarind. Rice and most fruit and vegetables (except mangoes and the leaves of chick-pea) are imported, mainly by travelling salespeople; such produce includes potatoes, aubergines, artichokes and bananas. Malwa is considered to be a relatively affluent area of north India. It is known as an area free of famine, the only known instance of which was in 1899 (Singh 1978: 6). There was a food shortage in 1942, but today, with rapid agricultural development matching population increase, the problems are distributional rather than productive. The rural population density for the Ujjain area was 92 per square kilometre in 1971 (Singh 1978: 42). The last cholera outbreak was in 1942, and the eradication of smallpox was a major boon to villagers, many of whose faces bear the ravages of the disease.

Almost all the villagers are involved in the two-season cycle of *kharif*, the main October harvest dominated by sorghum, and *rabi*, the March harvest dominated by wheat. At the harvest period even the artisan households either work their own land or take on work as labourers for the large landowners. The third season is the monsoon period; the rainfall between June and October accounts for over 90% of the annual total in this area (Singh 1978: 11). Day-labour wages are low, at 2–3 rupees (r) for female and 3-5 r a day for male workers. Wages are slightly higher for monthly and annual contracts. The village includes enormous disparities of wealth, since these wages may be set against the 40,000 r which a wealthy landowner would be expected to pay out for his daughter's wedding. Most households own some livestock. The wealthy have cattle and water buffalo, used both for traction and to supply the flourishing, co-operative-sponsored village dairy, which sends about 500 litres of milk daily to Ujjain. Poorer families, who also tend to be the meat-eating households, are more likely to keep goats and chickens.

Donkeys are kept by potters for transport, and some of the richest households have horses, mainly for display.

The village is divided into two areas, *puranagaon* (old village) and, at a
distance of around 300 metres, *nayagaon* (new village). The latter was
built after a particularly severe example of the annual floods, in 1959. As
can be seen in Fig. 2, the layout of the new village shows an increased
concern with cardinal orientation, and the focus is now on the road leading to the two principal cities of Malwa, Indore and Ujjain. Each section
of the village is divided into wards, each with its own character, and often
centred on a recognised shrine or 'sitting place'. A few houses are large,
courtyard-centred structures, some built of fired brick, surrounded by

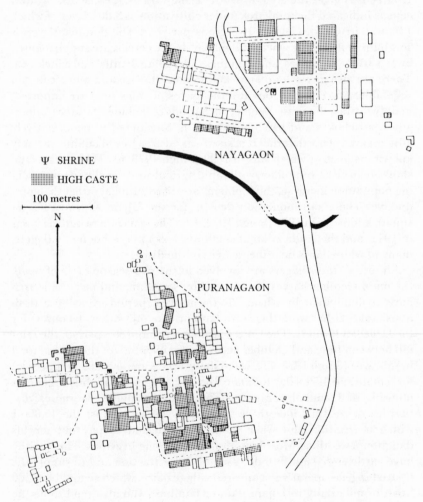

Fig. 2. Areas occupied by high-caste households in Dangwara

high walls and roofed with fired tiles; they often include the separate
households of once-joint families and their livestock. At the other
extreme are houses consisting of a single room with a front verandah and
a thatched roof. Most houses are of mud and typically have a linear form
– for example, three rooms in a row. An area for livestock is often incorporated within the house or in the courtyard. The front of the house is
associated with male activities: men sleep on the verandah and artisans
conduct their work there. The back of the house includes the hearth, and
is associated with female activities. This gender differentiation is one of
several separations which ideally should be respected (Jacobsen 1973),
but, while they may generate separate rooms in a larger house, in the
smaller house they tend to be marked by simple divisions, such as a step
up in the floor level, or a row of stakes.

The 'form' of the village in social terms is more problematic. The
major factor imparting character to the village, according to the perception of the people of the area, is the dominant position of the *jat* caste.
Srinivas suggests that, 'For a caste to be dominant, it should own a
sizable amount of arable land locally available, have strength in numbers
and occupy a high place in the local hierarchy' (Srinivas 1966: 10). The
jat clearly manifest all these attributes. They represent the most popu-
lous farming caste of north India, one of a number that were relatively
mobile up until the nineteenth century. Towards the centre of their distribution, in the states of Punjab and western Uttar Pradesh, they still
have a reputation as a martial caste, over half the Sikhs being of *jat* caste,
and their complex corporate political organisation and strong degree of
factionalism have been extensively studied (Pettigrew 1975, Pradhan
1967). Their main attributes as noted by Bayly (1983: 22) are 'a set of
religious beliefs which tended to depress if not eliminate hierarchy' and
'the capacity to assimilate pioneer peasants and families from poorer
areas'. Dumont also comments on their unorthodoxy (1972: 179). In
Malwa, on the periphery of their distribution, they are known as a
'liberal', pragmatic group.

According to local opinion, Dangwara is considered a good deal less
orthodox and less observant of caste, *purdah* and other forms of discrimination than the villages in the region dominated by castes such as *rajput*
and *brahman*, which have reputations for pride or orthodoxy. This is significant for a study of categorisation, since the formal order of Hindu
society and rules of behaviour are more relaxed and less clear than is
probably the case in other such villages. This study has not, then,
selected the most rigidly subdivided village in the area: many examples
illustrating a more rigid use of categorisation as the basis for social order
may be found. Dangwara villagers are also less inclined to display
wealth, except at marriage feasts. There are no motorcycles or tractors
(which, according to informants, tend to be purchased for display rather

than practical use) in the village, although these are found in villages of equal wealth in the area. On the other hand, agricultural development is highly impressive. Electricity was introduced eight years prior to the fieldwork, by which time there were reputed to be eighty-two electrically-driven wells and tube-wells supplying water for irrigation.

This pragmatic attitude is further reflected in the political climate. The village had formed part of the fief of a *brahman thakur* landlord, prior to the emancipation which followed independence from the British. Today the village is run by an elected village council and a headman. This council forms a tier of administration between, on a lower level, the family and caste, and, on a higher level, the government. The village has a certain degree of autonomy in administration – collecting taxes, for example, and imposing fines for straying livestock – but any major crime would nowadays be reported to the police based at a nearby crossroads. The village receives government support for its school, the council, the dairy and some agricultural schemes. Political dominance appears to have passed from the *brahman* to the numerically superior *jat* and particularly that faction within the *jat* which employs the ideology of the Congress Party and Gandhi's liberal attitudes towards untouchables and other issues. These castes continue to form the basis for any potential factional divisions. There appeared to be a considerable level of open political discussion.

The focus on the peasant village as a unit of analysis in regional ethnographic study has been the subject of severe criticism in recent years (e.g. Ennew 1976: 54). Marriot summarises lucidly the multitude of factors which indicate the 'reality' of the village, and those which transcend it (Marriot 1955). As a unit, the village is of much greater significance to the patrilocal, male population and the farming castes than to the female and artisan members. Although, as a location, the village exhibits extreme stability, extending over two or even four millennia, the same cannot be said of its population. The overall village census indicated that around 10% of all households had arrived within the last generation, while the second, in-depth census, the results of which are probably more accurate, suggested that 25% of the households had arrived within the last two generations and 14.3% had arrived within the previous twenty years. This mobility was particularly evident in the case of the artisan castes. For such castes, it is often the case that only one or two households can be supported in the profession by any one village, and this factor of limited demand, combined with the high child-mortality rates, has created a need for mobility in order to accommodate demographic fluctuation. There is also more mobility amongst the landless.

Although there is no rule of village exogamy, almost all of the married women of Dangwara were born outside the village. A group of twenty women, who were asked for the location of their natal village, were found to have moved an average distance of 39.5 km at marriage. Villagers are constantly in search of potential marriage partners for their kin, and this virtual village exogamy results in the maintenance of regular contacts over an area of some 10,000 sq km. This is a slightly larger area than that suggested by the pan-India study of village exogamy by Libbee (1980: 95).

According to the terminology of central-place theory, in which settlements are analysed within a hierarchy of functions, services and their hinterlands (Haggett 1965, Singh 1978: 98–105 for a local example), Dangwara as a large village with a number of small shops may be considered first as a node within a circle, looked to by other settlements for first-order services. These include a hamlet inhabited entirely by the *gujar* caste. At the next level in the settlement hierarchy there are several nearby villages, including the local weekly market. The next level embraces the local town at a distance of 10 km which holds cattle markets and supplies the village with many of its metal goods, clothes and other commodities. The apex of the local hierarchy is the town of Ujjain, a centre of major historical and ritual importance, which is the centre for less common commodities and, in particular, for entertainments. The villagers tend, however, to regard the towns with suspicion, and, despite the proximity of Ujjain, very few marriages are conducted with the urban population.

The village is not economically self-sufficient, and the importation of commodities is a major reason for the high frequency of visits to such centres. Most fruit and vegetables, festival foods, ceremonial paraphernalia, and all clothes and metal goods are imported. On any day, a number of itinerant castes may be found selling the cheaper goods in the village or working as travelling entertainers such as musicians or transvestite dancers. The importance of these external contacts and dependencies is, nevertheless, limited; most goods probably derive from the same 10,000 km hinterland which forms the pool for marriage arrangements, and I do not recall many objects in the village which appeared to be imported from abroad.

Caste and society

In discussing village society, a number of criteria may be employed for discriminating social units, including wealth, caste and family. In South Asian ethnography, it has been caste, standing for the common segmentary, endogamous groups often associated with particular occupations, which has maintained a pre-eminent position in analysis. The best-known synthetic account is that by Dumont (1972), who argues that caste society is based upon a number of classical conceptions, including the fundamental dimension of purity and pollution. This dimension manifests as an evaluative principle the nature of hierarchy, which is not reducible to power and social stratification, and therefore preserves a radical distinction between status and power. It provides the structural basis of a society in which the position of any one caste is derived from its interrelation with all others.

Social organisation is thereby intimately bound to a set of religious ideals and values. These are discussed by Mathur, with reference to a nearby village, in his book *Caste and Ritual in a Malwa Village* (Mathur 1964: 78–120). The most important of these religious principles are *karma*, the belief in rebirth in a form dependent upon the merit or demerit earned during the present life (pp. 80–3), and *dharma*, the belief in intrinsic duty (pp. 83–95). These are major legitimatory ideals, since the social position held by the individual can be explained in relation to his or her behaviour in previous lives, while the duty of the caste, *jati dharma*, implies that each individual tends to act naturally according to the behaviour expected of a member of that caste. A general exposition of these principles and their implications may be obtained from any member of the village. The more detailed elucidation given in Mathur's book, however, reflects the stance of the higher castes and especially the *brahman*. Religious principles are intrinsic to the social organisation of the village as a set of discrete categories, and to the means by which their separate nature is maintained. Pottery will be found to be implicated in a number of ways in the symbolism of pollution and purity: for example, in constraints on transactions, and the carrying out of religious traditions, whether regular prayers or annual and life-cycle ceremonies.

'Caste' is the translation of the word *jati*, which has, however, a much more flexible reference than the English term. *Jati* is essentially a segmented system working at a number of ideological and practical levels. The discussion of different topics will find the word used to describe different groups of people, including those divided by language, region and religion (Parry 1979: 87–92). Recent work (e.g. McGilvray Ed. 1982) has emphasised the actual heterogeneity of practices, with caste principles dependent upon the playing out of strategies and interests in a relatively flexible manner. Nevertheless, Dumont's normative analysis may stand for a number of these transformations, and the existence of endogamous groups, aligned hierarchically according to the principles of purity and pollution, and employing a whole series of dimensions for differentiation, is still the primary base for village social organisation in much of South Asia today.

The caste system relates to a pan-Indian hierarchical structure in which, as analysed by Dumont, at least the two poles of *brahman*, at the top, and certain untouchable castes, such as leatherworkers, at the bottom, remain fairly constant. The actual nature of these two groups, and their degree of perceived purity or pollution, may vary greatly, however (Parry 1979). There have been many critiques of Dumont's structural presentation (e.g. Madan *et al.* 1971) and other reviews of Indian social organisation emphasise extended kin groups (Kolenda 1978), agrarian social structure (Beteille 1969) and class (Gough 1981).

Caste is often associated with a given traditional occupation. This does not mean that the members were ever exclusively bound to that particular work, although the historical details are unclear (Ghurye 1950). This relationship is still of some importance, however, and Mathur found that, out of 283 adult males in the village where he worked, 173 followed, exclusively, their associated occupation. An alternative origin for some castes is found in the various 'tribal' groups, who are thought to have been the 'original' inhabitants of the area, but who have become incorporated into the dominant social organisation. Each caste is divided into smaller units, called sub-castes (*biradari*), which are entirely endogamous. Every individual is born into a sub-caste and can only marry another member of that sub-caste. I was unable to find any examples of inter-caste first marriage in Dangwara.

In Dangwara, such groups do seem to be established as the basic reference-point for social relations. It is the local sub-caste which serves as the actual unit of endogamy and prescribed ritual behaviour, and the family which is the focus of immediate relations, but when villagers refer to each other it is caste which seems most strongly to influence their identification. Caste is taken to indicate wealth, so that a poor household of the *jat* is taken as relatively anomalous, to be explained by the profligacy of the previous generation. All castes have associated with them stereotypic images of personality which appear to have considerable practical effect in daily interaction. It is of particular significance to villagers that the *brahman* is expected to be arrogant and obfuscating, the barber to be cunning, the *jat* to be an amoral pragmatist, the *gujar* to be rough and the *rajput* to be proud. All of these expectations are understandable in relation to the position of the respective group in the caste hierarchy and caste relations. A further indication of the effectiveness of caste is the spatial separation, especially of the lowest untouchable castes. In Figs. 2, 3 and 4, particular note should be taken of the area to the south-west occupied by the leatherworkers and weaving castes, whose separate nature is emphasised by the orientation of their houses, facing away from the main village. Further evidence of continued untouchability will be given with reference to pottery in Chapter 8.

Compared to caste, agrarian class structure is a much grosser form of classification: the large landowner, landless labourer, small farmer and artisan constitute the main groups, but these are not discrete or stable. The ideals of familial organisation are relatively homogeneous throughout the village society. The ideal 'joint' household is one in which all the married sons' families remain under the roof of their parents, who maintain complete financial and administrative control (Mathur 1964: 40–1). Usually at least one son does remain in the parental house, but others may split away before the deaths of their parents, and such joint families do not usually last long after the death of the father. These partitions are commonly highly acrimonious (Mayer 1960: 241). With this developmental cycle, the majority of families at any one time are nuclear. Inheritance is partitive and usually patrilineal. Kin relations are discussed in detail by Mayer (1960), who includes a number of topics, such as the precise nature of exogamous groups, which I do not propose to discuss here.

There are thirty castes represented in Dangwara, although again this

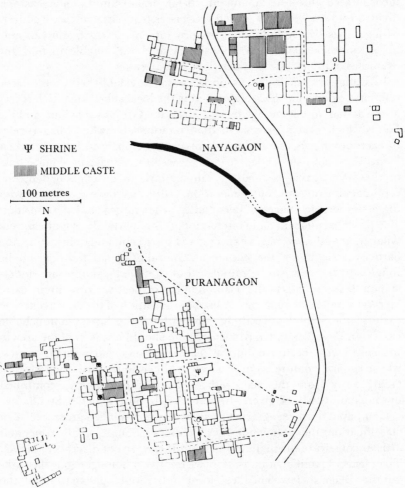

Fig. 3. Areas occupied by middle-caste households in Dangwara

was not constant; an oilpresser family had recently left, and a merchant family came and went again during the fieldwork. Table 1 presents details of caste and landholdings for the whole village. The traditional occupation of each caste is that given by the members of that caste in Dangwara. Some of these may be open to dispute; for example, the *balai*, described here (and also by Mathur 1964: 27) as weavers, are described in the 1931 Census of India (vol. XX: 228) as village watchmen. Ten castes no longer have any households engaged in the occupations traditionally associated with them, a major reason for this being the disappearance of weaving in the village. Many of the weavers and paintmakers now provide the main pool of agricultural labour. Some castes

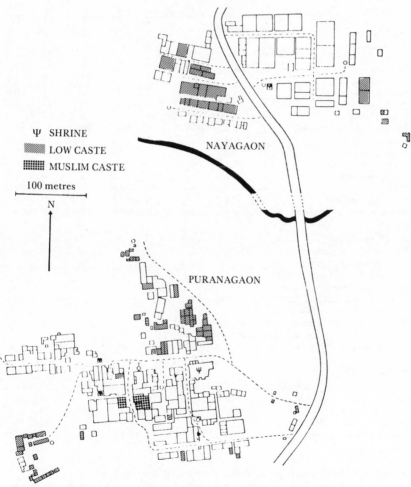

Fig. 4. Areas occupied by low-caste and Muslim households in Dangwara

Artefacts as categories

Table 1 *Caste and landholdings*

A	B	C	D	E	F	G	H	I
Jat	60	22.6	3222.5	560	254	5	4342	72.4
Balai (weaver)	24	9.1	168	10	59	6	188	7.8
Bhambhi (blanket-weaver)	16	6.0	172	27	90	7	226	14.1
Gujar	16	6.0	510	86	120	1	682	42.6
Brahman (priest)	14	5.3	491	124	170	4	739	52.8
Dhobi (washerman)	14	5.3	349	27	136	2	403	28.8
Bhil	13	4.9	4.5	1	4	11	6	0.5
Kacchi (paint-maker)	12	4.5	242	1	95	3	244	20.3
Gayri (shepherd)	11	4.2	193	10	53	1	213	19.4
Rajput	10	3.8	137	24	60	3	185	18.5
Bairagi (mendicant)	8	3.0	84	13	22	0	110	13.7
Musulman	8	3.0	398	37	116	1	472	59.0
Nai (barber)	7	2.6	58	15	27	1	88	12.6
Vagri (mat-maker)	7	2.6	67	2	32	3	71	10.1
Dholi (drummer)	7	2.6	8	0	8	6	8	1.1
Kumhar (potter)	6	2.3	34	0	6	0	34	5.6
Chamar (leatherworker)	5	1.9	16.5	2	17	2	21	4.3
Darji (tailor)	4	1.5	70	0	70	3	70	17.5
Sutar (carpenter)	4	1.5	5	0	5	3	5	1.2
Bargunda (basket-maker)	3	1.1	16	0	13	1	16	5.3
Phakir (mendicant)	3	1.1	27	0	20	1	27	9.0
Sunar (goldsmith)	2	0.8	31	7	0	1	7	3.5
Kumavat (tobacco-grower)	2	0.8	31	0	16	0	31	15.5
Kharol (wall-builder)	2	0.8	0	0	0	2	0	0.0
Bhaat (genealogist)	2	0.8	55	13	81	1	81	40.5
Gusain (mendicant)	1	0.4	0	0	0	1	0	0.0
Kalar (wine-seller)	1	0.4	0	0	0	1	0	0.0
Mina	1	0.4	26	12	50	0	50	25.0
Luhar (blacksmith)	1	0.4	0	0	0	1	0	0.0

KEY

A = Name of caste
B = No. of households
C = Percentage of village
D = Unirrigated land (in bigars)
E = Irrigated land (in bigars)
F = Maximum holding (calculated as wealth index)
G = No. of households without land
H = Wealth index (1 bigar unirrigated land = 1 point)
          (1 bigar irrigated land = 2 points)
I = Average landholding per household (calculated as wealth index)

Summary chart

	Total landholding	Total households	Average holding	% landless
Group 1 castes	6058.5	108	56.1	12.0
Group 2 castes	823	57	14.5	33.3
Group 3 castes	940	89	10.6	42.7
Group 4 castes	499	11	45.4	18.2

Note: (1) One household of potter's caste is not included in this table.
      (2) The figures for landholdings are based on a verbal census and no independent check of landholdings by measurement has been attempted.

such as the *gujar*, *mina* and *bhil*, whose traditional occupations included pastoralism, shepherding and, in some cases, hunting, have now become arable farmers. The *mina* and *bhil* are two examples of groups who have developed as village-based castes through the process of 'sanskrit-isation', the process by which groups not previously a part of the caste system evolve the classic attributes of a Hindu caste (Srinivas 1966: 7). This leaves sixteen castes in which at least one household is still engaged in the occupation with which the caste is traditionally associated. In some of these castes, such as the basket-makers, carpenters and black-smiths, all the households of the caste are engaged in these occupations.

It is noticeable that, although some artisan professions, such as blanket-weaving, have disappeared, most of the occupations related to religious practices have survived. These include the priests, barbers (who remove a bodily substance considered polluting), drummers and the *bairagi* mendicant, who goes around the houses of the middle and high castes every morning collecting offerings of grain. There were originally three mendicant castes, the *bairagi*, associated with the wor-ship of the god Vishnu, the *gusain*, associated with the worship of the god Siva, and the *phakir*, a Muslim caste, but the latter two are now following secular pursuits. The occupations of non-farming castes, such as these, should not be viewed as necessarily alternative to agricultural involve-ment. The possession of land is an important symbol of status for all castes, and the majority of non-farming households still hold some land, even when they are also carrying out their traditional occupation. All the potters who produce pottery also farm their own land.

Caste is commonly used to provide a generalised hierarchy by which commensal and other social relations within the village are thought to be organised. Mayer found, however, that, while there was a general hier-archy in caste relations, some groups of equivalent castes appeared to have emerged, particularly amongst the middle-ranking castes, in which there was little evidence of the avoidance relations or attempts at assertion of ritual superiority that otherwise characterise inter-caste relations (Mayer 1960: 37). He terms these the 'allied' castes. A similar situation was found in Dangwara with the most pronounced avoidance behaviour amongst the lowest castes (compare Moffatt 1979). Mayer's tabular form of presenting the hierarchy of castes has been followed here (Table 2). The evidence in this table is based on the second census, in which each informant was asked to rank all the castes in the village. Although informants tended to 'displace' their own caste, the overall results could be collated into a relatively consistent framework. Marriot (1968) found that even the most sensitive transactional criteria, such as inter-caste commensal relations, still provided a ranking which merely reflected that stated by most members of the village, and this therefore seemed a reasonable basis for its construction. Although some of the

Table 2. *Caste hierarchy*

Group 1
Brahman
Bairagi
Rajput *Jat* *Gujar*

Group 2

	Genealogist	Goldsmith	*Gusain*		
Mina Paint-maker	Shepherd	Blacksmith	Carpenter	Potter
Tobacco-grower Tailor	Barber	Wall-builder	Wine-seller
	Fisherman			

Group 3

| *Bhil* |
| Drummer   Washerman |
| Basket-maker   Blanket-weaver |
| Mat-maker |
| Leatherworker   Weaver |

finer discriminations between castes may be open to dispute, the basic division into three main groupings seemed firmly established.

There are some unusual elements to this local hierarchy – for example, the high position of the *bairagi* mendicants, the only caste in Dangwara other than the *brahman* to wear the sacred thread (the symbol of the twice-born and therefore ritually superior castes). The *mina* of 'tribal' origins is also relatively high in Dangwara. The two Muslim castes represent something of an anomaly. Whilst the principles underlying caste are Hindu, caste appears to have survived conversion into a number of other religions, and in village practice the Muslims are treated as much in accordance with caste principles as any other group (Dumont 1972: 251–4). Theoretically, the Hindus see Muslims as lower than themselves and there is no formal equivalence, but in practice the *phakir* caste are treated as borderline untouchables, while the *musulman* caste, as major landholders, would be ranked at the lower end of the group 1 caste, on a level with the *gujar*.

Caste, for all its importance, is not the only form of social division characterising village social organisation, and criteria such as wealth and family are also employed here. As a first approximation, wealth may be equated with landholdings. These were recorded during the census, and, by giving a score of one unit for each bigar of unirrigated land (there are nearly two bigars to one acre), and two units for each bigar of irrigated land, which can yield two crops per annum, a wealth table was constructed. This was then divided into five wealth classes as follows:

Class 1   less than 3 units
Class 2   3–10 units
Class 3   11–50 units
Class 4   51–150 units
Class 5   more than 150 units.

The third main criterion for subdividing the village was the form of family unit. Kolenda (1968: 339–96) has provided some definitions of such units, based on a synthesis from a number of village ethnographies, which used such terms in disparate ways. On the basis of her article, families in Dangwara have been divided into three groups, the first representing 'partial' families – that is, less than a nuclear family, for example a widow with her children (Kolenda's groups 3 and 4), the second representing 'nuclear' families, which can include unmarried relatives (Kolenda's groups 1 and 2), and the third representing 'joint' families, including both lineal and collateral linkages (Kolenda's groups 6 to 11).

One of the major factors imparting character to the village is the relationship between these three variables of caste, wealth and family. In order to demonstrate the strength of these relations, a cross-tabulation with the chi-square statistic was used with the SPSS package (Nie *et al.* 1975) to test the level of association between them. The three ranked classes of caste, the three ranked classes of family size and the five ranked classes of wealth were all found to be significantly associated at the 1% confidence level.

These associations may be further inspected using Table 1. Although a glance at this table reinforces the impression of a strong association between caste and wealth, this is clearly not a simple relationship. There are five *jat* and four *brahman* households without land, while a washerman scores 136 and a blanket-weaver scores 90 on the wealth index. Artisan castes are amongst the lowest landholders, but this must be offset against their income from their professional activities. It is, however, significant that seventy-two households, that is, 27% of the total, are landless, and this includes 42.7% of the Group 3 castes, as against only 12% of the Group 1 castes. All of the eight households in the wealth class 1 are also in Group 1 castes. The strongest indication of caste association with wealth is provided by the summary chart of Table 1, which indicates that Group 1 castes hold a total of over 6,000 wealth units, as against only 2,262 for the whole of the rest of the village. Members of the *jat* caste

Table 3. *Caste and family type by household*

| | | Family type | | |
		Partial	Nuclear	Joint
Caste	High	6	46	56
	Middle	8	24	25
	Low	10	44	35

alone, although only 22.6% of the village population, hold over half the land.

The general association between caste and family type (Table 3) supports the conclusion of Kolenda (1968), who suggested that there was a tendency for members of the high castes to live in joint families. In fact 52% of the high castes, as against 39% of the low castes, live in joint families. This finding has to be set, however, against the much stronger relationship between joint families and higher wealth classes. All of those in wealth class 1 and 2 live in joint families, while 72% of the partial families are in the lowest, virtually landless, wealth class. This relationship would be expected, *a priori*, given the division of land on inheritance.

This pattern of alignment, based on wealth and caste, is evidenced in a number of other variables. For example, the highest percentage of adult literacy was 97% for the *brahman*, and the lowest was 7.6% for the *bhil*. Again, the relationship is not exact, since the *gujar* were only 30% literate, against 50% for the drummers. There is also a strong gender distinction; the 1971 Census of India for the village gives 255 literate males, as against 22 literate females.

The material presented in this chapter serves as a framework for the discussion of pottery variability which follows. The major points derived from the material relate to the heterogeneity of the society when considered as the context of the study. This diversity is clearly patterned, as shown by the association between general characteristics such as caste, wealth and family form. These patterns relate to much wider structures, but take on a particular local form. All these variables are analytical classes of the 'fuzzy set' form discussed in Chapter 1. The result is highly complex, creating multivariate qualifications for any ethnographic assertion. Discussions of these relationships will involve some simplification of the contextual background, but in Chapter 9 an attempt will be made to confront directly some of the implications of this complexity. Using these variables to establish the social 'context' for the interpretation of the pottery is not to imply the potential reduction of one to the other. As will be made clear the pottery has as much analytical potential, as a dimension characterising an aspect of village society, as these more usual variables. It is no more reducible to them than they are one to another. Each is employed to capture some aspect of the organisation of social practices.

A movement parallel to that from normative models to issues of variability will be that from reductionist to constructivist approaches. The dimensions of caste, family form and wealth, used here to characterise the village, can become a base-line against which other material is measured. The problem with such analysis is that it tends to reify a notion of 'society' of which these are directly representational, as against a series of cultural forms which are secondary reflections of this society. This is common in archaeological approaches to material culture which take the objects found as symbols for the unobservable dimensions assumed to be the goal of archaeological reconstruction. Correlations are then postulated between these two. This volume will attempt to move from such a position towards a view of both material culture and these dimensions as equally constructive of social relations. Objects provide evidence for social divisions and relationships which are not reducible to caste, class and family form, but have their own active place within the overall reproduction and transformations of society.

3
Creating categories:
the manufacture of pottery

The central concern of this chapter is the physical creation of material categories, that is, the relationship between the process of pottery manufacture and the variability of the resultant pottery forms. Although this may appear to be an obvious relationship to investigate in a study of manufacture, it is one which is rarely discussed and still more rarely systematically described in the accounts of pottery manufacture for South Asia. This is not to say that both components of this relationship are not presented. The most basic ingredients of an ethnographic account of ceramic production are the descriptions of the various processes of pottery manufacture and a list of the various types of pottery produced. Yet, although the two may be placed in juxtaposition, how precisely the latter emerges from the former is often quite unclear.

This problem is not confined to South Asia, but should be seen in the general context of ceramic ethnography. Many of the advances in this field have been stimulated by the specific interests of archaeologists, a factor which has been largely responsible for the plethora of descriptions for the manufacture of contemporary ceramics, in comparison to those available for other materials. The current archaeological interest has been demonstrated by three recent, large-scale conferences on ceramics at Southampton (Howard and Morris Eds. 1981), Leicester (Woods forthcoming) and London (Picton Ed. 1984). Such archaeologically orientated interests include:

(1) The study of ceramic manufacture in order to reconstruct prehistoric technology (Arnold 1971, Franken 1974, Rye and Evans 1976, Van der Leeuw 1976)

(2) Technical studies of minerals in order to establish patterns of ceramic exchange (Shepard 1965, Peacock 1977)

(3) The ecological context of ceramic production (Mateson 1965, Arnold 1975, Toll 1981)

(4) Analysis of the functional associations of pottery shape, either with a view to reconstructing pottery use (Braun 1983) or to the location of certain activity-specific areas in archaeological sites (Rubertone 1979)

(5) Perhaps still dominant, the analysis of stylistic variation to identify cultural groups, for seriation, or for the possible identification of
social interaction (Plog 1980, 1983).

Studies of contemporary pottery-making have tended to reflect these
developments within archaeology, producing case studies which focus
upon learning-networks (Longacre 1981, Stanislawski 1978), social
boundaries and exchange (Hodder 1977) and ceramic ecology (Arnold
1975). None of these approaches requires a specific concern with the
relationship between production and variability in form (except where
this is related directly to function, or to the archaeological reconstruction of the technology itself (e.g. Van der Leeuw 1976)), and this may
account for the lack of systematic study. Of the South Asian studies,
only Allchin (1959) and Dumont (1952) discuss the implications of the
structure of the technology.

The detailed study of the processes of pottery manufacture represented a major component of the fieldwork, but was not undertaken
solely for the purpose of investigating technology. When viewed from the
perspective of this research the usual conclusions drawn from the study
of manufacture may be reversed. Clearly, since the pottery is produced
by a series of physical processes, it may be argued that the resultant
shapes are in part the product of the tendencies of the technological processes, which may lend themselves to the creation of certain shapes
rather than others. Suggestions of just such possible determinant factors
will be examined here. If, however, the pottery is investigated as a series
of material categories, it may equally be argued that, for reasons related
to the further use of the pottery in the society, such as their function or
their symbolic order, a certain pattern is required of this series of shapes.
This leads to the much more rarely posed question as to the kinds of
technological methods required by the demand for a particular type of
material object. In practice, neither technology nor product should be
regarded as 'given'; rather, the dynamic of the relationship between
them needs to be explored.

The nature of this relationship may be examined under the notion of
'style'. This term, much used since the emergence of modern archaeology in the last century, may refer to numerous aspects of a set of
material objects (Plog 1983), but all of these may be subsumed under the
general idea of that which makes possible the recognition of an individual item as a member of a group, which in turn is associated with a
given place, time and people. There may be a number of such styles
having different boundaries with respect to any such social or temporal
correlates.

The factor which allows style to operate in this manner is the structured relationship between attributes of the members of a set of material
objects. It is not the case that two objects have to share the same attri-

butes to be members of the same style, even if these attributes are analysed polythetically (Clarke 1968); rather, the term may refer to the use of the same dimensions to create both similarities and differences. For example, a given ceramic ware may form a recognisable series through its differentiation in terms of ringfoot and shoulder decoration, and its common retention of a plain rim. This definition of style, based upon the selection of a series of dimensions which are used to structure variability, will be used throughout this book. The concept of caste, discussed in the previous chapter, is clearly a case of style, since it is precisely the creation of difference along particular dimensions such as food exchange or occupation which enables ethnographers to study it. As David notes (1977: 192) 'Symbols defining diversity are not themselves diverse. That is, the system of symbols used to define caste identity does not vary from caste to caste.'

This notion of style provides a perspective from which to investigate the processes of manufacture. Each stage in the manufacturing process may be considered as contributing its measure of differentiation, by creating a dimension upon which variability, as style, may be structured. The first step in this analysis will therefore be to detail these contributions. This will be followed by an investigation of the nature of the resultant variability through the study of the pottery morphology as material categories characterised in quantifiable terms. The technology can then be examined within a wider framework, including its temporal and spatial parameters. The pan-India study of pottery production by Saraswati and Behura (1966) and several other more localised studies allow some assessment of the generality of the methods found in Dangwara. Finally, any suggestions that the technology might have a determinate impact upon the pottery will be examined.

Chapter 5 will provide details on the background of the producers. There are six households actively engaged in ceramic production, all members of the potter caste. Throughout this volume, the term 'potter' will be used to refer to the main male producer of pottery in the household, and the term 'painter' will refer to the main female painter in the household. Although now all separate, the households derive from two original families, one consisting of the four brothers here termed A, B, C and D, and the other of two brothers here termed E and F, with their respective families. These terms are used to preserve some anonymity and for convenience.

The precise details of the equipment used by the potters, their place of work and the methods used at each stage of the manufacturing process, will be of more specialised interest, and these are therefore given in an appendix to this volume (pp. 207–32 below). This provides a detailed description of the main methods employed, and a table which summarises the procedures used for twenty-seven common and twenty-four less common pottery forms produced by the potters. This appendix may be referred to for evidence substantiating the claims made for the manner in which the final variability is produced. Here only a brief summary will be given of these methods as they pertain to the overall argument.

The production of pottery vessels comprises four major stages: throwing on the wheel, the beating out of the base, decoration and firing. When analysed from the perspective of the production of variability, they contribute in markedly different ways to the final product. The initial element of differentiation comes from the selection of raw materials. Although there are three types of earth and inclusion combination used – that is, yellow clay with donkey dung, black clay with sieved sand and mixed clay with donkey dung – this in effect represents only a single dichotomy since the latter two varieties are always used in the same vessels (Fig. 5). For pots which are going to be used base down into the hearth, the mixed clay and donkey dung are thrown on the wheel, following which the black clay and sieved sand are added to the base and the two joined firmly during the beating process. It should be noted that this aspect of difference is not evident in the morphology or appearance of the final vessel, since pots which are fired black include forms made both in this combination and in the more usual yellow clay with donkey dung.

The first stage of production – throwing on the wheel – is more significant in creating difference in shape; indeed, all vessels are to some extent differentiated at this stage, although not as markedly as might at first be thought, since most of the morphology of the container vessels is later altered by further stages of production and only the shape of the rim and neck is retained right through to the finished vessel. The production of difference comes through the quantity of clay used, the manner in which the body is drawn up, and the use of the fingers as templates held against the top of the vessel as it turns, to produce the shoulder and rim. This

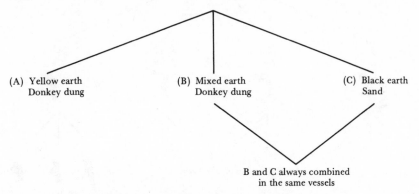

Fig. 5. Variability created by choice of raw material

results in some generalised classes of rim (Fig. 6) but each pot type represents a specific category within these. Such classes include a variety of 'rounded' rims in which the top of the rim has been folded in upon itself to produce a thickening which then receives only slight additional shaping into more circular or angular varieties. There are the 'split' rims in which this thickened section has to some degree been parted into two. Another common class is the sloping rim in which this section is elongated at a diagonal to the main body. This stage of manufacture thereby represents the creation of a particular dimension upon which is developed some elaborated differentiation.

The second stage of manufacture comprises the beating out of the base of the vessel by simultaneously striking it with a wooden beater held on the outside and a stone 'anvil' held on the inside of the vessel. It is at this stage that vessels obtain the characteristic rounded base exhibited by most. The specific dimension of variability created through the exploitation of this stage is illustrated in Fig. 7. Either by the retention of the angle between two stages of the beating process or through the creation of a horizontal flat facet (the details are given in the appendix, pp. 222–6 below), a division of the vessel into three classes of body shape is created. These are termed the possession of no *parti* (rounded base), one *parti* (base with carination), or two *parti* (base with flat facet).

The third stage in the production of differentiation is the decoration of the vessel. Some pots are given a form of indented decoration through the use of a cogged wheel during the throwing on the wheel. After beating, some additional incised and indented decoration may be applied to vessels which are going to be fired black. These vessels are also slipped and burnished. Most of the vessels which will be fired red are painted at this stage. In most cases this is done in red ochre, but the vessel may be

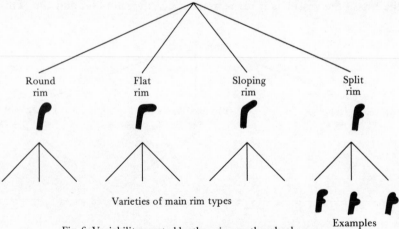

Fig. 6. Variability created by throwing on the wheel

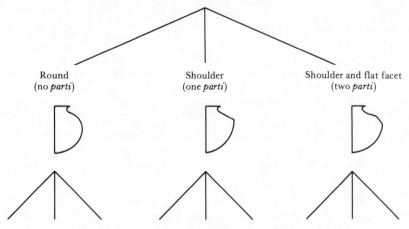

Varieties of proportional height of shoulder, etc.

Fig. 7. Variability created by beating with a paddle and anvil

entirely slipped in red ochre and a white paint then applied. Painting is not coincident with morphology; that is to say, vessels of the same morphological type may be given a large variety of paintings which overlap with those on other pottery forms. This is therefore best treated as an area of differentiation separate from the construction of morphologically defined categories and, along with the description of the painting process, is discussed in detail in Chapter 6. This stage of production can, however, be generalised as adding a further dimension, which divides the pottery again into three major classes (Fig. 8):

(1) vessels termed 'black ware' which will be fired black having been slipped with a self-slip and burnished and which may have incised or indented decoration;

(2) vessels termed 'painted red ware' which are painted in red ochre or white paint;

(3) vessels termed 'red and buff ware' which are slipped with red ochre on the top third of the vessel.

The final element of differentiation is contributed by the fourth stage of production and provides a simple dichotomy (Fig. 8). The 'painted red' and 'red and buff' wares are fired in oxidising conditions. The 'black' ware receives an alternative form of firing in which the pile of pottery is covered over in wet ash after it has reached the point of maximum temperature and is left until the following morning in this reduced condition (i.e. in the absence of oxygen).

The result of these various processes of manufacture is to produce a large variety of distinctive forms. There are around fifty-one such categories depending on how precisely they are defined. The majority of these forms are round-based container vessels, but there are also a

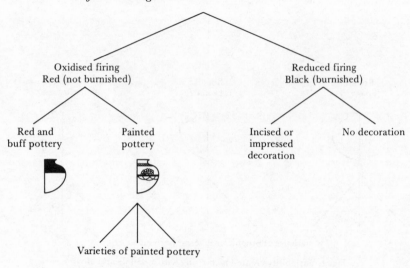

Fig. 8. Variability created by decoration and firing

number of lids, musical instruments and other more individual varieties. Figurines and building materials such as roof tiles have not been included in this description, although they are also produced by some of the potters. It is assumed by the villagers that a given pottery form comprises a consistent morphological range which would be distinguishable by any villager from any other material category, and that each is associated with a particular name, and in most cases a particular function also. It is, however, necessary to investigate how far such distinctiveness is determinable from the forms themselves. The paintings could have contributed to such distinctiveness, but they are not used in such a manner, since the application of design is not exclusive to particular morphological categories. The villagers are therefore reliant on morphological distinctiveness itself to create their full variety of forms. As a first stage towards the investigation of the degree of such distinctiveness, the actual quantitative variability of the pottery categories was investigated.

Quantitative variability in the pottery

Villagers assumed that a label applied to an individual pottery form would be consistent with those recognised by other villagers as members of that category. This implies sufficient internal coherence for equivalence between members of the category to be assumed. The question of the ethnographic reality of the 'types' identified by archaeologists has provided one of the most sustained debates within the discipline. The distinction noted in Chapter 1 between categorisation and classification must be asserted here. The term 'categorisation' implies that the potters have, through the process of manufacture, created a particular cultural order embodied in the variability of the resultant pottery forms, the precise nature of which is open to investigation.

If, in this particular instance, such investigation confirms this impression of discrete categories, this does not imply a fixed relationship with a given set of semantic labels. It was clear after a short period of fieldwork that many forms may be given a variety of names. Overall, there is a far greater number of words for pots than there are actual discrete pottery categories. The terms given in the list of drawings which preface this volume (pp. xi–xiii above) represent the common labels, which most villagers would recognise, but few of them are exclusive. One of the main conclusions drawn from the material presented in Chapters 8 and 9, where word–object relations are investigated more systematically, is the high degree of variability in the cultural significance and interpretations of these forms. This is not inconsistent with the existence of discrete morphological categories, since the 'text' at any given time allows for a variety of readings.

Most of the attempts to discriminate forms in archaeological practice have been made on the basis of nominal variables, the clearest being the variety of decorative classes, or by using qualitatively defined attributes such as the rim form. These nominal variables do appear to be the major discriminating features of the pottery. This does not mean, however, as recently suggested by Spaulding (1982), that all classifications which intend to reflect cultural choice should aim towards characterisation in terms of nominal variables. One of the points of Rosch's work (e.g. 1978) is to indicate how ordinary human categorisation often employs gradations and continuous variables, and is opposed to the assumptions of more traditional logic. When measurements of pottery are used, nominal differences are always converted into statistical clustering. This may on occasion be merely the natural variability of production, as in Fig. 9 which shows the variability in rim form made by an individual potter attempting to produce identical vessels. Gradation may, however, as in the paintings (see pp. 113–16 below), be an integral part of the categorisation process.

The array of attributes along a particular variable may signify a variety of processes. Fig. 10 illustrates the variation in maximum diameters of the *divaniya* (oil lamp). One hundred examples were taken from each of the six potters. There appeared to be sufficient difference between the resultant histograms to warrant a further investigation on a topic that has recently come to the fore in archaeological research: whether the products of the individual producer are so markedly different from one another as to make it possible to ascribe a given artefact to a particular maker (Hill and Gunn Eds. 1977). For this investigation, ten of the most common pot forms were selected, and six measurements were taken – on ten examples from each of the six potters, in eight cases, and from five potters in two cases.

The six measurements used were: rim diameter, mouth diameter, neck diameter, maximum diameter, height of maximum diameter and overall height. A principal-components analysis (from the SPSS package, Nie *et al.* 1975) was run on these measurements and lines were drawn around the products of the individual potters on the resultant ten plots. Out of a possible total of forty-eight, there were only two cases of totally discrete distributions, representing a particular potter, and a further six cases of a distribution in which only one pot lay within the distribution of another potter.

Dohni

Dhakan

Mamatla

Matka

Fig. 9. Variation produced in selected rim forms by one potter during a single session. Scale 1:2

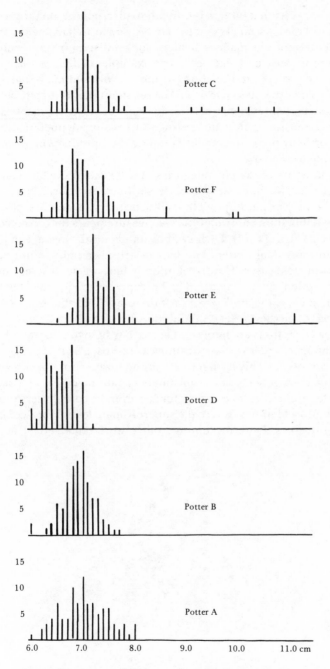

Fig. 10. Histograms of maximum diameters of 100 *divaniya* of each potter

This suggests that pottery is difficult to discriminate on the grounds of the typical measurements that tend to be used in archaeological analysis. A final attempt was made to achieve such a discrimination, employing the same six measurements, on thirty examples of *divali matka* from each of the six potters, and analysed using the discriminant-analysis programme from the SPSS package. The resultant plot is illustrated in Fig. 11. There is some evidence here for the separate identity of, for example, potter D, but these plots do not suggest that any deliberate attempt is being made by the potters to differentiate their products on the grounds of morphology or size.

The integrity of the pot categories may be established by comparing this evidence for internal coherence with evidence for differences between the various pot forms. This is illustrated with simple scattergrams using combinations of two of the six measurements for eleven common pot forms (Figs. 12–14). Each symbol stands for the average of ten pots from an individual potter. The pots clearly discriminate into discrete clusters in most cases. The distributions which are not discrete are (with one exception) pots which might be expected to be morphologically similar, such as the *divali matka* with the *matka*, and the *chayra dohni* with the *dohni*, since they are essentially sub-varieties within a class.

These exceptions are important since they help to illustrate the effect of hierarchical order in classifications as in Rosch's (1976, 1978) notion of the prototype. This notion refers to the fuzzy nature of categories in which instead of being either members or non-members of a category, examples are treated as closer or further from its core. In semantics this may fit into a hierarchy where the superordinate level 'table' connects in varying degrees the terms 'dining-table', 'work table', etc. The pottery

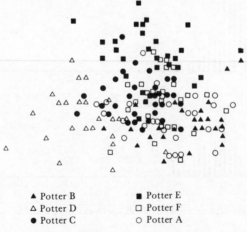

▲ Potter B	■ Potter E
△ Potter D	☐ Potter F
● Potter C	○ Potter A

Fig. 11. Discriminant analysis of 30 *divali matka* of each potter

also exhibits the comparative closeness between pot categories which are variants of the same prototype at a superordinate level. Gradation as an integral part of category conception may be observed either by taking part of the pottery corpus as a series (see Fig. 50, p. 153 below) or as in the paintings, where gradation was discovered in what might otherwise be taken as a homogeneous category (see Fig. 38, p. 114). These elements of categorisation, while discoverable from quantified studies, are only explicable in terms of the contextual information which will be presented later on.

Analysis

The processes by which these simple technological procedures create a series of discrete categories may now be considered in their temporal, spatial and social contexts, which provide alternative approaches for the understanding of the 'style' of the Dangwara pottery. The earliest good evidence for ceramic production in South Asia comes from the site of Mehrgarh in the Kachi plain of Pakistan. From there, in the levels of Period VI, dated to around 2900 B.C., a firing was discovered, abandoned because of overheating, with 140 jars still in position. The excavators reconstructed this as follows: 'Sitting upon a heterogeneous floor, the jars were piled upon one another in layers, being propped up when necessary by sherds of older vessels. Having been covered by a layer of sherds and straw, the mass of jars was in turn buried under a covering of clay designed to trap the heat within the pile' (Audouze and Jarrige 1979: 217). The temperature reached is said to have been between 750° and 1,000°C., but the latter represents an overfiring with vitrification, so that the intended range was probably much as in Dangwara. There was also evidence for 'ventilation chimneys' using the broken mouths of pots.

This early pottery firing is, then, remarkably similar to that observed in Dangwara today (see appendix, pp. 228–32 below, for details). Simple continuity cannot be assumed, however, since the early levels of archaeological pottery from Dangwara itself, that of the Jorwe period around 1000 B.C., is associated at the site of Inamgaon with highly sophisticated closed kilns (Sankalia 1977: 131). Pottery of this period is of interest, however, in that, in common with much of the prehistoric ceramics, it shows evidence of having been built in two stages, a feature which Allchin (1959, 1978) has used to link the modern and prehistoric material. Of the Ahar period ware, which is the earliest to be found on the main Dangwara mound, Srivastava says 'The neck and upper parts were wheel-turned but the rest were hand-made' (1969: 36). The illustrations of pottery from the Dangwara site (Wakankar 1982: pl. 25/2–3) suggest that this was also true locally. Unfortunately there are no analyses of the

KEY

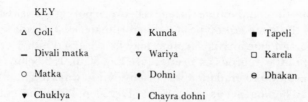

△ Goli	▲ Kunda	■ Tapeli
▬ Divali matka	▽ Wariya	□ Karela
○ Matka	● Dohni	⊖ Dhakan
▼ Chuklya	∣ Chayra dohni	

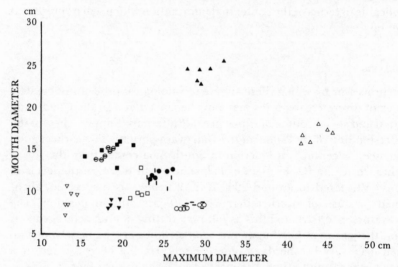

Fig. 12. Scattergram of mouth diameter and maximum diameter for common pottery forms. Each symbol represents the average of 10 pots of one potter

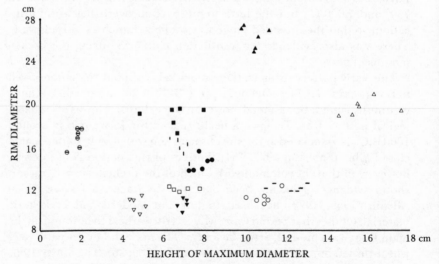

Fig. 13. Scattergram of rim diameter and height of maximum diameter for common pottery forms

medieval and other intermediary ceramics which would allow for the demonstration of continuity from the prehistoric to the modern period.

The existence of a nationwide survey allows the Dangwara technology to be placed within the regional traditions of pottery making, and, in most details, the Dangwara evidence accords with the report by Saraswati and Behura (1966) on the Ujjain district and the north-west region. The main fault of that work is the degree of generality, which is contradicted by Behura's own later publication, which shows that many of the variations in technique described for large regions of India can be found in the single state of Orissa (1978). In the local state of Madhya Pradesh there is evidence for hand-moulding techniques that are not found in Dangwara (e.g. Saraswati and Behura 1966: 57).

Surveys of this kind can be used as the basis for a discussion of possible relationships of a deterministic nature between different aspects of the technology. Saraswati and Behura themselves claim a possible link between the use of dung as an inclusion and the distribution of the 'black cotton' soils (1966: 46). In Dangwara, however, other reasons for the

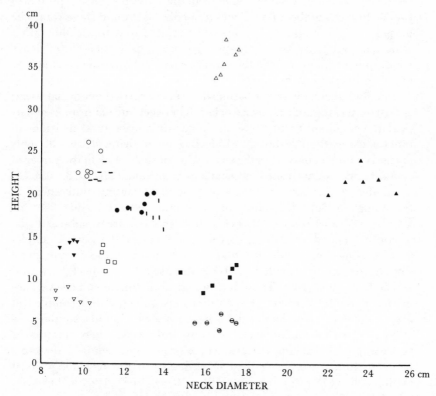

Fig. 14. Scattergram of height and neck diameter for common pottery forms

use of dung have been given (see appendix, p. 213 below), and the dung is used in conjunction with alluvial soils and not with the black cotton soils. A further possible example is Nicklin's suggestion (1971), following Freed and Freed (1963), that there is a relationship between the simple wheel, as used in Dangwara, and the use of hand-finishing techniques, such as paddling, as opposed to the kick wheel, in which the vessel is finished on the wheel. The abundant evidence from Pakistan provided by Rye and Evans (1976) contradicts this, however, with many examples of the kick wheel being used in conjunction with paddling the base. The Pakistan evidence may be used to counter a further argument which employs physical factors to explain, in this case, the spatial distribution of potting. Arnold, in his approach to 'ceramic ecology', illustrates cases where the natural location of clays seems to have strongly influenced the location of pottery making (1975). Rye and Evans, in contrast, state that 'Evidence suggests that the location of the potter's clay deposit is determined by the location of his workshop, rather than the opposite' (1976: 168). The close proximity of the clays used in Dangwara and the village's exclusive use of two out of three are supportive of this latter case. Further evidence comes from the active presence of potters in twenty-four out of the forty villages immediately around Dangwara. The presence of these potters appears to be related to demographic rather than to material factors (see Chapter 5). In summary, then, the evidence for any determinant cause of the use of the particular forms of technology found seems to be rather slight.

A major conclusion of the nationwide survey carried out by Saraswati and Behura is the lack of any association between the main zones of particular technologies and the main linguistic and cultural divisions of India, such as the Dravidian to Indo-European divide (1966: vii). This presents a direct contrast to the suggestion of such a link in the survey of ceramics and languages in Guatemala by Reina and Hill (1978: 205). On a smaller scale, however, there is evidence relating differences in technology to social differentiation as summarised by Nicklin (1971: 29–30; also Behura 1978: 21). It is clear that, in some areas, sub-caste distinctions depend on technological variation, so that, for example, potters using donkeys do not intermarry with those who do not, and a similar distinction is made by potters who use the fast wheel (Saraswati and Behura 1966: 182). These technological distinctions, however, are probably merely markers of such divisions, along with a complex of features of dress, food habits and other contrasts. I found a similar situation in the Central Moluccas, Eastern Indonesia, where differences between pottery-making villages, which produced essentially the same range of forms, were exhibited in variation in the technology itself (Miller 1976 MS., Spriggs and Miller 1979). In Dangwara, however, social differentiation of this kind was not evident.

A final approach to the linkage between technology and style is that most comprehensively stated by Boas (1955: 17–63), who related the motor habits involved in craft activity to the notions of rhythm and pattern. Similar relationships have more recently been posited by Steadman (1979: 234–6), who sees the inheritance of craft tradition as the learning of discrete technological patterns rather than the conceptualisation of the overall objects produced. For this reason the exact observation of finger and hand positions in wheel throwing was observed. It was found (see appendix, pp. 215–21 below) that the movements used are generalised and subject to variation, and cannot be equated with the expected precise sequences of action, at least at this detailed level.

Conclusion

The approaches outlined in the last section help to put the manufacturing processes in their context, but they tell us little about the use of particular techniques in relation to the general 'style' of Dangwara pottery. The perspective advocated at the beginning of this chapter provides an alternative viewpoint. The techniques do not determine the form of the distinctions used in creating the pottery series. Rather, certain 'dimensions' may be viewed as having been selected, and used as a focus for differentiation, exploiting particular aspects of the production process. A clear example is the *parti* system which exploits the methods of beating. The use of such 'dimensions' is one of the strongest arguments for analysing the material as a corpus rather than as individual forms, since, as in most structuralist studies, it is the very elements which divide the categories that also unite them in the creation of a distinctive style. This is because it is the use of the same divisive dimension, such as in the rim forms or the *parti*, that is common to so many of them.

When the pottery is analysed as a structure which generates the observed variability, some forms are evidently more closely integrated than others. Many container forms may vary only with respect to those particular dimensions discussed here, while some lids possess much more specific features which are more difficult to incorporate into a simple schema. It is this overall high degree of integration which allows the observer to recognise particular pots as members of what is commonly called the 'style' of the area.

In summary, this perspective begins by taking the need to produce a large variety of different pottery shapes, and investigates how the various stages of manufacture are exploited to create the requisite differences. The resultant picture of a set of forms produced by variance along few dimensions, with a certain number of more specific variants, is an arrangement which will recur in a number of subsequent chapters. Its implications will be developed in Chapter 9 in a comparative analysis of technology, form, use, distribution and symbolism.

This perspective establishes the production process as the creation of categories. It requires a quite different understanding of the material from that favoured by recent work on archaeological classifications. The positivist tradition, exemplified by papers such as Hill and Evans (1972), appeared to deny the notion of categories as indicating equivalence for the users of the pottery (although they further simplified categories by a tendency to associate them with an inappropriate notion of the 'emic'). Their proposal to construct classifications only through attributes selected for their relevance to the particular 'problems' identified fails to acknowledge the order that is created by production processes. The dimensions emphasised here may not be 'emic'. Although there are words for *parti* and for some of the rims, these are restricted to the potters, and for most other dimensions, including major groups, such as the red and buff ware, there are no terms at all. The categories are only observable in the variability of the actual pottery. This means that the identification of significant dimensions of variability is accomplished by precisely the same activity in ethnography as in the archaeology of prehistoric societies. The perspective adopted here seems, therefore, much closer to the notion of 'key attributes' advocated by Clarke (1968: 137) and recently espoused by Redman (1978) in his analysis of medieval Islamic pottery, where multidimensional analysis is applied to archaeological ceramics on the assumption that co-variation is itself an argument for significance. Still more appropriate seems to be qualitative but systematic observation and characterisation of discriminating dimensions.

4
Form and function

From one perspective the entire project of this book is redundant. It is a perspective often associated with the notion of 'common-sense' explanations. This assumes that the determinance of form lies almost entirely in the realm of function. As 'common-sense', this assumption is as likely to be met with in a London street in the justification of shopping as in an Indian village in the justification of the form of village objects. It received academic approval of the strongest form in the dictates of modernist theory. This chapter is concerned with the relationship between form and function and in particular with the extent to which this relationship appears to have relevance to an understanding of the specificity of form. The first section will explore the way in which archaeological approaches to artefacts have examined function as a constraining or determining influence on form. The second section will examine, in detail, the evidence for functional constraints in the Dangwara pottery. In the third section the results of a census of pottery carried out in sixty-three households will be considered for information about the position and contents of pottery, and the association between distribution and function.

The notion of function has played a peculiar role in archaeological description and explanation – always an important one, but fluctuating between highly explicit and implicit positions in archaeological discourse. In traditional excavation reports function plays the role primarily of a label. Although major textbooks, such as Hole and Heizer (1973: 203–4), attack the use of functional labels, a general survey of British prehistory would reveal that most stone tools and pottery forms have such labels (e.g. Renfrew Ed. 1974). Usually, in British archaeological reports, functional labels are no more than convenient terms for morphological ranges. In surveys of Indian archaeology, however, divisions between 'serving-vessels', 'eating-bowls' and 'water containers', as well as the local terms such as *lota* and *kunda*, are often assumed to have more direct implications for the kinds of functions demanded by particular kinds of society (e.g. Sankalia 1974: 456–7). The important implicit role of functional description has rarely been discussed. Shepard's major textbook on ceramics (1956) virtually ignores the concept. It is a major achievement of the New Archaeology of Binford and others to have made such basic, but generally implicit assumptions, more explicit (e.g. Binford 1962).

In practice, the close relationship between form and function often assumed in archaeology has reflected more general underlying preconceptions in society. The adage 'form follows function' has been central to modernist design (Benton and Benton Eds. 1975, Papernek 1974), and the positivist and technocratic developments of this century, represented in the creation of modern artefacts such as architectural modernism (Habermas 1982), have their counterparts in romantic assumptions of the embedded ability of 'traditional' cultures to have perfected this relationship between people and their environment in some 'natural' manner. This is very apparent in accounts of contemporary South Asian pottery. Typical is Coomaraswamy's comments on Singhalese pottery: 'I scarcely ever met with aberrant or unusual forms; in other words there is a great fixity of type, and we do not find individual potters experimenting on their own account probably because the fixed types exactly fulfil the purposes for which they were required, and it would not occur to the potter to work for mere amusement or for the production of beautiful forms apart from practical ends' (1908: 228). The link with classification is expressed by Saraswati and Behura – 'The form is so much related to the use that the classification of pottery is actually based upon it' (1966: 168) – and also by Birmingham, who provides the most detailed description of function for any corpus of South Asian earthenware. She states: 'In fact function remains the dominant aspect of the pot for both potter and consumer. Classificatory terms used by the consumers and potters themselves are predominantly functional, with minor complications' (1975: 384). I have found these to be the usual sentiments of informants in both Indian villages and British cities.

As a result of the more explicit emphasis on such factors in the New Archaeology, there have been moves towards a more general theory of function, employing notions derived from functionalist anthropology and indirectly from behaviourist psychology. The progression of this theoretical development has been from the more general principles of human–environmental relations, within an evolutionary and adaptive framework which demanded relations of efficiency and adaptation as the key to the survival of variability, to their more specific implications, which suggested the separation of those particular attributes of morphological variability which contributed directly to these tasks. Systems theory provided a linkage between adaptation and variability.

In explicit statements of these principles, Dunnell suggests that 'Style denotes forms that do not have detectable selective values. Function is manifest in those forms that directly affect the Darwinian fitness of populations in which they occur' (1978: 199), and Sackett writes that 'Just as an artefact has an active voice which connotes function, so it has a passive voice which connotes style' (1977: 369). These build on Binford's earlier characterisation of 'technomic' artefacts as those having their primary functional context in dealing with the physical environment (Binford 1962), and on the critique of all-purpose typologies in favour of classifications based on those attributes deemed to have functional or behavioural significance (Hill and Evans 1972, Schiffer 1976). In practice, however, there has been little work on the precise implications of these ideals for the detailed analysis of artefact variability. Binford's original work on Mousterian stone tools emphasised function as the key element in the explanation of artefact variability, but employed the relative proportions of tool types in an assemblage, which was assumed to be associated with particular functions, rather than a direct morphology–function relationship (Binford 1973). Direct functional analyses of ceramics have been rare, and those which exist depend on very general associations (e.g. Plog 1980: 85), an exception being the work of Braun (1983) who has also noted the lack of systematic attempts to explore the nature of prehistoric ceramics as 'tools', and has employed a barrage of analytical techniques to uncover evidence for the causal connection between intended function and pottery material and shape. The general assertions on the relevance of adaptation and system have only once been related closely to a theoretical study of the detailed variability of artefacts and their specific attributes and dimensions of difference (Clarke 1968). Most attention today is focused either on gross features of materials, such as building form (Hunter-Anderson 1979), or on the intrinsic properties of natural materials, such as bones (Binford 1978).

There are three levels at which form–function relations may be conveniently analysed. The first is a general level which indicates the usual purpose for which a form is used. This is a very common attribution, whether for British archaeologists or for Dangwara villagers. It is easy to confuse this level with the wider implications of function. When asked why a pot is of a particular shape, most people, including the people of Dangwara village, will almost always reply with some version of 'It is because of the use of this vessel', but, on further questioning, it will become clear that the precise relationship between the two has not been considered. The term remains a label. Labels may themselves be subjected to elaborate formal analysis, in which function is understood as a stage of classification that is analysed for its formal properties and practical implications, as for example in the componential analysis of cooking terms by Lehrer (1974). Lehrer describes the classes of cooking terms used in several societies and compares the semantic 'spaces' occupied by each. This approach analyses the structure of function as a labelling device.

The second level of functional relations is based on the premise of efficiency, which suggests that a form is the way it is because it is particularly well suited, by some stated criteria, to that function. Even this premise has been rarely demonstrated in detail. One possible form of evidence would be a strong correlation between form and function over space or time. In a study of pottery in several villages in Indonesia, I found that in different islands the same form would be used for quite different purposes, while quite different forms might be used for similar functions (Miller 1976 MS.). The general variability in forms used in contemporary British and other societies for the tasks with which pottery is normally associated should be a warning against simple assumptions as to the relationship of efficiency to form. The Chinese *wok*, for example, represents a strong contrast to British frying pans as a utensil for cooking in oil.

The third level of the relationship is the assumed adaptive role of functional efficiency. This implies that the efficiency of these artefacts is such that they contribute, if only in a minor degree, towards the maintenance and survival of the society that uses them. The New Archaeologists insist that this level is crucial for the first and second levels also, if they are to have any explanatory significance. Assertions as to the importance of this relationship by Dunnell and Sackett were given above, but, as suggested earlier, these tend as yet to remain at the level of a general principle, rather than a detailed analysis. This level is closely related to the premises of cultural materialism (Harris 1979).

Archaeology is not the only discipline to be concerned with the form–function relationship. In a recent critique of the notion that the design of an artefact is necessarily linked in a relationship of efficiency to its function, an architect, Steadman, indicates clearly the way in which this relationship has been embedded in wider applications of Darwinian and other evolutionary models to the study of design change (Steadman 1979). The easiest area for examination is represented by local constraints – the postulation of certain attributes, such as the sharpness of a stone tool or the impermeability to water of a pot, which appear to relate the form directly to its proposed function. In the theories under discussion, this function is deemed to constitute an 'environment', to which the artefact is adapted, but Steadman argues that 'If the "ecological" analogy is developed in any detail . . . the question arises as to what exactly the "environment" of a building or other artefact consists of, or refers to' (p. 59). Such environments are usually fairly immediate: 'The design of a nut must fit into an environment which is very largely constituted by some given size of bolt' (p. 204). They can rarely be studied as autonomous, deterministic relations; rather, each level of function is dependent upon the *cultural* creation of that 'environment'. Steadman's conclusion, quoting the anthropologist Sahlins, seems hard to contest: 'All the "economic" activities, of agriculture, the manufacture of agricultural tools and cooking utensils, the trading of foodstuffs, and so on, which are created to supply the alimentary "needs" of society, all stem from what are at bottom a set of *cultural* choices. Instead of there being a deterministic relation between biological necessity and the cultural form, biology serves only to set extreme limits on the cultural; it provides a "negative determination", as Sahlins puts it, of the realm of cultural possibilities' (p. 224).

A corollary to these recent developments has been the attempt by some archaeologists to use the distinction between style and function, not to dismiss style as 'remnant' variability (i.e. what remains after all that might be significant has been extracted), but to see it as a further functional parameter of variability. The strongest exponent of this approach has been Wobst, who has employed functionalist studies of boundary maintenance and communication to examine the role which style plays in society (Wobst 1977). Binford's original division of forms of variability also assumed a functional role for ideational attributes (1962). More recently Sackett has attempted to develop an independent role for this notion of style (1982). Hodder has exemplified a functional role for stylistic attributes used in boundary maintenance, in his work in the Baringo area of Kenya and amongst the Lozi, but in the same work is equivocal about their 'functional', in the sense of adaptive, implications (Hodder 1982a), a disquiet echoed in his critique of functionalism published elsewhere (Hodder Ed. 1982). Some of these questions about the nature of style will be discussed in Chapter 6.

In this chapter some terms used in the debate over function will be subject to a more detailed analysis in terms of one set of artefacts. Society will not be treated as synonymous with an environment with which cultural form interacts and adapts; there will, on the other hand, be a study of the forces which generate both society and the cultural environment, including ceramic form. This chapter also directly examines relations of efficiency and function, the discussion of which is essential, given the strength of such associations in our daily interpretation of the material world, and its importance also in contemporary archaeological literature.

Dangwara pottery (see Table 4)

The difficulty in deciding whether pottery is to be considered 'well-designed' may be illustrated with relation to the non-container forms of Dangwara. The *chhapa* seems appropriate to its purpose; it has a series of

Table 4. *Primary functions of Dangwara pottery*

Cooking pots	*barnai, bhartiya, chayra dohni, dohni, jhawaliya, karela, kareli, tapeli*
Food preparation pots	*dhatri*
Food serving pots	*brahman dohni, harawla, kap-plaet*
Food storage pots	*barni, dabba, kulhra, kundi, wariya*
Lids	*bujhara, dhakan, dhakni*
Money box	*galla*
Musical pots	*damru, dhol, nagara*
Potter's work	*pawanda*
Ritual pots	*chhapa, dhupana, kalash, kulhri, gorni ki kundi*
Oil lamp	*divaniya*
Tobacco pot	*kundali*
Toys	*anar, pahiya*
Tree-planting pot	*jhar ka kunda*
Water pots	*akhartij gagra, batloi, chuklya, divali matka, gagra, goli, keliya, kunda, lota, maman, matka, surahi*
Wedding ritual pots	*katwa, mamatla, patya, tolro, wari*
Wine-making pot	*sharab ka kunda*

concentric ridges, separated by depressions, and a convenient protuberance for holding. It appears to serve its function, which is on a particular day of the year to imprint a decoration consisting of concentric circles on the bodies of the village cows (although dogs, goats and people may also be subjected to similar decoration). I do not propose to study the exact gripping-qualities of the handle, or the skin curvature of the cow, but superficial observation suggests that the shape performs well enough. Clearly, as in the example of a nut and bolt described by Steadman, we are dealing with a notion of function that implies an adaptation to a highly specific 'environment', particular to the society being studied. In such cases the term 'well-designed' approximates closely to 'specific to a given task'. Other 'specific' forms are the musical instruments, such as the *nagara* drum, if it is assumed to achieve the correct sound, or the *dhakni* lid which has a small knob which helps it to act as a convenient closure for a number of the container forms. The very specificity of form to a particular function found in the case of the *karela*, for wheat, and the *kareli*, for sorghum *roti*, may also be thought suggestive of efficiency.

There are, however, examples which suggest that specificity does not necessarily imply efficiency of design. The lid usually placed on the *goli* is the *dhakan*, which is of a shape that would normally be associated with a small carinated bowl, rather than a lid. It requires beating with a paddle and anvil, and this demands more effort in manufacture than the *dhakni* or even the *bujhara* lid, whose high degree of elaboration would not suggest a design based on instrumental efficiency. The *dhakan* is also part of the annual distribution of pottery under the *asami* system (see pp. 82– 93 below), yet it is relatively bulky and clumsy for its normal task, especially when compared to the *dhakni*. If the *divaniya*, used almost entirely as an oil lamp, is compared to lamps in other regions, it is found to possess neither elongation, nor partial closure, nor any form of provision for the wick. Indeed the wick was often observed to slide beneath the surface of the fuel and extinguish itself. These forms, then, appear to be comparatively badly designed, despite their specificity.

Rather than taking individual pot forms, it may be more instructive to explore the whole range of shapes used for a field of utility. The container forms may be divided into two main fields, those associated with cooking and those associated with water. Much of the discussion will consist of arguments for a lack of association between form and function in this material. This is difficult to demonstrate, since, while a positive association can be exemplified, the lack of such an association can only be postulated as an absence of evidence and is always more open to contradiction.

Cooking pots

In Chapter 8, the social and ritual importance of the organisation of cooking will be discussed. Here, the focus will be only on the practical demands presented. Nevertheless, one of the distinctive features of Indian earthenware is its status as a ritual substance. This factor is responsible for the lack of vessels used for eating in the village. In Dangwara the single eating-vessel is the *harawla*, a relatively rare form. The majority of food-associated vessels are used in cooking, and these, in turn, may be divided into two main groups, those used in the preparation of the daily *roti* (unleavened bread), and those used in the cooking of the food which accompanies them.

The making of *roti* is one of the most time-consuming activities for the women of most households. Ideally, *roti* should be prepared separately for the two daily meals, but women who work as day labourers usually have it cold for their evening meal. Grain may be milled on the day of use in the rotary stone mill, which is found in all houses, although the electrically driven mills are becoming more common. Flour and water are mixed either in a *dhatri* (usual for sorghum or maize flour) or a metal dish called a *parat* (usual for wheat flour). A ball of dough is patted between the hands to make a thin disc and is baked on a *kareli*, if it is sorghum or maize, and a *karela*, if it is wheat. After the dough has been baked for a minute on each side, it is placed for half a minute near the hearth mouth where the trapped air expands, bubbling and then browning the surface. Fig. 15 depicts sorghum *roti*-making; Fig. 16 shows another flour preparation, the *barfla* roll of wheat flour, here being cooked for a short time on the *karela*. It is then placed within the ashes in front of the hearth to bake.

Fig. 15. Cooking sorghum *roti* in a *kareli*

Fig. 16. Cooking wheat *barfla* on a *karela*

At the meal, which is taken first by the men, and secondly and separately by the women, *roti* are served in a metal dish and taken as individuals require. Each diner has his or her own dish, in which are set metal bowls or china saucers with an accompaniment, usually either a vegetable or a pulse. Some of the wealthier households may have vegetables, pulse and curds at a single meal, and eat three times a day, but these are a minority. The most common accompaniment is lentil, followed by aubergine, flour or chick peas, potato and leaf of gram. Curd is seasonal and its consumption has also been much reduced as a result of the success of the co-operative dairy. Most of the items which accompany the *roti* are cooked in variants of a basic formula, in which vegetables are first fried with spices, water being then added to complete the cooking by boiling. Meat is eaten by a few high castes, such as *rajput*, but mainly (if rarely) by lower castes.

This description applies to ordinary meals. The preparation for feasts represents a marked contrast. A number of elaborate recipes for sweets were collected. Lentils, which are soaked once for daily cooking, are soaked and dried nine times over the course of three days when being used for a feast. On these occasions the *roti* is cooked with clarified butter or vegetable oil substitute, and rice may be served with raw sugar or chilli, or boiled in sweetened milk.

Both earthenware and metal vessels may be used in the preparation of any of these foods. With respect to the pottery forms, *roti*-making provides the clearest case of the specificity of form and material in relation to function. During manufacture a disc of sand-tempered black clay and inclusion mixture was added to the base of the *kareli* after it had been thrown on the wheel. This is spread out during beating but is still concentrated around the base, which is then cut away from the remainder of the form to produce the final shape of the vessel (see appendix, pp. 223–4 below). It follows that, although other cooking vessels include this mixture, the highest proportion relative to other clays is to be found in the *kareli*, which consists entirely of a pot base. In use, the *kareli* is placed with its convex side resting below the surface of the hearth mouth (Fig. 15). The *karela*, by contrast, is made of dung-tempered yellow clay and is placed the other way up, facing away from the flame, its surface pricked with holes allowing the passage of hot air, which lifts the edges of the lighter wheat *roti*. The difference in material between the *karela* and all other cooking vessels used on the hearth is associated with its increased distance (about 12 cm) from the flame.

The majority of the pots in the range of cooking vessels are containers, used for boiling and frying vegetables, pulses, meat and milk preparations. Here again we find a specificity of pot form to function; the *bhartiya* and, to a degree, the *dohni* are associated with milk, the *chayra dohni* with vegetables and pulses, and the *jhawaliya* with meat. Equally, marked

Table 5. *Average neck and orifice diameters of cooking pots*

	No. of cases	Neck (cm)	Mouth (cm)
Bhartiya	14	12.2	14.0
Dohni	57	12.8	14.4
Chayra dohni	55	13.4	15.8
Jhawaliya	23	15.2	17.7

differences are found in rim shape and orientation, and in the degree of angularity of the shoulder. Cooking was observed frequently and in detail, including the stirring of foods with the common long metal spoon, and the lifting and serving of food. No association could be found between the variation in morphology and functional requirements. For example, it is clear that a longer rim is easier to grip and lift, but the form that appeared to require the most rapid lifting off the flame, the *dohni*, used for boiling milk, has the smallest and most inconvenient rim (a horizontal distance of 2.4 cm in an average of 57 cases, as against 4.3 cm in an average of 55 cases for the *chayra dohni*). The *dohni* also has the least angularity at the shoulder, a feature which would also have facilitated lifting.

Another feature which was investigated, since it has been much used by archaeologists, is that of mouth and neck orifice. This attribute has been selected by Braun (1983) and also quoted and applied by Plog (1980: 85) to prehistoric materials. The argument has been that the size of vessel orifice, as a restriction at the mouth, should co-vary with frequency of access and the need to secure the contents. These cooking pots exhibit a relationship between function and neck size precisely opposite to what might have been expected. It is the rarely used *jhawaliya*, associated with meat, that has the largest mouth and neck diameter, while the more commonly used pots have a smaller diameter, as shown in Table 5. No relation could be found between the angularity of the body and any functional constraints. In Britain, although there are quite similar cooking requirements, such as milk boiling, and vegetable frying and boiling, none of the forms used exhibits the partially closed morphology of the Dangwara vessels.

Water pots

The largest group of pottery forms used in Dangwara is associated with the same basic function, the carrying and storage of water. This uniformity of function represents a crucial distinction between these and the cooking pots. In the previous example, it was the specificity of the morphology–function association that was suggestive of some relationship of functional efficiency, even when, in most instances, this proved to be illusory. In this case no such argument would be possible. Over 50% of Dangwara pottery consists of essentially round-bodied vessels, with short and narrow necks and with extended rims. Any of these would suit the traditional use of pottery to draw water from the well. This used to be performed with a rope tied around the neck (as is frequently shown in medieval miniatures, the well being a popular scene for the arranging of a lovers' tryst), and is still occasionally practised by villagers who cannot afford a metal bucket. The aspect of water-carrying that is most likely to be suggestive of functional differentiation within the pottery is the range of finger grips used for holding and lifting pottery. These were recorded on a number of occasions. Empty vessels are usually carried in the hands, with the four fingers of one hand held inside the pot mouth and only the thumb outside, or the pot is supported in the area above the hip by the elbow. Fig. 17 shows the common method of lifting full water pots at the well on to the head, and Fig. 18 illustrates the grip for keeping the top vessel in position; the hands may then be dropped to the lower vessel, and finally to the side. It is considered auspicious to carry two pots known as a *bera*, rather than an individual pot, although young girls may only be able to carry one. A cloth is rolled into a ring and placed on the head to support the vessels and is also used as a filter when taking water from the well.

The water pots exhibit considerable rim variation, ranging from the split rim of the *matka*, or the flat rim of the *divali matka*, to the vertical rim of the *batloi*, but none of these variations is in any way implicated in the uses to which pottery is put. It was found from detailed observation, and may be seen from the illustrations, that the finger positions are unaffected by rim shape, and, since the rim extends out from the neck in all of these forms, the suitability for lifting by rope is also unaffected. The one pot which does show considerable morphological variation that might potentially be related to function is the *kunda*. The ordinary *kunda* is used to catch the water dripping from the water-table, and then used for the washing of hands (Fig. 19). A larger, but morphologically identical, version is used to feed cattle. A quite different shape is used to grow fruit trees in, and a very large, rounded version, observed but not recorded, is used for the fermentation of the *muar* flowers, which are distilled to produce alcohol. Finally, the *pawanda* (which is also thought of as a variant of the *kunda*) is used by the potters for holding their slips and paints. This series will be more fully considered in Chapter 9, but even with the *kunda* it is difficult to equate morphological variation with efficiency. All the forms are relatively wide-mouthed, but otherwise the curves and body shapes which distinguish them are not closely related to their specific functions. This is more evident if a wider focus is taken, since, for example, in Udaipur in Rajasthan the *kunda* forms noted were based on straight-sided vessels with different rims, although they might be used for similar purposes.

There are two areas of variability which, although not especially accentuated in this particular corpus, are of interest in that they are often quoted in studies of variability in ceramics. The first of these is the relationship between accessibility and orifice size, to which reference has already been made. The pots in the Dangwara household which are most frequently used during the day are the water pots on the water-table (*pirendi*) (Fig. 19). There are three main ways of taking water from these pots, and they all appear to illustrate the difficulty found with the narrow mouth, especially of the *matka* varieties. Either a hand-held cup is dipped into the pot, which is a tight squeeze and unpopular, since it involves possible pollution of the water, or alternatively the vessel itself is tipped,

Fig. 17. Lifting water pots on to head

Fig. 18. Holding water pot on to head

Fig. 19. Pottery on the water-table

which is difficult with the large *goli*, and none of the pots has a spout, so that the water splashes. The third way is to have a metal *lota* welded to a long metal handle, and this is a very common possession in the houses. Even this, however, is rather ineffective, since the *lota* is itself 10 to 11 cm in height and when fixed to a long straight handle cannot be manoeuvred within these vessels with restricted necks. It cannot therefore be used once the vessel is half-empty.

The final distinction often assumed by archaeologists to indicate function is the division between black reduced wares and red oxidised wares, the former being associated with the dirty work of cooking and the latter with cleaner work (e.g. Plog 1980: 18). At first glance, these expectations seem confirmed in the Dangwara corpus. Red pottery is never used for cooking and is ritually pure (see p. 143 below). If the range of pottery is examined more closely, however, the association is found to be less simple. The ordinary words for clean and dirty are *saf* (clean) and *ganda* (dirty). According to Mathur (1964: 98), who quotes a number of examples of their use, these words may refer either to ritual or actual cleanness and uncleanness. This is often the case in Dangwara, but in this instance an inverse relationship is found between their practical and ritual associations. The red pottery is that painted with red ochre, which is often fugitive, especially as it is usually wet when being carried, and so tends to rub off against the clothes. It therefore contrasts with the burnished black ware, which is considered less likely to dirty one's clothing. Therefore, although red pottery is ritually more pure, it is more likely to be called dirty (*ganda*). Equally, there is not the close association between black pottery and cooking that might be expected. Although the pots used on the hearth are black, most black pots are not used on the hearth. Vessels such as *barni*, *wariya* and *dhatri* are associated with food preparation, but not with cooking, so that the majority of black vessels do not receive the soot of the flame (see Table 14 in the appendix (p. 216 below) and Table 4). As will be shown in the next chapter, many of the water pots found on the water-table, which were first obtained on secular as opposed to ritual occasions, are black. So, whereas the association between clay, inclusion types and use on the hearth is very strong, that with pottery coloration is not.

In summary, while Dangwara pottery performs a wide variety of functions, it can hardly serve as an exemplary corpus, indicating the 'evolution' of forms adapted to their 'environment'. Much of the observed variability bears no evident relation to the variety of tasks to be performed or to any criterion of efficiency. This is particularly the case with those dimensions which most express that variability, body shape and rim form. There are numerous ways in which the efficiency of the forms might be improved with little additional manufacturing work: a slight depression to aid pouring, for example, or other devices such as handles and spouts, which are well-known from other media. The only vessel with a spout in the corpus is the *wari*, whose sole function is the pouring of *ghi* (clarified butter) on to the bride's plate at the wedding of the shepherd's caste.

Overall there is massive redundancy: a single, narrow-mouthed pot in a range of sizes could replace virtually all the water pots and many of the vessels used to serve and present at ceremonies, and could serve for most storage purposes with minimal loss of efficiency. Such a pot could replace virtually half of the entire corpus – that is, the *akhartij gagra*, *batloi*, *barni*, *brahman dohni*, *chuklya*, *dabba*, *divali matka*, *gagra*, *goli*, *kalash*, *keliya*, *katwa*, *kulhri*, *kulhra*, *kundi*, *kundi* for funerals, *maman*, *mamatla*, *matka*, *patya* and *surahi*. Equally, the container cooking pots could be replaced by a single sand-tempered, black clay form, and only a single lid form is needed, which would result in another eight forms being replaced by two. Most of the other pottery forms, such as musical instruments and toys, are relatively rare earthenware products. Although there are no studies in South Asia on a corpus of pottery comparable in detail with that reported here, there is some evidence that the Dangwara pottery is not unusual. In Gujerat, for example, Fischer and Shah (1970: 121) note thirty common forms, and Bose (1980) notes nine forms used for water in Surat.

The redundancy of the pottery is further emphasised when the more general provision of container forms and, in particular, the number of skeuomorphs are taken into account. The range of metal vessels can be matched in most cases by similar earthenware forms. The main metal (brass or bell metal) water pots are the *batloi* and *gagra*, the former having the same body facets and vertical rim as its earthenware counterpart (Fig. 20), and the latter is close to the earthenware *akhartij gagra*. There is also a metal *dhakan* lid, in the form of a flat disc, which makes the peculiar shape of the pottery *dhakan* even less explicable. It is not possible to see either metal or pottery as the clear 'original' form, although the more angular of earthenware forms probably indicate the influence of metal technology, while the common beaten round base of the metal may well indicate the reverse influence. However, as has been pointed out in Chapter 2, technological considerations generally defer to the demands of style. The metal water vessels have an identical function to the earthenware forms and, alongside the *matka*, *goli* and other pottery vessels, are mainly kept on the water-table.

The aluminium or steel *bhandia*, also called a *handi*, is as common as the earthenware cooking vessels. The equivalent in shape to the *chayra dohni*, it may be used to cook any substance. The pottery *bhartiya* is identical to the heavy brass version also used for boiling milk (Fig. 21). The *tapeli* is another common metal cooking pot, which may be in brass or aluminium, and has a pottery skeuomorph, although the iron double-handled *kerai*, which is used for frying, does not (except in the very uncommon *barnai*). The functional equivalent to the *kareli/karela* is the iron *tawa*. Even the brass *lota* has a pottery version, although this is very rare. The one range of metal vessels which is not usually copied in earthenware is the brass *parat* dish, and the small steel *katora* bowls, which are used for eating. The only pottery eating-vessel is the *harawla* (sometimes called a *pyala*) bowl.

China ceramics are not common in Dangwara, but both the forms found have been directly copied in earthenware. The *kap-plaet* (cup and saucer) is the only form of china found in most households. The rare earthenware copy is looked upon with some amusement by villagers. The china *barni* is imported as a pickle jar, and in this case the earthenware copy is probably as common as the original. Glasses are more common in the tea-shops than in the domestic kitchen. Basketry forms made by the basket-weavers' caste come in three sizes of open basket (*topli*). These have orifice diameters of 26 cm, 44 cm and 55 cm and heights of 15 cm, 30 cm and 39 cm respectively. The baskets are found in all households and are used for collecting dung, keeping uneaten *roti* and other tasks not performed by earthenware. The corpus of container forms is completed by a papier-mâché bowl (*batwo*), which is an uncommon form, made by the women of individual households from newspaper and clay, and used for storing fruit or vegetables. Unlike the metal and basket forms, which

Fig. 20. Metal and earthenware *batloi*

have minimal surface decoration, these may have raised triangles and finger-impressed decoration in vertical and horizontal bands.

This enormous degree of redundancy in container forms suggests that, except as wide constraints, the notions of function and efficiency play little part in any detailed explanation of the specifics of variability. That such a conclusion would be evident for most industrial commodities was demonstrated in the campaign by the Friends of the Earth against the variety of glass bottles used in England. Yet in carrying out this project, the continued assumption, both of the majority of British academics and of the Dangwara villagers with whom I discussed the explanation of variability, was that it was on this relationship that the weight of explanation was bound to fall. A villager, asked why a pot is of a particular form, will almost always reply in terms of function and efficiency.

The census of pottery

The lack of any precise association between pottery function and morphology does not, in any way, detract from a possible relationship between pottery function and distribution. Once a firm association between form and function is established by convention, as is the case with all of the Dangwara pottery forms, then functional considerations may dictate the actual distribution of pottery to households and within the household, unless other factors, such as the particular mechanism of pottery distribution (to be considered in the next chapter), intervene.

To investigate the distribution of pottery, a census was carried out of

Fig. 21. Metal and earthenware *bhartiya*

Table 6. *Secondary uses of Dangwara pottery*

	Examples noted during census									
	Sorghum	Wheat	Flour	Pulses	*Jigri*	Maize	Salt	Chilli	Seeds	Cloth
Batloi	1	0	1	1	0	0	1	0	0	0
Divali matka	2	0	1	4	2	3	0	0	0	0
Dohni	2	0	1	5	0	0	0	3	1	1
Gagra	0	1	0	3	0	0	0	0	0	1
Goli	35	11	15	11	15	6	15	6	1	0
Kalash	2	0	1	2	1	0	0	2	0	4
Matka	2	1	2	0	2	1	1	2	1	2
Wariya	0	0	0	1	1	0	5	0	1	0

sixty-three households, in which all pottery in use, either for primary or storage purposes, was recorded. The census was carried out on two occasions. The first included ten high-caste, nineteen middle-rank-caste, thirteen low-caste and three Muslim households. This was designed to include at least one household from each of the thirty castes represented in the village. Such a selection results in a bias towards the middle-ranking castes, which are often represented by very few households (Table 1). A second census therefore was carried out of nine high-caste and eight low-caste households, in order to produce a result more in keeping with the actual demographic composition of the village. In total the pottery census included 23.3% of all village households.

There are many kinds of information which might be obtained from a census of pottery. In this chapter only certain general inferences will be drawn, but further reference will be made to the census in later chapters, when the more specific associations of particular pottery forms are considered. Three aspects of the census will be considered here: the evidence for secondary storage functions, the position of the pottery within the household and the general distribution of pottery in relation to the dimensions of caste, wealth and family size.

The discussion of function has so far referred only to the use with which a vessel is primarily associated. Even here, there is a certain degree of flexibility: a *goli* may be used to churn butter (Fig. 22), a *dhatri* was once seen in use as a lid for a *tapeli* of boiling water, and a *dhakan* was noted collecting the dirty water under the water-table. In general, however, the pots are used, in the first instance, for their associated function, as listed in Table 4. Virtually all pottery forms will, however, after a period be taken out of their primary functional context and used for general storage purposes. Although all houses have niches in their walls, there are very few closed cupboards, and vertical piles of pottery, together with biscuit tins, provide the major form of household storage (Fig. 23).

Table 6 provides details of the most common items stored in container vessels. It will be evident that there is no restriction on what might be put into a given pottery type, and at this stage the great variety of specific associations is abandoned for a generalised container function. The items listed represent only a selection of those noted during the census of pottery; other contents included lime, turmeric, peanuts, fertiliser, small metal vessels, a fishing net and black earth used for washing hair. Some of the smaller vessels such as *kalash*, *dohni* and *dhakan* often contain small pieces of cloth, light-bulbs, bottles and glasses. Pots are often found with their lids sealed in clay, preventing any inspection of the contents. It is probable that a number of these contain jewellery and other valuables, which are said to be commonly stored in pots. Villagers are quite clear about this secondary use of pottery, as a potter noted: 'You

Fig. 22. *Goli* used for making whey

say you know sixty kinds of pot, each has its first use, and it has a name, so with a *goli*, its first use is to be filled with water, after that it can be filled with anything.'

Most of the household pottery is found in one of five areas. Table 7 gives the number and proportion of some of the more common varieties of pottery found in each of these areas. As might be expected, virtually all of the *dhatri* and *karela/kareli* are found in the area of the hearth, these pots being used for the making of *roti*. The other cooking vessel, the *dohni*, is divided between the hearth and storage purposes. The *wariya*, often used for keeping salt and chillies in, is also often found on the hearth edge. The water vessels are associated either with the water-table or with storage areas. The high proportion of *divali matka* on the water-table reflects the time of year when the census was carried out, soon after a distribution of these vessels (see p. 83 below). The *kunda* are not placed on the water-table, but below it, since they catch the water which drips first from the porous water pots on to the water-table, and then from the table itself. This water can be used for washing the hands. There are two main storage areas: the area around the *koti* (the large, clay grain-storage bins) and the main storage area, which is usually situated along the back wall of the house. *Koti* are almost always closed at the top with a *goli* (Fig. 24). Only the *kunda* is found in any quantity outside the house, in the court-

Fig. 23. Pottery in use for general storage

Table 7. *Position of pots in houses*

| | Area of house | | | | | | | | | |
	Cooking %		*Koti* %		Water-table %		Exterior %		Storage %		Total
Divali matka	0	0	9	9	43	43	0	0	47	47	99
Dhatri	11	73	0	0	0	0	1	7	3	20	15
Dohni	11	17	15	24	0	0	4	6	33	52	63
Goli	4	1	90	30	50	17	20	7	132	45	296
Karela/kareli	35	83	0	0	0	0	0	0	7	17	42
Kunda	1	3	0	0	14	42	13	39	5	15	33
Matka	1	1	12	13	18	21	7	9	45	54	83
Wariya	11	26	7	17	0	0	0	0	24	57	42

yard area, since this is used for giving water to the animals. Table 7 relates only to pottery actually in use, either for primary or for storage purposes. Most houses also have unused and abandoned pottery, especially in the rafters. Many also have piles of abandoned pots outside the house. One blanket-weaver had such a pile containing at least forty vessels (Fig. 25).

The third aspect of the pottery census to be considered here is the general distribution of the ceramic forms in relation to the major dimensions of village society considered in Chapter 2. In Table 8 only those pottery forms occurring in some quantity have been included, and some of the water vessels have been omitted, as they are essentially similar in distribution. During the first census, the distinction between the various *dohni* types was not understood, and figures for these types have therefore been presented only for the second part of the census. The sample size is therefore sixty-three households for the association with family and wealth, fifty-nine for the association with caste, and seventeen for the *dohni* and *chayra dohni*.

The metal vessels have been divided into three groups: (a) the large vessels, including the major water-storage forms such as *batloi* and *gagra*; (b) the medium-sized vessels, including the cooking vessels, such as *tapeli* and *bhandia*, and also the *parat* eating-dish; and (c) the small vessels, including the *lota*, lids and small bowls.

Statistical tests were carried out using the SPSS package (Nie *et al.* 1975). The programmes used were cross-tabulation, scattergrams and non-parametric correlation. These tests were mainly of numbers of pottery per household, as against wealth and family size. Caste, with only three main classes, could not be represented by a ratio scale, and was therefore harder to test for significance. The results of these tests were only partially instructive. Most factors were found to be significantly correlated with each other.

Fig. 24. Pottery used to close *koti* (grain storage bin)

Fig. 25. Pile of used pots outside house

Table 8. *Average number of pots per household by caste, wealth and family size*

	Caste group			Wealth group				No. of adults		
	1	2	3	1&2	3	4	5	6+	4&5	1–3
Total pots	23.4	16.0	22.1	25.3	24.6	18.4	13.7	26.4	20.1	16.2
Goli	7.1	4.7	6.0	8.3	6.4	5.5	3.9	7.5	6.6	3.9
Matka	1.4	1.8	1.7	1.7	1.9	1.6	1.5	1.9	1.8	1.4
Divali matka	2.0	2.1	2.1	2.5	2.4	1.9	1.4	2.4	2.2	1.8
Kalash	1.0	1.0	1.7	1.6	1.1	0.3	0.4	1.2	0.6	0.5
Kunda	1.0	0.7	0.9	0.8	1.3	0.7	0.3	1.3	0.6	0.5
Dohni	1.2		0.5	1.0	1.7	0.4	0.7	0.4	0.2	0.1
Chayra dohni	0.1		1.0	0.2	0.2	1.0	0.7	0.2	0.2	0.1
Dhatri	0.2	0.2	0.5	0.1	0.5	0.3	0.2	0.4	0.2	0.2
Karela	0.7	0.6	0.4	0.7	0.6	0.4	0.6	0.7	0.4	0.6
Kareli	0.7	0.4	0.7	0.6	0.6	0.5	0.6	0.7	0.4	0.6
Big metal	3.1	1.8	1.8	3.4	2.5	1.8	0.7	3.5	1.9	1.2
Medium metal	9.4	7.0	5.4	9.9	8.3	5.7	4.4	10.1	6.5	5.7
Small metal	8.8	7.4	7.2	10.0	9.9	7.1	8.0	9.9	9.7	7.5

These results reflect the general tendency of pottery and other material items to associate with the major social dimensions of the village. A similar result was found with measurements of house size, both as covered area and enclosed area, which again appeared to be significantly associated with both the various forms of pottery and the major social dimensions. The data have therefore been presented, not in terms of statistical significance, but in the form of the average number of particular pottery forms per household for the three major dimensions. Caste is divided into three analytical classes, and wealth into five, as defined in Chapter 2 (wealth classes 1 and 2 have been combined because of their low frequency of occurrence). Family size has been divided into three classes, reflecting the number of adults rather than the type of family or overall size, since this was found in the statistical tests to be a more significant variable.

The strong association between the three major dimensions of caste, family size and wealth, demonstrated in Chapter 2, is important as the context to these results, because each can be understood as mediating the relationship between pottery and other dimensions. Presented alone, one of these dimensions might be seen as the major positively associated variable, with an implication of cause, when, in reality, each is only an aspect of the fundamental hierarchical principles that generate the form of village society in India (Dumont 1972).

Using Table 8 as a guide, it may be seen that the dimension which shows least sign of an association with the number of pots is caste. There is neither a clear association with the overall number of pots, nor with the particular types of water vessel. Amongst the cooking vessels, there is some suggestion that high castes tend to have more *dohni* and *karela* and fewer *chayra dohni* and *dhatri*. The significance of these observations will be considered in later chapters. The metal vessels, in contrast to the earthenware, are strongly associated with caste. Wealth appears to be closely related to the total number of earthenware vessels and with the number of *goli*, *divali matka* and *kalash*. The association with cooking pots is less clear, except for a general tendency among poorer groups to have fewer *dohni* and more *chayra dohni*. There is a clear association with metal vessels. The very low numbers of all vessels recorded for the poorest of these classes is striking. The number of adults in the household seems to be positively associated with all earthenware and metal vessels with the exception of the *karela/kareli*. These and the *kunda*, which is another exception, tend to occur in small numbers, but are essential possessions of every household. There may also be a tendency for water pots to be more closely associated with wealth, and cooking pots with caste, some cooking pots tending to a negative association with these variables.

In conclusion, there is a marked difference between, on the one hand, the apparent relation of function to form and, on the other, between function and distribution. The precise morphology is not easily related to function, which appears to act only as a wide parameter for variance, but the vessels are closely associated by convention with particular functions. Function, then, acts as a label for form, without implications of efficiency, but this is sufficient to have a marked effect on the distribution of the pottery, being a major factor in the number of particular pots per household and in the position of particular pot forms within the household. This conclusion assumes that the demands for water, cooking and other actions with which pots are associated, are themselves associated with the size of the family and with wealth, which seems probable both *a priori* and from observation. Larger, wealthier families in village India eat a greater variety of foods, and eat more often. That the demand for water rises with wealth is clear from the demands on potters as drawers of water, discussed in the next chapter. This is, however, only raising the implications of function from the first level, of associated label, to the second, of efficiency. There is nothing in this material to suggest that pottery will impinge in any way upon the third level, of functional explanation – that is, the adaptation of the community to its environment in such a manner as to affect its capacity to reproduce itself. This seems equally the case for morphology and distribution. Distribution cannot, however, be adequately assessed without a consideration of the mechanisms by which it is conducted, and this is the subject of the next chapter.

5

The Dangwara potters and the distribution of pottery

The last two chapters have indicated the limitations of explanations of variability dependent upon deterministic criteria derived from the study of manufacture or of function. An additional perspective derives from the analysis of the corpus of pottery as a variable set of symbolic categories within a social context. In this chapter, a first step will be taken towards such a perspective by examining two elements of this social context. The first is the social and economic conditions of the six pottery-making households, and the second is the mechanisms by which the products of these households are distributed to the remainder of the village.

The history of the Dangwara potters

There are two partilineages present in the village. The older, now represented by potters E and F, claims to have been in the village for nine generations, although detailed genealogical data could only be obtained for four. They trace their origins from a town in Rajasthan, via another, 41 km to the west of Dangwara, which is still a preferred area for the selection of wives. The second group of potters came to the village only one generation ago, when their father was invited in, owing to the lack of anyone of the right age to produce pottery within the village at the time. He was later joined in pottery production by E and F's father's mother's brother's son, but this potter later retired and his three sons have not taken up pottery-making. These constitute the single non-pottery-producing household, of potter's caste, in the village. Initially E and F's father and father's brother did not make pottery, although they later learnt a limited range of forms, and it was the active potter of their line who taught them most of their pottery-making skills. Since their father's brother is childless, potter E was adopted by him as his heir.

Several points emerge from this account. Firstly, there is a confirmation of the high degree of mobility suggested for artisan castes in general in Chapter 2. Given that an approximate ratio may be determined between the social demand for pottery and the potter's productive capacity, there is an optimum number of active potters required for any given village size, and this number is likely to be small. Fig. 26 shows the number of potter households in the surrounding villages, all of whom are of the two major sub-castes, and most of whom are engaged in active pottery production. This is an area of high birth-rate and high infant mortality, and the actual numbers of active potters may fluctuate rapidly; the accounts of previous generations tell of rapid changes between a surfeit and a dearth of active potters owing to the high birth-rate and the incidence of early death. Mobility is one response to this problem; another will be discussed below in considering the nature of the *asami* system.

A second factor highlighted by this history is the responsibility laid upon the village leaders to ensure the presence of a working potter. Under the old system of landholding, the potters, on their original settlement, had grants of agricultural land from the landlord. When in the previous generation the village lacked a potter, it was the headman of the

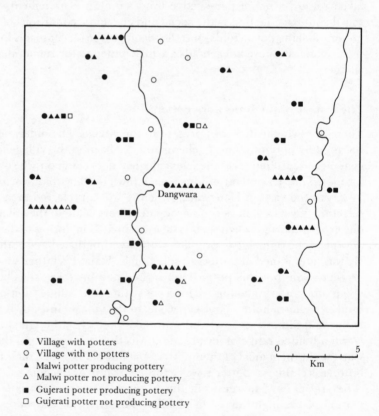

● Village with potters
○ Village with no potters
▲ Malwi potter producing pottery
△ Malwi potter not producing pottery
■ Gujerati potter producing pottery
□ Gujerati potter not producing pottery

Fig. 26. Pottery production in villages around Dangwara

time who, after consultation, brought in a potter, with a grant of housing and five bigars of land. It is this potter's four sons who represent the second line of active potters. The potters were under a theoretical obligation to supply the landlord and at least a moral obligation to supply the village. In return for this relatively formalised establishment in the village, the potters also received some further rights, which are the basis for their claim to precedence over any potter from outside the village (a claim known as *hak*).

There is probably a large variety of alternative relationships between village and potter. Saraswati mentions the existence of numbers of villages consisting largely, or entirely, of active potters, which might permit greater specialisation (1979: 56–8). Another strategy, an instance of which was recorded in the genealogy of one of the potters, is the importation of husbands against the prevailing virilocal pattern, and one potter is at present attempting to find land for his sister and her husband within Dangwara.

Childhood and learning to make pottery

This account will refer mainly to the training of males, as painters will be treated separately in the next chapter. Young children are more a liability than an asset in pottery production; whilst they may help in fetching materials and adding fuel to the fire, their play at throwing and painting may often damage the vessels. All sons and some daughters will attend the village school. The length of time they remain there seems to depend on whether they appear likely to be successful at obtaining waged employment: the eldest son of the only non-pottery-making household has now become a postman. After school, boys will attempt to find employment in town, or more commonly will work as shepherds. Such wage labour is considered preferable to village work, but is rarely obtainable, and the males generally return to the village to learn pottery manufacture. This training occurs at a relatively late age: one potter's son, having given up work in a shop in the local town for lack of pay, is now, at the age of twenty, learning to make *chuklya*, the simplest container form, having previously made *divaniya*, *bujhara* and *kulhri*. He will learn the remaining forms over the next five years, but may never learn *dhatri* if he does not prove adept. The techniques for making black pots are usually learnt after those for making the red painted pots. Generally, help in firing, preparing clay and sometimes in beating will have been given by the older children, and these tasks are learnt before the techniques of throwing clay.

The typically late age of learning pottery manufacture means that the chances of the father failing to pass on his knowledge are high, and in another village a family recounted at length how they had been 'ruined' because the potter had died before he could pass on his skills. There are, however, alternative sources of instruction. Many young potters take up at least a short period of apprenticeship with someone other than their father; the most common model appears to be the mother's brother, but there were also cases of learning from a brother, or from the father-in-law. The reason for the late age of learning seems again to stem from the balance between the number of potters and of the available clients. The trained son is immediately a potential rival. Equally, however, if there are a large number of clients, the newly trained potter may find himself with a considerable amount of work within a short period.

Marriage and the division of labour

The arrangement of marriage is a crucial strategic task for the parents, as affines may become the means for engaging in economic transactions of mutual advantage, as well as for possible demographic moves from potter-rich to potter-poor areas. Discussion of marriage arrangements was one of the most common reasons for absence from the village. The males admitted to a preference for importing females from long distances, in order to limit the possible protective influence of affines over the new daughter-in-law. Within the potter families, the average marriage-distance was 25 km (17 cases) although this is less than the 39.5 km average of a group taken from all castes. Young brides clearly find the move to the husband's village traumatic, and tend to spend about two months of each year back in their natal village, always having their first child there (compare Jacobsen 1977). Marital relations are highly asymmetric, a state of affairs symbolised by the wife's relatives' reticence in accepting gifts from the husband's relatives, even to the extent of refusing to drink from streams running from the latter's village, in contrast to the elaborate hospitality which they area expected to provide. As described by Selwyn (1979), the symbolic representation of the inferiority of the bride's family is a prominent feature of the wedding ceremony.

Jacobsen's study (1973) details the effective, if different, purdah systems of Hindu and Muslim households. In Dangwara, purdah is most pronounced for *brahman* and *rajput* households. The potters observe a number of restrictions typical of Hindu purdah, the most noticeable being the avoidance of any relations between husband and wife in public. All economic and social decisions of any importance appear to be dominated by the husband, and there was no evidence, from the daily observation of life in the households, to suggest that the husband's public authority is complemented by the wife's authority within the home, although this was sometimes claimed.

Details of the sharing of expenditure and responsibility varied greatly between the six households, and this is also true of the relative contributions to pottery manufacture. In Dangwara, only one of the painters regularly and substantially assists in clay preparation and kneading. All painters beat the earth and donkey dung, remove stones, look after donkeys, slip, burnish and paint the vessels and help in the firing. The division between potting and painting, and the simultaneity of requisite tasks during firing, require that the basic unit of production should be a minimum of one male and one female. The male appears to dominate in work on the fields owned by the potters, but both spouses appeared to take on wage-labour work with equal frequency. The painter is responsible for all domestic labour and food preparation, and females only eat after the males of the household. Ideals expressed about female status suggested that, theoretically, this should improve on bearing male children, but, in observed practice, relations within marriage seemed to depend almost entirely on the vagaries of the personal relationship between husband and wife, which often shifted radically from month to month. The wife who is not on good terms with her husband or his family is extremely isolated within the village.

Sons almost always stay with their parents for some period after marriage, but often leave before the death of the parents. Officially, the father controls all income into the household until death, and this may be a cause of conflict. Cases were found of splits resulting from acrimony, but this was not always the case. At the beginning of fieldwork, two potters were still sharing a house (though with a partition wall) and pottery-making facilities. By the end of fieldwork, a house had been purchased in preparation for a formal split, but this was due merely to the lack of available space. Most other kin relations are as those described in detail by Mayer for a nearby village (1960: 222–7). Potters continue to participate in the range of kin and ritual relationships and the mutual obligations described there. Certain differences were noted, but most of these do not bear directly on pottery production. The most pronounced difference was the importance of second marriage (*nathra*), which is a very common phenomenon in the Dangwara region. Two instances were found amongst the potters' families.

The economic background of the pottery-making households

The details of income and expenditure represent a popular subject of discussion and are no cause for embarrassment. They are, however, enormously complex. Members of middle-ranking castes such as the potters seem, at any one time, almost all to be both substantial debtors and substantial creditors, with respect to the size of their annual income. All potters possess land, which is essential for their status and an important supplement to their income. The actual area of land being farmed

Table 9. *Estimated annual income for 'average' potter household*

Service provided	Estimated annual income (r/kg)
Provision of ritual vessels	510
Provision of secular vessels	280
Services at life-cycle events	375
Sale of pottery at markets	150
Drawing of water	60
Agricultural labouring	700
Crops of own land	500
Total	2,575

varied from none, for two potters whose land was being cropped by a creditor owing to the debt on payments made for their father's funeral feast, to a potter who was farming twice the area of his own land, having invested in the use-right of another plot for a three-year period.

It is not only in land that apparent ownership may be but a poor reflection of actual control. Potters frequently borrow money, despite the local interest-rate of 2% per month charged by large landowners. These same potters also lend out cash, or take in metal vessels on pawn from their neighbours. As an example, one potter, who claimed to spend 7,000 r on a funeral feast plus 500 r on presents to his daughter's prospective affines, still decided, when over three bigars of land came up for sale near his own land, to buy them at 5,500 r plus 800 r expenses for taxes, registration, etc. At this stage he had debts of 15,000 r. He then sold his buffalo and bought a pregnant goat, and made some money through speculation on commodities purchased in one area and sold in another through his affines (goods which he never actually saw). The debt was then 13,000 r, which he hoped to pay off on his nine bigars with good crops of quick-growing chick peas, and with a loan borrowed at high interest from a landowner. He knew he might well fail, but decided it was worth the risk. The effective value of land and the value of labour input varied greatly. One potter who saw himself primarily as a farmer obtained 600 kg of grain from his land, while another who saw himself primarily as a potter obtained only 250 kg of grain from a landholding of the same size. All potters own between one and eight donkeys, two have a buffalo and one has a pair of oxen. In general, the apparent ownership of resources differs radically from the subtlety of actual control and obligations.

The calculation of potters' income (Table 9) is based upon the comparison of a number of sources of information. These include details of yearly payments given to potters by twenty-eight households (including the weighing of some payments in flour), detailed discussions and attendance at several markets. These estimates were then averaged, and,

Table 10. *Estimated annual expenditure for 'average' potter household*

Goods	Estimated annual costs (r/kg)
Pulses	300
Vegetables	200
Milk	60
Additional foods (not grain)	600
Fuel for potting	400
Materials for potting	60
Tax and schooling	32
Cloth	250
Travel accommodation	150
Total	2,052

given the varied results for each household, a 'typical' potter's household was created, which was assumed to have one-sixth of the village as its clients. Estimates are given in rupees which are also equivalent to kilograms of sorghum. At the time of fieldwork there were 18 rupees/kg sorghum per English pound.

If to this total one adds free meals given while working for clients, various minor payments and profit on investments, one arrives at the reasonable estimate of around 3,000 r per annum for an average income. This would give the potters an income twice the national average. As the potters are probably around the median in income for the village and Malwa is a relatively fertile area, this result would not be surprising. The income derived specifically from pottery would be slightly more than the 955.45 r estimated by Freed and Freed (1978: 91) for a village near New Delhi.

In comparison to this may be set the estimates of expenditure (Table 10). This is calculated for a nuclear family, such as most of the households represented during fieldwork. These estimates are based on much weaker evidence than that for income, being mainly reliant on an averaging of the suggested requirements of four households. This calculation does not include other expenses, such as interest on debts (which are more difficult to calculate) or the sale of grain when a surplus has occurred, but, overall, it appears that on these annual costs the potters' income exceeded their expenditure. My impression was that as a calculation of normal annual income and expenditure, this would be true of most households in the village, including those who work only as labourers. Yet all the potters, like almost all the villagers, are in fact in debt. The reason for this lies in the expenses of life-cycle ceremonies. These represent a curious oversight in the treatment of South Asian ethnography, where such expenses are usually mentioned only in passing, even though their significance is evident. Dumont, for example, states that the cost of weddings 'is known to be the main cause of debt among Indian peasants, so imperative are the dictates of prestige, even for the poor' (1972: 152), but makes no further comment. Mayer (1960: 225–6) merely records the large expenditure with relatively little comment as to its economic significance. Given all the kin relations and obligations that are activated on these occasions, as documented by Mayer, this lack of emphasis is remarkable, especially in contrast to the extensive literature on ceremonial feasts and exchanges in Melanesia, where I worked previously.

The dowries and the feast expenses of the wealthy *jat* families are notoriously large. One wedding attended during the fieldwork was estimated to have cost between 40,000 r and 50,000 r, and another *jat* gave 4,000 r worth of gold for his only daughter's engagement. The expenses for the parents of the bridegroom are also considerable, often equalling half that of the bride's family. Potters' expenses at weddings and funerals were closely observed, and 5,000–7,000 r seemed a reasonable estimate for total expenses. The cost of such funeral feasts are a major cause of dispute between brothers, and often the immediate cause of splits between them.

In summary, the distribution of pottery, which will be described in the following section, is based within a social and economic context in which customary obligations play a major part. The social position of the potters, symbolised in their account of original settlement, includes a responsibility to the village. Although the provision of ritual pottery and attendance at life-cycle events probably involve less overall work than the provision of secular pottery through the year, they generate more than double the income. But if ceremonies provide an exaggerated income, they also represent by far the greatest expense, often ensuring a lifelong state of debt.

The distribution of pottery

In Dangwara, as in villages throughout India which contain a range of castes, the relationships between castes, involving the exchange of goods and services, may be formalised through a contractual system, known in the ethnographic literature as the *jajmani* system. The term *jajman*, which, as Dumont (1972: 139) notes, originally referred to the relationship between a priest and his patron, is not commonly used in Dangwara, except for priests. The term *asami* is used for the normal contractual arrangements and *ayath* for a stronger bond. *Asami* as used here does not seem to have the negative connotation it carried in other regions. Details will first be presented showing how this system works to distribute pottery in the village, and this will be followed by a discussion in more general terms. This will suggest that the equation commonly drawn between the *jajmani* system and the 'economic' system of the village may be misleading.

The provision of ritual vessels

The term 'ritual vessels', as used here, refers not to the use of these vessels, but to the context of their presentation. The provision of certain pots at fixed times in the annual cycle is taken by villagers to be the most essential service provided by the potter within the formal *asami* system. There are two main festivals at which pottery is presented. At *akhartij* the potter will provide for every client *asami* a *goli*, a *dhakan* and an *akhartij gagra*. At *divali* clients of most castes receive two *divali matka*, two *kulhri* and some *divaniya* (the *gujar* caste on *divali* receive two ordinary *matka*, two *brahman dohni*, two *dhakni*, an unfired *karela* and a *kunda*). Other annual presentations include a *matka* filled with water, placed on the fields of the larger landlords at the beginning of the agricultural year. The weaver and paint-maker castes receive a *karela* two days before *dashera* festival, and four small and one large *divaniya* at the festival of *garbah puja*.

The supply of these pots is fixed and does not relate to demand. If a household is still using the pots from the previous year (often, in effect, six months, as the main pots given on both occasions are water storage pots), it will nevertheless accept the new pots and consign either the new, or more likely the old, pots to storage purposes, to the heap of disused pots or to a general rubbish heap. The giving of these vessels symbolises the *asami* relationship. A potter when asked for a list of his *asami* replied, 'Wait until after *divali*, I have to see who will accept my pots.' Although the supply of secular vessels builds on this relationship, *asami* are not obliged to take these pots from the same potter.

The supply of the water pots is subject to only minimal variation. Larger joint families may take double the usual number. In the *divali* which I observed, only one family in the village was found not to have been supplied: a leatherworker, whose household was absent during the distribution and who never afterwards took steps to obtain the pots. There is more scope for the potter to respond to differences in caste and wealth in the supply of the *divaniya* and *kulhri*. Although everybody agreed that a family ought to receive two *kulhri*, Table 11, which is based on forty households, indicates that this was often not the case.

That the supply of *divaniya* should be associated so strongly with wealth is not surprising, since the oil lamps are used on the evening of the festival to light up the outside of the house and thereby act as a highly visible marker of prestige. Muslim castes also receive these pots and display *divaniya*. A *phakir* actually received the largest number of *kulhri* (one for each of his children, who wanted them as toys). The use of these various pots for religious purposes will be discussed in detail in Chapter

Table 11. *Distribution of* Divaniya *and* Kulhri *at* Divali

Wealth group	Average per household		Caste group	Average per household	
	Divaniya	*Kulhri*		*Divaniya*	*Kulhri*
1	40	4.3	1	22.6	2.6
2	32	2.8	2	20.9	1.7
3	16.3	1.7	3	15.6	1.5
4	19.6	1.7			
5	10.8	1.3			

7, as will the other major area in which ritual pots are provided, the life-cycle ceremonies.

Payments for the provision of these vessels and for all those services which are considered part of the formal system were made either once or twice a year, at *divali* and *akhartij*, which mark the distribution of the proceeds of the two harvests. In the case of a major landowner, the potter might obtain payments at the threshing floor. Often, however, the potter has to wait until a labourer has himself obtained payment before he can receive his due, which may be several weeks after the festival. Payments from the labourers seemed to average around one-third that of the major landowner. The smallest payment weighed was 2 kg of flour. For other service castes, the potter works by reciprocal services and receives no grain, but will obtain repairs for his wooden and metal objects, supplies of basketry, music, hair-cutting and other services. To have a reliable carpenter, for example, as a client is of great importance to the potters. The payments for services at life-cycle events (the details of which are given in Chapter 7) were calculated on the basis of 20 r for the funeral pots, and 50 r for the weddings. Even the poorest household has to give 21 r for its wedding pots, while the richest may give 150 r plus clothes and gifts, such as a watch.

The provision of secular vessels

The provision of secular (black) vessels is theoretically outside the *asami* system. The potters occasionally supply new types of pottery unbidden to their most prestigious clients in the hope of promoting the form, but in general the supply of these vessels is regulated by demand. The potter keeps in store many of the most commonly requested vessels, such as *kareli* and *matka*, following seasonal shifts in demand, and may make a special firing if he receives a series of requests for a particular vessel, such as *dhatri*, otherwise waiting until he is ready for a pottery firing of that colour. Fig. 27 shows how the changing emphasis on different pots is reflected in the annual cycle of production. *Barni*, for example, which

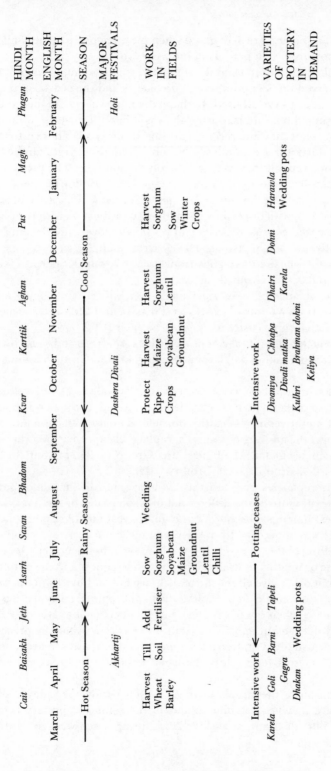

Fig. 27. Seasonal factors in pottery production

are used for pickles, are in demand when the mangoes are ripe, while the festival pots represent periods of intensive work.

The calculation of the supply of most vessels per annum is problematic. Observed rates of production, breakages and the census of pottery currently in use were all used. Perhaps the most successful method was simply asking households, during the caste-based census, how many of each type of pot they had received during the last year. These estimates, based on thirty-three examples, are probably more accurate for the commoner pots, though they may still be on the low side. The provision of pots on non-formal occasions was averaged as the following per annum per household: *kareli* 2.5, *karela* 2.4, *kunda* 2.0, *matka* 1.8, *dohni* 0.8, *wariya* 0.5 and *goli* 0.3, with other pots in smaller quantities. As with the pots in the caste-based census, described at pp. 73–4 above, only certain forms are sensitive to caste divisions. The clearest examples were:

(1) *Dhatri*, whose intake goes from 0.1 for Group 1 castes to 0.2 for Group 2 and 0.4 for Group 3 castes.

(2) The balance between *kareli* and *karela*, which, while being nearly equal in ratio for Group 1 castes at 2.6 *kareli* and 2.7 *karela*, was quite unequal for Group 3 castes at 2.9 *kareli* as against 1.2 *karela*.

(3) A much higher intake of pots, such as *goli*, *kunda* and *matka* by high castes, Group 1 taking 5.0, Group 2 taking 4.6 and Group 3 taking only 0.76.

(4) As with the census of pottery, the overall intake of vessels is positively associated with wealth, despite the evidence for a much larger intake of metal vessels. Wealthy households tend to have many more vessels overall, and do not simply replace cheaper earthenware with more expensive metal. The figures are: Group 1 – 21.3, Group 2 – 23.4, Group 3 – 8.4, Group 4 – 5.9, Group 5 – 9.8.

The discrepancies between this evidence and the census of pottery give some measure of the differential breakage-rates of the pots. These are highest amongst the *kareli/karela* and lowest amongst pots, such as *goli*, which are not moved from their stand when in use.

The selling of these vessels is a familiar event in the potter's house. A high-caste or wealthy householder will send a request and the potter will deliver, but otherwise either the male householder buys from the potter or, often, the female householder from the painter. Payment is not usually made when the pot is given but is collected at a later date. This is usually in cash but may be in grain. Price is established by precedent and is not usually a matter for argument, although there are 'special' requests, such as for slightly damaged pots at a nominal price for a widow.

In addition to the supply of these vessels within the village, all the potters are involved to some extent in the selling of pottery through markets outside Dangwara (Fig. 28). During a ten-week period, one potter went to the market five times, two went twice, a third once and the remaining two not at all. Potters generally sold between one-third and two-thirds of the vessels taken to the market, earning an average of 21 r for each visit made. The total pottery sold in ten visits was:

matka 40	*kareli* 40	*dohni* types 28	*goli* 20
dhatri 19	*karela* 17	*dhakni* 16	*batloi* 11
small *goli* 8	*kunda* 7	*gagra* 4	*kulhra* 4
tapeli 2	*keliya* 1		

In addition, an uncertain quantity of lids and oil lamps were sold. Taken but not sold were *chuklya/kalash, bhartiya, kundi, harawla* and *dhakan*. A potter may also travel around the villages close to Dangwara, selling pottery carried by his donkey. Both these forms of marketing by Dangwara potters reflect the active manufacture by six households in a village of 265 households and the resultant over-production of pottery. A generation earlier, the Dangwara villagers had themselves purchased their black pottery at the market, when the single active potter was unable to supply all the pots needed by the whole village.

Fig. 28. Black pottery on sale in market

Other services performed by the potter

A variety of obligations other than the provision of pottery has accrued to the potters, although they are mainly obvious extensions of that role. The duties of potter and painter at ceremonies will be described in Chapter 7. It is considered extremely courteous, when an important guest arrives, to have the potter come and present a *kalash*, and assist in serving the meal. Potters help arrange ordinary *puja* (prayers) and *yagna* (sacrifices), for example, placing the red *tilak* mark on the foreheads of those attending, or distributing *prasad* (sweets previously offered to the deity). They may assist at a social party, serving food and water. After the drummer caste, they appear to be the most common musicians and singers at the frequent evening singing of sacred songs around the shrine of the mother goddess. They may have special tasks at festivals related to Shitala Mata (the goddess of small-pox) or the elephant-headed god Ganesh, with whom the potters are particularly associated. These tasks may all be seen as extensions of the potter's major duties, either at ceremonies or in his provision of the vessels in which food and water are presented.

The most onerous (and rewarding) additional task is the drawing of water. Three of the potters had long-term engagements for water-drawing, one for a *brahman* and two for *jat*, all amongst the wealthiest members of the village. This task, which is usually undertaken by the potters when the women of the household are unwell or absent, requires the cleaning of all water vessels and their replenishment in the early morning. In a typical case, this required four visits to the well, taking two pots each time. The *brahman* family required twenty pots but, as the potters commented, 'Brahman wash a great deal.' The one household of the potters' caste which did not manufacture pottery nevertheless had contracts to undertake this work. Payments averaged 10 r per month. In addition, potters were required to fetch water on festivals for certain prestigious families, mainly *jat, rajput* and *brahman*, although the household of a lower caste, which was attempting to raise its caste status, also required this service. This duty reflects favourably on the status and ritual purity of the caste, since it is unlikely that high castes would allow a low caste to perform this function. The status of the *kumhar* (potters' caste) varies; in some areas the association with the donkey and its dung is used as a marker for a lower ranking (Saraswati 1979: 47–50), but these factors are not considered significant in Dangwara.

Forms of client relationship and their inheritance

The two terms used for the description of clients are *asami* and *ayath*. The first indicates a relationship of the kind which has already been described, but there is also an additional, still stronger bond, called the *ayath*. This term appears to be flexible in use, but generally the potters refer to a proportion of their clients as such. One potter claimed eight *ayath*, another claimed twenty-three. The potters enthused about their *ayath*; one noted: 'If an *ayath* breaks a *kunda* today, we will will supply him with a new one tomorrow. If we take a *myna* [another word for *matka*] in the morning and they want another in the evening, we will bring it to their doorstep.' One formal difference is that while the *asami* is not required to take the black pots from the potter who is his client, the *ayath* is bound to take all the black pots, which he requires, from that potter. Another difference is that the relationship should ideally be over a longer term, holding through the generations. In effect, then, the *ayath* is an extension of the same principles which bind the *asami*.

A generation earlier, the village households appear to have been divided fairly equally between the father of the four brothers and, once he was old enough to work, the potter of the other line. Today, the number of clients per individual potter who could be ascertained varied from 13 to 71.

It should be noted that the association of a particular *asami* and potter is liable to dispute from both sides of the relationship. Some *asami* were found to have been served by more than one potter. The four brothers were found to have 135 clients as against 94 for the other line. An examination of the castes and wealth of the known clients reveals a different picture. Using the wealth index, the total landholdings of the 94 clients came to 4,120 bigars, as against only 3,880 bigars for the 135 clients; the smaller group also tended to be higher in caste.

Changes in *asami* relationships occur quite slowly. Only three clear cases of a change in association were noted during the year between the two periods of fieldwork. Of 13 who were asked the question, 12 were found to have a potter of the same line as in the previous generation. The occasion of a split is hard to document, since villagers avoid overt conflict and will not openly inform the potter that they are changing, but merely note that another potter has already supplied them. Equally, a potter dissatisfied with payments will simply not supply vessels on the next customary occasion.

Although the reasons given for changes are entirely economic (i.e. disputes over payments), a more subtle basis for change may be deduced from analysis. One potter tends to be known as the '*jat*'s potter', even though he does not, in fact, have the largest number of *jat asami*. In effect the association refers to the factionalism that may be found in Dangwara, as in most similar Indian villages. The *jat* have a particular reputation for factionalism (Pettigrew 1975, Pradhan 1967). Power in the village depends on the gathering of support, which can be brought to bear on elections and decisions relating to the village. Dominance appears to have moved in the last few decades from the minority *brahman* who may have enjoyed the support of the major landlord of the area, to the majority *jat*; but within the *jat* there are now divisions based on national political affiliation. To be known as the '*jat* potter' is to be associated with the dominant group within the *jat* that is, at present, associated with the dominant Congress Party and certain 'liberal' attitudes towards untouchability and other such issues. The same potter appeared to be expanding his numbers of *asami* essentially within that group. This general political stance was dominant in the village, and all potters except one were Congress supporters, although not as closely involved. From general discussion, I obtained information on the stated political affiliation of most of the households in the village, and two-thirds of the *asami* of the one potter who supported the nationalist wing of the Janata party were found to share that political allegiance – the highest proportion for any potter. Therefore, although change is slow, a gradual coherence appears to be emerging between the major factional leanings of the households and the service castes with which they associate. Any morphological or decorative attribute which discriminated between these potters and painters would therefore be loosely symbolic of these social divisions.

Disputes over *asami* appeared to occur as often between the brothers within a family as between the two families, although there is a difference in perspective here, in that the *asami* themselves often regarded the potters more in terms of the larger patrilineage. Disputes were especially strong over *asami* in other villages. In 1981 the potters claimed a total of 59 *asami* outside of Dangwara. If these are added to the 259 households of the village, we obtain an average of 53 clients per potter. This is comparable to the evidence of the survey of Surat by Bose (1980), which gives 25.6 clients within the village and 31.5 in other villages, i.e. an average of 51 clients per potter.

Interpretation of the *asami* system

The *asami* and *ayath* are clearly examples of the *jajmani* system found in diverse forms throughout most of South Asia. In many areas where it is not prevalent it is reported as having died out, but there may be as much spatial as temporal differentiation. In Gujerat, for example, Bose (1980) reports only 3.5% of the potters surveyed as engaged in a formal *jajmani* exchange system, but Pocock (1972: 35) reports that potters exchanged entirely on a cash basis during his fieldwork in 1953–6, and it may be that the system was never strong in that area. There has been a considerable literature on the nature of this system and it has been doubted recently whether there really exists a common phenomenon which should be described in this manner.

The popular (and, outside of academic papers, almost ubiquitous) presentation of the *jajmani* system is that it is virtually synonymous with the internal village economic system. According to the older, functionalist interpretation, it was held to provide the supportive relationships which balanced the disruptive caste system (Wiser 1958); that is, caste was seen to split the village into units which were rendered cohesive again by the *jajmani* system. The main focus of village economics was said to be the contracts between the major landowners and the remaining members of the village. The *jajman* was the wealthy patron, who used the system to procure the services he required, exploiting the divisions of labour represented by the caste system. In the division of his harvest, he provided recompense and subsistence for those who did not grow their own crops. Some analyses have concentrated on questions of exploitation as against integration (e.g. Beidelman 1959, Orenstein 1962). A recent textbook (Malone 1974: 230–2) provides a typical description of the simplified and economistic kind, emphasis being laid upon the services which the artisan castes provide and the proportion of the harvest they may expect to receive, a model also implied by Saraswati (1979: 37) for potters. More recent academic analysis has tended to present a critique of the normative view which represented a constant and simplified system of relationships, pointing rather to the regional diversity and the differences in contractual arrangements for particular groups within any one village (e.g. Good 1982, Pocock 1962, Parry 1979: 59–83. For a critique of these positions based on the Dangwara material see Miller forthcoming b).

The potter's main task is the supply of pottery, but it is only in so far as this task can be represented as the supply of pottery beyond functional need and as a ritual service that it is included within the *asami* system. Furthermore, the general assumption of the dominance of the major landowners is not evident. The potter supplies all households in the village, whatever their caste or income. This supports Gould, who sees the identification of the system with service to landlords as 'one of the most persistent over-simplifications which students of Indian society have perpetrated over the years' (1967: 40). When I first discovered the *ayath* system, I thought that perhaps this bond, with its stronger obligations, might represent the 'real' link to the landlord, which was absent in the ordinary *asami* relationship. There is some association with wealth. The average landholding for *ayath* is 52 bigars, as against 44.3 for *asami*. There are, however, many low-caste *ayath*. One potter has three households of weavers and three of washermen, not necessarily the wealthiest of their caste, and also a landless, labouring paint-maker and a landless tailor. Another potter has two washermen with 8 and 10 bigars respectively, while his richest client is not an *ayath*. *Ayath* is significant in understanding the *jajman* system, but not primarily as a landlord-service relationship.

The separation of the provision of secular and ritual vessels emphasises the division between a 'formal' and 'informal' system of exchange. The formal system may be closely related to certain more general conceptions about the proper relationship held between individuals and society. The concept of *dharma*, which also generates, in part, the system of caste, is central here. At a recent conference on the concept of duty in South Asia (O'Flaherty and Derrett 1978), a major conclusion was that the Western concept of duty emphasises the external pressure which society brings to bear on the individual to perform certain actions that he or she might otherwise be inclined to ignore. The concept of *dharma*, by contrast, emphasises the natural inclination of the individual to perform those actions which are intrinsic to one's birth and therefore character, but which might not be followed because of the influence of society.

Through the *asami* system, the members of the potter's household are able to perform their *dharma* in accordance with their natural inclination, which derives from their birth as members of this caste. This concept is known as *jati dharma*. The potters' relationship with other castes, then, takes a form which represents their work as ritual activities, from which merit will accrue to both giver and receiver. These relations work within the nexus of kind, rather than abstract cash, and through fixed, formal obligation, rather than *ad hoc* utility. They represent a clear example of an embedded system of exchange. In return the potters' service to the village is recognised in *hak* which are their rights to supply the village as against any external potters.

The *asami* system is both embedded and normative. It is to be understood more in the tradition of the work of Mauss (1970) on the fundamental properties of the exchange process, in terms of the relationship thereby created between the giver and receiver. A useful parallel is the work by Munn (1977) on exchange of canoes in the Trobriand system, in which she shows how we can construct a model of exchange which counteracts the property of alienation, intrinsic to the process by which we give away something we have produced. This links with the recent discussion in South Asian anthropology of the non-duality of transaction and person emphasised by Marriot (1976, Marriot and Inden 1977).

This approach treats the *asami* relationship as an ideal system. However, when the relationship is realised as a scheme of practical action, some of the complexity of those other social dimensions, with which it is involved, must be taken into account. The model will distort in the direction of these various practical and contextual forces. In Dangwara, for example, there is the actual inequality of the distribution of the *divaniya* and *kulhri*, associated with the disparities of wealth and caste, and there is the articulation with relations of power expressed through a coherence with village factionalism. It is these factors which account for the different ways in which an ideal model generates different forms specific to their context.

This break into the more informal and variable exchange also allows for a different interpretation of the relationship to the market. The exchange of pottery for cash through the market need not be opposed to the *asami* system, as a more 'rational' modern system replacing a more embedded, traditional system (as might be suggested by the dichotomous approaches which followed the work of Polanyi *et al.* 1957, and most 'evolutionary' models). On the contrary, the market may be understood as assisting in the maintenance of the *asami* system. The potter has a dual responsibility, to work both in the arena of the ideal and also in the arena of the practical. There is a clear demographic constraint. Since a village does not need a large number of potters, the ideal ratio of potter to village requires few families in any single locus. This problem is compounded by the high infant-mortality rate and the late age at which potters learn their trade, so that at any given time a number of villages may be without a potter, despite the relatively high mobility of artisan castes. This acts as a major practical constraint on the ideal system, as does the demand for pots to be used in secular contexts and the need to replace pots in the case of ordinary breakage.

All of these considerations imply that the *asami* system with its formal mode could not, by itself, fulfil the practical needs of the Indian villager, and for this reason a complementary system of exchange on a more *ad hoc* basis is required. In this context, the market system can be seen to provide the flexibility required and thus to help preserve an embedded system from the challenge of utility (compare Bloch 1977). The two modes are, then, complementary, and not opposed. Where possible, exchange is incorporated into the formal mode. A generation earlier, secular pottery was purchased in the market, but now that the village is comparatively 'potter-rich', an increase in the number of *ayath* may be discerned, indicating the extension of formal reciprocal obligations to the secular vessels. Chapters 8 and 9 will show how this division between the formal and informal modes of exchange is closely related to that which is expressed in the morphological and decorative variability of the pottery corpus itself.

6
An analysis of the paintings

On first encounter, the paintings of the Dangwara pottery present as bewildering an array of variability as the shapes. Such an impression is reinforced by observing the rapidity of execution and the subsequent 'loose' style. The term 'style' is nevertheless appropriate here, since any individual example can be recognised as characteristic of the region. As in the analysis of the pottery shapes, the task is to locate those dimensions of variability which underlie and permit the identification of such a style, to look for patterns in the way these dimensions are exploited to generate the observed paintings, and then to attempt to find evidence for the further manipulation of these designs in relation to cognitive and social codes. This chapter therefore includes approaches already applied in the previous discussion of pottery production, use and distribution, but it also introduces some further concepts to be discussed in later chapters. These approaches are applied to a relatively discrete field and one that appears less rich in the manner of its exploitation than the variability of form; nevertheless, it provides some interesting additional examples of the nature and use of visual categories.

The analysis of paintings on earthenware has tended to become subsumed under the general problem of 'style'. In this book the term is used only to denote the characteristic dimensions of variability that establish the place of an individual within a series, but the term has been employed far more widely by others. This is especially the case in archaeology, but to a degree it is also true of a tradition in the anthropology of art, best exemplified by Boas (1955), Gombrich (1979) and Steadman (1979). In archaeology there are two main branches to this enquiry. The first, termed formal analysis, is the investigation of the structure of designs, and the way in which they are 'generated' from elements. There is a long tradition of such analysis and Boas (1955) not only provided an aesthetic theory, relating the manner of production and representation to style, but, in his extended analysis of the art of the American north-west coast, exemplified the method of formal analysis. More recently, Muller (1977), Shepard (1956), Mead *et al.* (1973), Washburn (1978, Ed. 1983) and others have expanded the possibilities of formal analysis, mainly under the influence of its success in linguistics and semiotics. Most studies have as their objective the reduction of variety to simple elements, rules and transformations, sometimes identifying principles employed in the transformation of designs, such a bilateral symmetry. Others attempt to show how, on the model of Chomsky's grammars (1957), rules can be discovered which generate the space-filling of a field by a design (Hodder 1982b: 174–81, Muller 1977). There is also a strong heuristic tradition in ceramic analysis by archaeologists attempting to discover systematic descriptive procedures (Gardin 1965, Plog 1980, Redman 1977).

A second branch of enquiry is concerned with the relationship between the variability of the material and the society which produces it. This relationship has tended to be presented in archaeology in terms of a general notion of social information or interaction, rather than as an analysis of material in its specific context (Hodder 1982b: 212–29). This approach achieved its modern form in the 1960s with the study of prehistoric pottery as an indicator of social or, more specifically, kin interaction (Hill 1970, Longacre 1970). It has been met with several criticisms (Allen and Richardson 1971), and has been investigated in various ethnographic contexts (Graves 1981, Lathrap 1983, Longacre 1981, Stanislawski 1978). The approach reflected a rather passive view of the artefact (Braun and Plog 1982: 509, Plog 1980: 5–8), and there has since been a shift towards an emphasis on style as the exchange of social information (Wobst 1977). Most recent work (e.g. Plog 1980: 136–8, and Wiessner 1983: 256) is strongly influenced by this approach. This new approach, has in turn, been the subject of recent criticism from Hodder (1982b: 191–3), whose ethnographic work (1982a) challenges the assumptions underlying both the social-interaction and the information-exchange theses. At this point, there is some re-articulation between the two branches of the enquiry, because Hodder's own analysis relates the structural principles underlying style in a variety of media, in order to construct a more genuinely contextual approach (1982a: 212–29).

Plog (1983) has recently reviewed the large number of archaeological analyses of stylistic variability in pottery. This suggests that a large number of different analytical units have been used as indicators of an equally large number of temporal, spatial and cultural variables. Apart from these inconsistencies, ethnographic enquiries designed to investigate these relationships have produced often contrary results (p. 126). In one recent volume (Washburn Ed. 1983) divisions in pottery decoration have been taken as directly representative of features ranging from ecological zones (Arnold 1983) to the division of labour (Faris 1983). Two very different conclusions have been drawn from this evidence. Least satisfactory are Plog's own recommendations (pp. 129, 139–40), which are essentially for more of the same. He wants rigorous 'testable' hypotheses for both prehistoric and ethnographic enquiries, with more consistent analytical units selected. Underlying this is the continued positivist assumption that, if we try hard enough, eventually the 'right' analytical unit will be located from which 'correct' cross-cultural or even universal associations may be drawn and applied scientifically to the archaeological record. Hodder (1982a), by contrast, has abandoned any such research aim, and argued that his contextual analysis, which treats any particular trait as having meaning only in relation to the other material variability which is its context in specific historical situations, is a better basis for archaeological analysis.

In general, most of these approaches are a continuation of a rather outmoded debate. They concentrate on style as information about ethnic identity, in the tradition of the discovery of 'cultures', although some use a more sophisticated concept, sensitive to variability and to the polythetic quality of groups, which could replace the culture concept (Hodder 1982a: 2–12, 186–90). The stress is on how similarity in design or design structure relates to identity in groups. The nature of this relationship, like the terms 'interaction' and 'information', is theoretically underdeveloped; a term such as 'information' in particular has become autonomous and detached from any social analysis. Nor has much attention been paid to what the groups identified as a result of this work imply in relation, for example, to current discussions on ethnicity (e.g. Cohen 1974). One of the rare alternative approaches to style, termed by Hodder the 'chamber pot' approach (Braithwaite 1982, Hodder 1982b: 185–9), follows Douglas (1966) in an emphasis on the special treatment of that which is considered dangerous by virtue of its ambiguous position between categories. Such an approach should not be spuriously generalised into a deterministic rule. It may or may not be applicable to a given body of material, depending on the strategies employed in societal reproduction.

At this stage the term 'style' itself should be called into question; even Hodder employs this concept in such a manner as to reify a nineteenth-century abstraction, which is still often defined in opposition to a notion of 'real' function, and which thereby replaces a creditable goal, the study of social relations, by an illusory one based on the assumption that objects will behave in a generalisable way, effectively outside society. Equally problematic are the assumptions about representation implied in these approaches, which employ a simple signifier–signified relationship between cultural traits and society. The manner in which culture constitutes social action as a series of often contradictory material ideologies (Miller and Tilley 1984) is ignored.

The application of formal analysis has indicated both its limitations and its appropriate use. Most of the formal analyses of the structure of design no longer purport to uncover general properties of the mind. They are mainly derivative (for example, from linguistics and semiotics), and virtually any of them may be used to provide the basis for a reorganisation of bodies of material for further analysis. In fact, their heuristic nature, as merely a stage towards a contextual analysis, is suggested by both the more theoretically inclined approaches (e.g. Hodder 1982b: 181) and the more logistically orientated kind (Redman 1977). Ethnographic research (Friedrich 1970, Wiessner 1983) suggests that the various levels revealed by formal analysis relate to corresponding levels in an investigation. This conclusion seems true of formal analysis in general (Lévi-Strauss 1977: 115–45), but this is also relative to the specific enquiry. As a first stage, formal analysis provides a description that may be more informative and parsimonious than the mere listing of motifs, and may provide alternative levels at which to examine the articulation between form and society. This is how it will be employed in this chapter, which begins with a formal analysis and proceeds to investigate the social context of paintings. Style as the term is used here implies a strictly formal analysis which may also assist in determining the degree of formalism embedded in a particular body of material. The dimensions which are used by the analyst to characterise the variability of the material are only a selection, the criteria for which should be heuristic.

The situation in much of India is quite different from that assumed in approaches which are primarily concerned with style as a means for the identification of social groups. In the Dangwara area, there are no language boundaries, only gradations between different dialects of Hindi; there are no clear cultural boundaries, there are no important political boundaries, there is no clear reference point for a spatially defined group-identity, and the same would be true for several hundred miles in any direction from the village. The vertical differences developed within one village are often more pronounced than the differences encountered for a given group over an enormous area. The lack of anticipated 'culture' areas was one of the conclusions of the survey of pottery manufacture by Saraswati and Behura (1966), discussed in Chapter 3. There seems no reason to expect marked plateaux of stylistic homogeneity. The question of stylistic gradation is not a focus of attention in this study. Such an investigation would require a more extensive survey. The critique of a gravity model that assumes a direct relation between distance and stylistic differentiation should, however, be noted (Plog 1976).

In this chapter a description will first be given of the paintings, detailing the elements and 'rules' which were found most useful in recording and comparing them. These will then be examined in relation to the method of painting and the learning of painting. The variability of painting will then be related to the variability of pottery morphology, both within a given pottery category and within the range of forms as a whole. After characterising this variability, its relation to the social context will be explored through examining the pottery distribution, the symbolic significance of the motifs and the structural principles that underlie their combination.

The nature of the designs

The basic corpus of paintings used in this description consisted of 30 *divali matka*, 10 *goli* and 10 *matka* from each of the six pottery-producing households, plus an additional 60 *divali matka* recorded in households during the census. This gave a total of 360 recorded paintings, although many more were observed during the course of the fieldwork. The paintings on smaller vessels, such as *chuklya* and *gagra*, are relatively standardised. In order to facilitate description, it was found that apparently complex paintings could be reduced to a relatively short sequence of symbols which allowed for swift recording. Initially these were developed heuristically, but it will be demonstrated in the description of painting and learning that they model a structure which has significance in other areas. Although reference will be made to some statements which were obtained from the painters, in general there is no verbal equivalent of the kind of analysis and analytical units that are employed here. Little verbal comment of any kind could be obtained from the painters about their products. Villagers appeared to attach even less importance to the paintings on the village earthenware than to the pottery itself.

Fields

Basic to the analysis of all the paintings is the division of the pottery into a series of 'fields' as opposed to the elements which are used to fill them (this is comparable to the distinction between analytic division and synthetic construction; see Hardin 1983). A field is a horizontal band around the vessel within which a particular range of designs may be employed. These exploit the shape of the vessel in a straightforward manner. The first field is the area immediately below the neck, the second is the shoulder down to the place of maximum diameter, which also represents the limit of the area which can be viewed from directly above the vessel. The final field is the area below the point of maximum diameter. The division of the pot is emphasised by the application of the red or white earth, used in painting, in two broad bands, one covering the neck itself, and the other painted on or near the place of maximum diameter (Fig. 29). The *divali matka* and other pots with two *parti* (i.e. a flat facet around the pot) present another potential field for painting, which

Fig. 29. Painting 'd' design on *divali matka*

would divide the shoulder field into two. No painter is consistent in her response to this, and, while the painters of the two brothers' households often create two fields (Fig. 29), this is rarely the case for the households of the four brothers. Where a division is employed, the designs used in both fields are of the range appropriate to the shoulder area, so that, in Saussurian terms, there are still only three fields that are in a syntagmatic relation. To represent a change in field down the pot, in the direction from neck to base, the symbol / was employed.

Elements

An element is a shape irreducible in terms of its use in the paintings, but not itself used in isolation, being elaborated upon in order to produce a motif. The first four elements listed below apply to the neck and shoulder field, the next three to the shoulder field only.

> l – a line
> q – a wavy line with a distance from peak to line centre of about 2.5–3.5 mm
> c – a wavy line with a distance from peak to line centre of about 4–5 mm

w – a wavy line with a distance from peak to line centre of about
    7–15 mm
r – a small circle
s – a spiral
b – a small filled circle (blob).

Procedures

There are two main forms of procedure. The first is 'elaboration' – that
is, the placing of one element around another. The second is the 'filling'
of a field by the repetition of a motif around a pot. The first procedure is
represented by the sequence of symbols, so that 'sc' means that a 'c'
element surrounds an 's' element (Fig. 30: 8). In the neck field, this
means reading down the vessel, since an 'l' around the neck is elaborated
by the 'q' below it. In the shoulder field, however, this means reading up
the pot since the central element often lies on the line indicating the

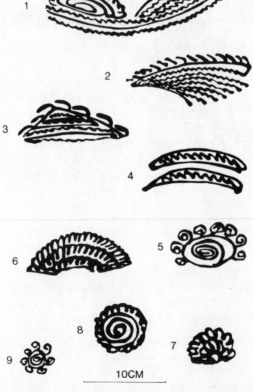

Fig. 30. Various designs used on shoulder of water pots

maximum diameter, as in r2½c where the 'r' has a semicircle of 'c' above it (Fig. 30:7).

Procedures indicating the filling of the field around the vessel are:

–	which means that the motifs before and after the – symbol alternate around the pot.
x3	which means the number of times the motif is repeated around the pot, in this case three (Fig. 31b), an alternative being:
to n	which means the repetition of the motif around the pot, usually at least five times, in order to fill the field (Fig. 31a).
to l or r	which means a motif (usually a 'd'; see below) placed to the left or right of the central motif, possibly linked by a line.
a	which means a motif or element added around the edge of a main motif (Fig. 30: 2, 3, 5 and 9).
,	which separates discontinuous sections of one field.

Motifs

There are two main kinds of motif: those representing mere elaborations of one element upon another element, and those which have to be described by unique symbols. In the first set, a common neck motif would read 'lqlw' (Fig. 32: 1, 2, 4 and 5); reading downwards, this means a line followed by a wavy line, followed by a line followed by a wavy line. All motifs on the neck fill the field, i.e. encircle the pot. For the shoulder field, basic elements such as an 's', an 'r' or a '½r' (i.e. a semicircle) are most often elaborated by a 'c' (i.e. a wavy line round it) or '½c' (i.e. a wavy line around half of it). Thus, Fig. 30: 6 reads as '½r3½c'. A very common motif consists of a 'q' line surrounded by an 'l' line. If this is a short discrete motif, it is called a 'd' and appears only in the shoulder field (Figs. 29, 30: 4 and 34). When the same motif is used in the neck field, it surrounds the field, so as to appear to give an 'lql' reading, and there it is called a 't' motif (Fig. 32: 3, 6). The neck and shoulder fields of Fig. 31b would therefore read: 't / s2½c–scorp,qlq' (which means that the neck has an 'lql' around it, the shoulder has a motif built up of a spiral covered by two semi-circles of wavy lines alternating with a scorpion, and beneath this, but in the same field, there is a line between two slightly wavy lines).

Pan-based motifs

Although the shoulder field may be filled by the simple repetition or alternation of one or two motifs around it, very commonly on *matka* and *divali matka*, and almost always on *goli*, there is an additional framework underlying the composition. A field consists of a circular band around the vessel; if a square or triangle is drawn within this, the curvature of the

Fig. 31a. Painting in white on *divali matka*

Fig. 31b. *Divali matka* with additional rim decoration and scorpion design

vessel produces a series of three or four ovals alternating with three or four inverted triangles. In Dangwara the triangles thereby produced are almost always filled with alternate, diagonal 'l' and 'q' lines. The resultant design is called *pan* by the painters, being said to resemble the leaf used in chewing areca nut (Fig. 33, lower vessel in Fig. 43).

The shoulder field of the *goli* usually consists of a *pan* x4 alternating with some other motif. The *divali matka* and *matka* have only three *pan*, again alternating with another motif. There are several other designs which may have been derived from a further abstraction of this same principle. Some *matka* and *divali matka* have shoulder fields consisting of either ovals 'o' or triangles 'tr'. The filling of these is more variable than that of *pan* and has to be symbolised separately in a round bracket following. This usually consists of 'q' or 'l' lines and a direction, so that 'tr(diagq)' means a series of triangles filled with diagonal 'q' lines (Fig. 31a). In addition, these motifs may have other elements or motifs added around them, which are placed after the bracket, resulting in, for example, 'o (horiz lq) filled d' (Fig. 30: 3). In the corpus recorded, all

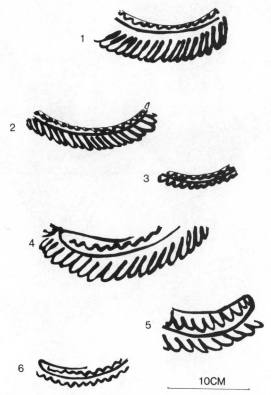

Fig. 32. 'tw' and 'tq' designs used on neck of water pots

except one of the *goli* of the six households had *pan* x4. For the *divali matka* the percentage occurrence of *pan* x3 and 'tr' or 'o' motifs is given in Table 12.

Table 12. *Percentage use by painters of selected motifs on* divali matka

Household of painter	*pan* %	'tr' or 'o' %
D	59	3
A	38	3
B	11	0
C	2	41
F	0	6
E	0	0

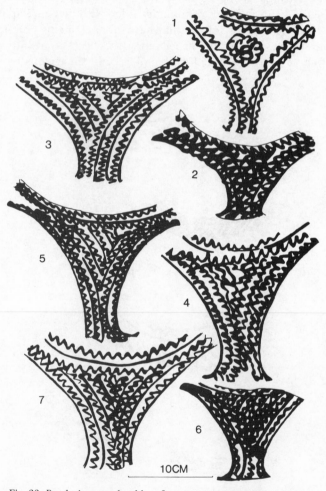

Fig. 33. *Pan* designs on shoulder of water pots

Representational motifs

The designs used on the shoulder include some which are clearly intended to be representational as opposed to those such as *pan* which may be so interpreted by informants, but which would not be evident as such to the outside observer. There are only two that are used with any regularity, the peacock (pea) (Fig. 35), and the scorpion (scorp) (Fig. 36: 4–7, Fig. 31b), and even these are not very common within the corpus, reaching only 13% for the scorpion in one household and 10% for the peacock in another. In Fig. 35, examples of the peacock are given from each of the main painters, and it is evident that, although these motifs are representational, they are, in most cases, derived from the same standard range of elements, such as 's' for the body of the peacock and 'd' for the tail. Other representational figures are very rare indeed. The elephant in Fig. 36: 3 is the only example of this animal noted, and the two fish (Fig. 36: 1, 2) are also single instances. Other motifs made up of

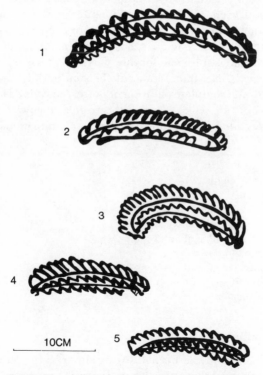

Fig. 34. Long 'd' design used on shoulder of water pots

element-combinations may be interpreted by both painters and other villagers as *phul* (flowers), in a general sense, and some are sufficiently 'naturalistic' to be perceived as such by a naïve observer.

Basal field

The designs applied below the maximum diameter are quite distinct from those used in the other two fields. Only four varieties are found in Dangwara and all are repeated around the field:

cr   intersecting semicircles (Fig. 37).

l   a series of short vertical strokes.

v   a series of angular lines produced with a slightly folded cloth (Fig. 29).

diag a set of diagonal lines from the maximum diameter to the base, usually augmented by a solid circle of colour at the base itself.

Some of the larger *goli* (e.g. middle pot of Fig. 24) are painted with a 'diag' below an 'l' design.

This account does not exhaust the distinctions that could be made or allow for every motif seen. The representations are sometimes schematic and do not include all variations. More unusual or complex designs had to be described in full. The code does, however, account for most of the observed variation and is sufficient for the analysis that will follow in this chapter. More precise discrimination would become unduly complex. As an example of how the complete painting of pottery may be described on the basis of this code, ten typical *divali matka* are given below; if read from left to right the coded descriptions generate unambiguous painted designs:

          t / *pan* x3–dd / cr
          t / *pan* x3–longdc / l
          tw / b to n /
          tq / sl/2cx6,lql,qlqlq / cr
          tq / *pan* x3–r2cd½ctol&r / cr
          qlq / r2½cx4–d½c,qlq,d½cx7 / cr
          qlq / dx6,qlq,d to n / cr
          qlq / ddx3–rc,qq,dx6 / v
          qlq / dx3–rc,qq,dcx3–rc / v
          qlq / w,dx5 / v

The method of painting

Painting is most commonly performed sitting either on the veranda or in the immediate vicinity of the house, where the pots have been left to dry after being beaten out. Since few instruments are needed, the choice of area is relatively unconstrained. Usually a piece of sacking is laid out for the painter to sit on and turn the vessel (Fig. 37). The paint is kept in a *pawanda* or occasionally in some other pot form. Since five of the six households only use red ochre, and the sixth uses white paint only on occasion, the description will be based on the use of ochre. Prior to painting, the pot is covered in a self-slip using the levigated clay from the clay pit, by running a cloth around the vessels or turning it against the cloth.

The 'fields' described above are established before painting by using a cloth, dipped in the *pawanda* of ochre, to rub around the neck and then the place of maximum diameter. This does not create a distinction between the shoulder and neck fields, which are separated in the course of painting. The first area to be painted is always the basal field. The painters of the households of the four brothers use a cloth to draw the 'cr', 'l' or 'diag' motifs. For their *divali matka* and *matka*, the painters of the other two brothers' household often slightly fold a piece of cloth and press it about forty times around the pot, to create the 'v' motif, but on their *goli* they use the same combinations as the other households. After the basal field

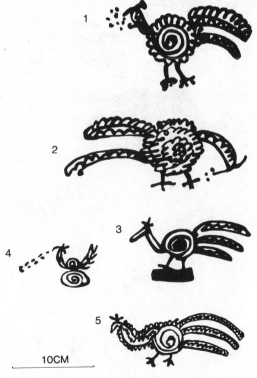

10CM

Fig. 35. Peacock design used on shoulder of water pots

has been painted, the rim is wiped with the cloth. This completes the first stage of painting, based on the use of cloth.

For the second stage of painting, the spine of a date-palm leaf is used; date-palms are plentiful in the area. The leaf is slightly blunted against the side of a metal vessel, or bitten. About two-thirds up from the tip, a small pad, usually of the painter's own hair, is wrapped around the spine, to act as a reservoir of paint. Initially the whole instrument is dipped into the ochre solution and then squeezed to remove excess paint. When paint starts to run dry the pen can be jarred or slightly squeezed to start the flow again. A similar instrument is used in many parts of India for this and other related tasks, such as cloth-painting. The first area to be painted with this spine is always the neck field. The painter runs the spine tip at an angle to the vessel, just under the neck, about half way round for a *matka* (less for a *goli*) and then doubles back, leaving a space. This is then repeated for the other side of the vessel, and a 'q' line is drawn between the resultant 'l' lines, with a slight finger movement to

10CM

Fig. 36. Fish, elephant and scorpion designs used on shoulder of water pots

produce the wave effect. This completes the 't' design, which is the most common form of neck motif (Fig. 31b).

For the shoulder field, the *pan* is usually drawn first, starting with the two outer crescents, each being drawn by a straight movement across the field, producing a curve on the surface. The painter then draws a 'q' line and then, doubling back beneath this, an 'l' line, and so forth, alternately. This is repeated on all three sides of the triangle to fill the entire *pan*. The painter may draw all three or four *pan* before the motifs that alternate with it, but often does not do so. For other motifs the order of painting is again as that suggested in the description of recording. The central element is drawn first and then the elaborative elements are drawn around it. Painters who divide a two-*parti* vessel into a double shoulder

Fig. 37. Painting the shoulder field

field tend to draw the two sets of motifs around the field before the lines (usually 'qq' or 'qlq') that divide them; the lower section may be left blank (Fig. 31a, b). The time taken to complete a painting varies from around three and a half minutes for a simple *divali matka* to ten minutes for a complex *goli*. Typically the first stage takes a minute to one and a half minutes and an individual *pan* motif takes half a minute. Other shoulder motifs, depending on their complexity, take between eight seconds and over a minute each.

Learning to paint

It will be evident that the order of painting – for example, the division of the field by *pan* and the development of a motif from an element – reproduces in most details the pattern developed for the recording of the paintings. The order of fields is different, since the basal field is painted first and described last, but in general the two accord well. The pattern is again found in the investigation of the order in which painting is learnt.

The social context of painting and learning to paint is extremely complex in Dangwara, despite the fact that there are only six households engaged in pottery manufacture. Firstly, while a consistency in potting may be assumed throughout, since there is only one potter per household, this is not the case with painting. This may be related to the dominance of the male in the society. Occupation is generally associated with the male, even when the female is carrying out as much, if not more, of the work. For example, in agricultural labour, what is seen as the 'real' work of sowing and threshing may be male-dominated, while the 'peripheral' work of weeding may be female-dominated. As the government report on the status of women in India suggests, 'what is important is that the tasks assigned to men are considered more prestigious in most communities and regions' (ICSSR 1975: 29). This clearly presupposes the male dominance in establishing status hierarchies, and does not deal with possible areas of female domination. This conflict will be discussed below. There are many examples of this in the descriptions of craft manufacture in the 1961 Census of India. While it may be important to villagers that a product can be associated with a particular male, it may be a matter of no consequence as to whether the part that is contributed by the female is associated with any particular female: the pot is still known as the potter's, and not the painter's, product. In all households where the potter is married, the main painter is his wife. In the case of the only unmarried potter, it is his mother. It is common for sisters to return to their natal village, often for around two months in each year, especially when they are relatively newly married. During their stay they are expected to work alongside the family, and in fact the paintings observed included a major contribution from potters' sisters, daughters and in one case a widowed mother-in-law who spent much time visiting her daughters.

Although the six households studied here are all actively engaged in potting, this does not make marriage into other families who are also active potters more attractive. On the contrary, one of the main reasons for not potting is the possession of sufficient land, or other employment, since farming or wage-labour is generally more prestigious than artisan work. Given the dominant ideal of hypergamy, the potters preferred to marry their daughters to wealthier families who did not pot. Of the marriages or engagements noted in potter families between Dangwara and other villages, there were six cases where a female from a potting household married into one which did not pot, five cases of a move between two households that potted, and the remaining four cases of a female coming to a household that did pot, from a household that did not.

Although information collected during the village census suggested that marriages were contracted at an average distance of 39.5 km from Dangwara, for seventeen members of the potters' households whose villages could be located the average distance was 25 km, one case being more than twice this distance. If styles of design shift gradually over distance –a possibility for which there is some evidence (see below) – this might be expected to reveal itself in the differences between the painters in the village who came from different areas. Such differences would not, however, be significant markers, since, although the area from which painters come is large, they are all from Malwa. There is no division within Malwa that appears to be of particular concern to villagers. This may, in part, account for the emphasis on learning painting from the affinal household, after marriage. Children in Dangwara, including a daughter of twelve, might play at painting, but were unable to paint. One painter claimed that she might teach her daughter some painting since she was marrying into a pottery-producing household, but this would not be a serious training. Engagements are arranged at a very young age, often before the child is six, and therefore the ability to paint is not a criterion in the choosing of the bride. Two painters claimed to have known something of painting before coming to Dangwara, but all painters claimed that their learning was dominated by their mother-in-law, thereby reproducing the styles of the affinal household and in turn the dominant status of the male.

This conclusion is supported by evidence from the paintings themselves. If prior knowledge of painting were important, we should expect to be able to detect the regional origins of the painters from the paintings; but while one painter comes from the south and another from the north, their style of painting is relatively similar. The main distinction between painters does not derive from their area of origin, but tends to express their social relations within the village. In particular, there is the major rift between the two patrilineages represented, who are often on bad terms. Table 12 shows the difference in the use of 'tr' and 'o', which are virtually absent in the paintings by the households of E and F. There is also a complete difference in the choice of basal field for the *divali matka* and *matka*. Close inspection of the paintings reveals the much looser-style *pan* on the *goli* of the households of E and F. In one case (Fig. 33: 4), there is no use made of the 'l', in another case (Fig. 33: 1), there is the employment of a separate motif instead of the complete filling up of the inside. The representation of the peacock (Fig. 35: 1, 2) also shows some similarity between these two households – for example, in portraying the head and tail, as compared to the other households. All of this is to be expected, given that there are only two main learning-sources, represented by the two mothers-in-law. There is an additional 'noise' above this pattern, reflecting the idiosyncrasies of all the painters in their particular interpretation of motifs. The clearest example of this is found in the representation of the scorpion. Some of these differences may be picked up on return visits to natal villages and incorporated, so that area may have some impact upon style, but such an influence is clearly secondary.

The painters all claimed that their designs were identical to those used in their natal villages, but this discrepancy between observation and statements was common in all discussions about paintings. My own observations suggested that change over distance, while certainly to be found, is indeed quite gradual. Even in Mandsour, at a distance of over 100 km, the basic elements and structure of the designs are the same, although the *pan* has pronounced differences and the shoulder motifs are built up towards much more representational flower forms. The most common of these was a long 'd' with 's' or 'r' below, and a flower including 'd' to 'r' and 'l' above. The base often had two thick 'q' lines between thick 'l' lines. Bose describes the common use of wavy lines between straight lines in Gujerati pottery (1980). Only in Udaipur, more than 200 km from Dangwara, in the state of Rajasthan, were both elements and processes observed to be quite dissimilar, though the division into fields was the same. More systematic transects would be needed to confirm this impression of gradual change. Changes in structure may have a spatial referent. *Pan* designs were common in Mandsour to the north, but the use of 'tr' and 'o' designs, which, as was suggested above, represent an abstraction from *pan*, was common in villages visited to the south. The only example of this phenomenon mentioned by the Dangwara painters was the dominant colour, certain regions being said to tend towards using only white, only red, or both.

The actual process of learning was observable from the daughters-in-law of painters in Dangwara. It was said that the initial learning commonly takes six months to a year depending on the interest of the individual. One daughter-in-law could only paint the basal design, although she had been living in Dangwara for four years. The description of the order of learning given by another woman is instructive. After learning to apply slip to the pot, she then learnt to apply the field divisions, followed by the basal-field designs. At the time of fieldwork she could paint the neck-field designs, but had not yet learnt the shoulder motifs, which would start with the *pan*. This sequence is identical with the painting of the individual pot and again suggests that the patterns made evident by the system of recording are not without significance. Learning begins with the *matka* and smaller vessels and ends with the more complex *goli*. Opinions expressed on the quality of designs always used the same term for good artistry: *barik*, which otherwise means thin. Opinions as to good quality, given in response to my questions, were consistent among villagers, particularly as to who were considered the best painters.

Paintings and pottery variability

Although the number of basic symbols required to describe the pottery paintings are few, the combinations and complete designs constructed from these elements are impressively varied. Only some of this variation is the result of differences between painters, since each painter uses a large repertoire of designs. To understand the ways in which the paintings are used, they may first be related to the variability of the pottery itself. Painting can be related to the variety of the shapes in the form of a general gradation between size and complexity. While a large *goli* may have 'lclc / *pan* x4–½r3½c / l,diag', a small water pot such as a *gagra* will probably have only a 't / b to n / l'. The *akhartij gagra* may have a 't / w / cr', while the *kalash* has only 't / w'. This relationship between size and painting is obvious as a glance, but, through measurement, a more subtle relationship can be found within the category represented by a particular pot form.

In Fig. 38a the maximum diameters of forty *divali matka* of one painter are shown and against them the presence or absence of an idiosyncratic decoration. This is the application of four sets of double dashes along the rim of the pot (Fig. 31b). The result is two quite discrete classes: all pots with a maximum diameter larger than 29.6 cm have this additional decoration and no smaller pots possess it. This decoration is only applied by this particular painter to these pots, but the same pots also show some association (Fig. 38b) between size and the use of the more common complex designs such as *pan* 'tr' or 'o'. As a non-potter, I had difficulty locating even the largest and smallest ends of this spectrum by eye, and would not have guessed at such fine discrimination. Fig. 38c–e provides details of the *divali matka* recorded for three other painters and in each case some appropriate measure of the complexity of the motif has been used, to set against size. While not as striking as the first result, all of the histograms reinforce this evidence for a close relation between decoration and size within the pot type, and an extraordinary ability on the part of the painters to judge size.

The *divali matka* was the only pot recorded in sufficient quantities to produce this kind of result. There are suggestions, however, that there may be a similar gradation within other pottery forms. Only one of the ten *goli* from one painter did not have *pan*, but this was also the smallest. Another painter used a kind of pseudo-*pan* (Fig. 33: 1) on three of her pots and again these were on three out of her four smallest pots. There is little evidence for the *matka*, except that two of the samples included a single vessel with *pan* decoration which in both cases was the largest vessel of the group.

This result indicates the creation of a hierarchical gradation within what might have been seen as homogeneous categories. The same gra-

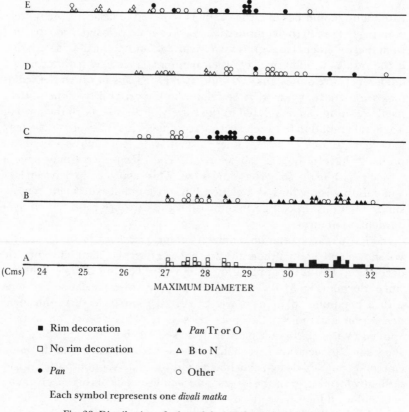

■	Rim decoration	▲	*Pan* Tr or O
□	No rim decoration	△	B to N
●	*Pan*	○	Other

Each symbol represents one *divali matka*

Fig. 38. Distribution of selected designs by size of vessel

dation is used across the painted pottery corpus as a whole. In part this must be related to the larger surface area presented by the larger pot, as is probably the case with the use of *pan* x4 on the *goli*, compared to the *pan* x3 on the *matka*. But this is only part of the explanation, since there is also a striking difference between the *divali matka* and *matka*, which are essentially the same size. The former tends to have more elaborate and more naturalistic paintings, the difference in this case being related to the context of presentation. Designs such as 'b to n' are more common on *matka* and there is more repetition. For example, one entire group of ten *matka* had 't / 2dx3–r2c / l'. *Batloi* are sometimes painted, although they are more usually solid red or solid black. When painted, the strong *parti* division is more likely to be marked by a dual shoulder field. *Gagra* and *chuklya* are almost inevitably decorated with 'tw / l' – that is, with no separate shoulder field – although some *gagra* may have 'b to n'. There is virtually no use of painting except for these water pots, though one potter has attempted a naturalistic palm tree on his *kunda* for tree-growing, and on occasion adds a design to his musical instruments. One of the clearest examples of a hierarchy in painting is the piles of pots used at a wedding. An example from a leatherworker's wedding at a village 25 km to the south was (reading upwards from the basal pot): (1) 't / *pan* x4–pea&dc / ldiag', (2) 't / longdcx5 / lcr', (3) 'tw / v', (4) 'tw / v', (5) *bujhara*.

There is, then, a complementary hierarchy both between pottery forms and within them. This example shows the creation of a dimension that is then open to exploitation by potters and painters in a variety of ways. On the basis of interviews it would have seemed that they were so exploited. Potters agreed that there was a gradation within a pottery category and that the wealthier *asami* would receive the finer pot. In a marriage, for example, they would obtain a more carefully decorated group of pots. In Chapter 5 it was found in the distribution of *divaniya* and *kulhri* that, while it was claimed there was an equal quantity given to all, observation revealed a gradation related to caste and wealth. In this case the opposite was found: the potter claimed that the gradation was exploited in precisely this manner, but in the census of pottery the results are not so clear. The only pot form measured within the houses in sufficient quantity to enable a search for such a relationship to be attempted were the thirty-two *divali matka* of one potter. When set against wealth classes there is at most a slight tendency to give less decorated pots to the very poorest households. General inspection of other pot forms, and comparisons with caste groups, all suggested a lack of association. On observation of the distribution of pots, I had the impression that the potters themselves may well modify their own ideal conception, which is that painting ought to be appropriate to *asami*, with more pragmatic considerations in that they compensate for a fine pot by pairing it with a less good example, so that no household received two poor-quality pots and criticism was thus forestalled. Given that it is the males who determine the distribution of the pottery, it is quite possible that more effort is taken to create the gradation than to exploit it.

The symbolism of painting

There are two levels at which the question of what the paintings 'represent' may be posed, representation being understood in the looser sense of patterns of evocation, rather than absolute signifier–signified pairs. The first is at the level of the motifs and designs, some of which are clearly naturalistic, and the second relates to the underlying structure that generates the paintings, which may also be shown to have a coherence with structural principles generating pattern in other media.

Representation in motif may be judged on two criteria; the first may be based on the statements made by members of the community and the second upon an analysis of the structure of the designs. I suggested in Chapter 1 that in studies of symbolism there is an emphasis on language, either as the direct determinant of the extent of representation or through the use of models derived from linguistics. Lévi-Strauss, even when considering relatively autonomous symbolic domains such as ritual and music, still emphasises the mediation of language (1981, final chapter). The Dangwara villagers ascribed labels to the peacock, scorpion and other animal or fish representations, and more generally to *phul* (flowers). Painters occasionally mentioned particular flowers, such as *gulab* (rose), but this was not done consistently and may represent *ad hoc* interpretation under pressure from myself. Most often painters and other villagers professed not to see any representational link with a given design.

It is possible, however, to apply additional criteria from external analysis to the degree of likely representation. These may be derived from the processes by which designs are constructed – motifs being formed, for example, from elements and procedures evident in the processes of painting and learning, and recoverable from the heuristics of recording. Some motifs are directly generated by this analysis, and are therefore easy to describe according to the system set out above; for example, an 's3c' motif is a simple way to describe a 'flower'. Most observed designs fall into this category, which is what enables formal description to reduce the observed variability so effectively. For the peacock, however, although the same elements are used, they are combined in ways that are more complex and are not immediately generated from these principles. It is easier to give this design a separate name than to use the formal description. The attempt at naturalism thus tends to break down the formal properties of the design system and distort it in the direction of the particular. It is an example of the more informal uses of style as defined here. Since most of the motifs that come under this general label of 'flower' seem to be more tightly based in the formal system, it seems reasonable to see them as essentially formal motifs subject to interpretation; their 'meaning' is thus a relatively separate and secondary process, whilst the 'meaning' in the case of the peacock is itself part of the process that generates the form. In short, the easier it is to describe a design in formal terms, the more likely it is that its interpretation as an evocative symbol will be secondary. The importance of secondary interpretation was clearly illustrated in the work of Boas (1955).

The figures that are represented by more naturalistic motifs are few, and they noticeably exclude the common village domesticates, such as cattle, which are represented in various forms in some festivals, but never appear on pottery. Peacock, scorpion and occasionally fish make up the repertoire, and the painters give no clue as to any link between them. This is, however, a woman's art, and literature on other women's art forms and folk song may be suggestive. In her work on henna decoration, which is used on the hands and feet in Rajasthan (and is found, although in a less elaborate form, in Dangwara also), Saksena (1979: 63) relates the motifs used to the content of village songs. She suggests that the scorpion represents love, there being songs about girls smitten by love as by a scorpion, while a peacock represents beauty, as does a fish which stands for the eyes of a beautiful girl. There may be a similar basis for the popularity of these motifs in Dangwara, but my access to information about women's art and interpretation was very limited. Whatever the reasons for the motifs, they come into conflict with another set of criteria which may account for the lack of domesticates on the pots. An anecdote collected not only by myself but also by Shri Wakankar of the Vikram University (pers. comm.) is about why the painters of Dangwara never paint peacocks on their pottery. The reason given is that the peacock is the national bird of India and it is forbidden to kill it. The potters fire their vessels after the painting and therefore they would be responsible for a kind of symbolic killing; it is therefore not possible to paint the bird, and when I first observed it, the adults refused to acknowledge it as representation, but the children, collapsing with laughter, screamed, 'Peacock! Peacock!' There may be more complex overtones to this radical dichotomy of verbal and visual expression. The ritual slaying of a peacock is performed at the village wedding ceremonies and Sahi comments on the polysemic symbolic quality of the bird (1980). They are in fact one of the most common creatures around the edge of the village.

The other possible level of symbolic interpretation is that of the structure of the designs, which essentially have two main characteristics. Firstly, there is the use of alternate motifs imposed on a radial symmetry, and secondly there is the use of triangles and squares, within and around circles represented by the *pan* motifs. There are, in Dangwara, very few other designs with which these paintings can be compared. There is a little jewellery decoration and a variety of designs are found on clothing, but there is no secular painting, and the main loci in which paintings are found are those used in domestic houses at the time of weddings and festivals and at other times only on shrines and temples. If the type of paintings found around the temple are compared with those on the pots, then they at first appear to be quite dissimilar (Fig. 39), in that none of the same elements or motifs is found. If, however, the paintings of the pots were transposed to a flat surface, then they would produce precisely the same form of radial symmetry with alternate motifs that characterises the paintings on the shrines. One of the most common symbols of Hinduism, the *swastik*, is based on this principle.

This basic structure is complicated by the *pan*, which is produced by the drawing of a square or triangle within a circle but on a curved surface. The most fundamental of all designs in Hinduism is the *mandala* which is defined by the dictionary of Hinduism as follows: 'Basically they consist of a circular border enclosing a square divided into four triangles' (Stutley and Stutley 1977: 178). The *mandala* is a ubiquitous element in

Fig. 39. Paintings on the wall of a village shrine

the analysis of Hindu art; it is the basis for the plans of the Hindu temple (Boner and Sharma 1972), it is basic to the henna designs mentioned above (Saksena 1979), and it is the essence of the *yantra* used in tantric art (Khanna 1979). The symbolic connotations of such designs are highly complex. The form mentioned by the Stutleys is only one variety; there are also complex arrangements of circles within squares within circles. Major rituals comprise the movement around a circle within a square, an example of which will be given in the next chapter, and it may be that the alternate motif, such as in the *swastik*, suggests this movement around the radial symmetry encompassed by the power of the *mandala* arrangement.

Conclusion

This chapter has developed a formal system of recording for the designs used on pottery. Although this was developed heuristically as the most efficient method of reducing the observed variability, it was found to accord closely with both the order in which painting is carried out and the order in which it is learnt. Once developed, this formal order can be used as a criterion for distinguishing primary representation from secondary interpretation of individual designs. Finally, it was found that some of the underlying structural principles may be related to Hindu devotional symbolism. These relationships are viewed as specific, and although a similar process from formal to contextual analysis may be followed elsewhere, the units employed here are unlikely to be appropriate in any other case.

The articulation of these paintings with their social context is strongly mediated by the sexual division of labour, and the tendency for female labour to be regarded as inferior to male labour. The products of this labour may then reproduce the basic asymmetry of gender relations. Several instances of this were found. The products of the painters, like their names, are most closely associated with their affinal rather than their natal origins. The product could be more easily associated with the potter's household than with an individual painter, and the similarity between paintings was dominated by affinal links, with learning acquired primarily through the mother-in-law. The attempt by the painters to create significant variability, in fine discriminations within a pot category, does not seem to be exploited by the potters in the pottery distribution. The naturalistic designs may be related to the sphere of women's arts, such as song and covert discourses on love, that tend to be practised away from the presence of males. There undoubtedly exists a complex alternative female discourse, which I did not study, but there is a question as to the degree to which it is objectified in this particular range of material variability. It may be that this conclusion reflects the inability of a male observer to tease out the ability of the covert female world to challenge that of the male, but the general impression was that paintings, as female products, do not penetrate into the dimensions strongly linked with power and status such as wealth and caste. Further analysis of this material in Chapter 9, including a discussion of the implications of this formal order in itself, will follow the more contextual analysis of pottery forms in Chapter 8.

7
The ritual context

Introduction: the potters' religion

The very extensive use of pottery in ceremonies became evident early on in fieldwork, and appeared a promising perspective which might provide insights into the nature of pottery variability other than the conventional approaches *via* technology and function. In this chapter a description will be given of some of these ritual uses, and it will be shown that this does represent valuable information – not because the pottery is found to be clearly 'symbolic', in the sense of 'representational', but because it provides information as to more complex ways in which the pottery corpus helps in the construction of particular forms of social actions and interpretations.

A brief account of the potters' own religious affiliations will be followed by a description of pottery use at the major life-cycle and annual ceremonies. This may serve to complement the description of the secular use of pottery in Chapters 4 and 5. The chapter ends with a preliminary model for the understanding of the material presented. The material on both secular and ceremonial use will be combined in the overall analysis of the pottery as a meaningful dimension, in Chapter 8.

In Chapter 5, it was suggested that the process by which pottery was distributed was embedded in certain religious ideals pertaining to the potter and painter by reason of their caste membership. The potters' caste have their own place in the complex religious tradition of Hinduism. In ethnographic analysis, Hinduism is conventionally graded, from the worship of the pan-Indian divinities of the Sanskritic tradition to the parochial and particular local saints and shrines (Harper Ed. 1964, Sharma 1970). In Hindu theology, lower-level deities are often thought to represent aspects of the higher divinities, which become more accessible to comprehension through their objectification in more mundane manifestations. Each caste tends to be associated in worship with aspects of those divinities appropriate to them. Thus higher castes emphasise the major deities, the *brahman* being associated with the whole pantheon, the *bairagi* with Vishnu and the *gusain* with Siva, while the lower castes emphasise local non-Sanskritic figures (Marriot 1955). The potters were found, however, to have associations with individual figures at every level.

At the very highest level they recognise and speak of a concept of god that is unity (*Ishwar* or *Bhagwan*). Of the high deities, they are most strongly associated with the elephant-headed god, Ganesh, and all six households have representations of Ganesh in their private shrines. One potter distributed to his *asami*, at the festival of *holi*, plaster of paris images of the god, purchased in Ujjain. The third level of deities is that associated with the various manifestations of the *mata* (mother) image, some of which are known only locally, but others, including the smallpox goddess, *shitala mata*, with which the potters are most closely associated, are well-known nationally. The potters undertake certain purificatory rituals at her shrine on behalf of the village, and, with the drummers, receive in return cooked food previously presented to the deity (*prasad*) and cloth. It is likely that the potters' link with the goddess is through their common association with the donkey, which is the conventional vehicle of the goddess. Finally, they have their own 'potters' saint',

Fig. 40. Religious painting showing miraculous preservation of kittens from pottery firing

known as Goraji, about whom they have many tales. Some of these stories are illustrated in a series of prints produced by a potter in the nearby town of Indore and displayed in the house of one of the Dangwara potters. These show, for example, how Goraji, as a disciple of Krishna, was saved from the sin of killing living creatures, when some kittens that wandered into his pots emerged unharmed by the firing (Fig. 40). This is similar to an ancient Puranic legend, which Saraswati records as being widely known amongst Indian potters (Saraswati 1979: 84). Another painting tells how Krishna saved Goraji's child, who was trodden into the clay during kneading because the potter was so intent upon his prayers (Fig. 41).

Myths of origin also exist for the potters' caste and for some of the instruments which they use. The myth of caste origin is the conventional story of Parasurama, common to many castes in the area (Mayer 1960: 61–2). More interesting is a story collected in Ujjain about the origin of the tools. The potter told of how, when dragons (*raksha*) still roamed the earth in large numbers, they caused concern to the gods. Brahma then made a doll from the dead skin he had rubbed off in cleaning himself, and Vishnu breathed life into it, in order to slay them. It was held, however,

Fig. 41. Religious painting showing miraculous saving of baby trodden into clay

that if the blood of a dragon should touch the earth, more would then be created, so it was necessary to create a bowl in which to catch the blood of the slain dragons. For this, Vishnu gave the wheel that revolves around his finger, and Siva his loin cloth to wipe the rim of the pot, his long stone used for grinding hemp as a stick to turn the wheel, the *pawanda* vessel for holding the water, and finally his *lingam* as a cylinder of clay (compare Saraswati 1979: 80). No such story could be found in relation to the paddle and anvil equipment, and any association with the wheel of Vishnu or the *lingam* of Siva was denied by the Dangwara potters, who claimed ignorance of this story.

The use of pottery at weddings and funerals

The importance of the two life-cycle events of weddings and funerals has already been discussed in terms of their financial implications, these ceremonies representing a major cause of village indebtedness. Their importance is further demonstrated by their complex nature as ceremonial occasions. Babb notes: 'It would be highly misleading to state that there is a particular marriage rite in Chattisgarh. In fact in most cases there is an elaborate sequence of rituals leading to the married state, and the nature of the sequence varies greatly with caste and family circumstance' (1975: 81). This point is exemplified by Gupta (1974), who provides details of thirty-seven separate ceremonies performed during the wedding (pp. 78–96), and a further six post-nuptial ceremonies (pp. 97–103). A detailed description of a wedding in a Malwa village is given by Mayer (1960: 227–35) with an emphasis on kinship obligations.

Although this is often not clear in ethnographies, descriptions of events in an Indian village cannot assume a homogeneous 'subject' as a basis for description, but only a spectrum of variability correlated with other dimensions, such as caste and wealth. The following description of the use of pottery is based on observations of three weddings, covering the range in caste. These were: a leatherworker's wedding in a village to the south of Dangwara, the marriage of a Dangwara potter and his sister's son to two sisters in a village to the north-west, and the marriage of a wealthy *jat*'s daughter in Dangwara. Not all the ceremonies are performed in any one wedding. Rather, the wedding is subject to 'telescoping' (Metcalf 1981); while there are many ceremonies that may be carried out to express caste, status, wealth or piety, there is a series of core rituals which are essential for all groups. In this case, as might be expected, it was the wealthy *jat* wedding which displayed the greatest degree of elaboration. I will not attempt to give here details of all the ceremonies observed, but will restrict the account to the part played by pottery.

The first occasion in the wedding which involves the use of pottery is the dispatch of the invitation from the bride's village to the house of the bridegroom. The invitation is placed in a *kalash*, and one or two *kalash* are then taken with singing and some minor ceremonies to the temple, where they will remain until the wedding itself. The first ceremony to mark the commencement of the actual wedding celebrations is the worship of the potter's wheel (*chak puja*) at the potter's house (for all but untouchable castes). The particular example of this ceremony which I observed was that of a merchant caste in Ujjain. The wedding party approached the potter's house preceded by the drummer band. The party consisted of women, mainly relatives of the spouse, but also some friends. The potter placed his wheel in position as though for throwing pottery. The wheel was given a fresh wash of cowdung paste, which is a common form of purification. Then a group of ten women entered the potter's house and sang short songs such as 'Oh Ganpati [Ganesh], a jewel and pearl be on your trunk' and 'Oh potter, did you make a *kalash* when Krishna was to be married? I made a *kalash* when Krishna was to be married.' The mother of the spouse then came forward and approached the wheel. Using a red paint (*kunku*) she drew a *swastik* on the wheel and next to it placed some rice grains, areca nut, coloured thread and one and a quarter rupees. Then she tied coloured thread (*laccha*) around the wrist of the potter, while another group of women presented him with rice and clarified butter (though any prepared food would serve). The party took away five large *divaniya*, five lumps of yellow clay, a drummer *kalash* and a *Ganpati kalash*, as well as four *wariya* which were part of their *warad* (see below). The wedding party spent ten minutes in the house of the potter, but most of this time was spent haggling over the price of the *cauri* (see below), which, as is the custom for richer families, was to be made of metal, but was nevertheless supplied through the potter.

Worship of the wheel has been recorded in other ethnographies. Freed and Freed describe a similar ceremony, though no *mantra* are sung and five *swastik* are drawn. They also describe additional ceremonies related to the doorposts of the potter's house (1980: 460–1). Although they interpret the ceremony as a fertility rite, as part of a general analysis of rites using models derived from Freud and Van Gennep, I observed no evidence in support of such interpretations. They also, however, note that Ganesh is the deity who marks wedding ceremonies in general, and it is as the worship of Ganesh that worship of the wheel can first be interpreted. In many other ritual performances, including the visit to the temple, the worship of Ganesh again symbolises the beginning of ritual activities, and the transformation of time and space. The potters are closely associated with Ganesh, and make an unfired clay figure of the god which they give to the wedding couple and which remains with them throughout the wedding celebrations until, at the end, it is thrown into the river with other ritual paraphernalia. Sharma's informants suggested

that this ceremony represented the casting into pure water of consecrated objects, which might otherwise become polluted (Sharma 1969).

Worship of the wheel presents a useful opportunity to take the *warad*,
which consists of virtually all those pots that serve a ritual purpose
during the wedding celebration, with the exception of one further group
known as *cauri*. The *warad* varies from caste to caste, according to the
details of the ceremonies enacted by each caste. The most important
single usage is the placing of the offerings in front of the representation
of the *mai mata* (mother goddess) during the wedding, but these pots are
also used for other rituals. An example is the *wariya*, used to hold the
turmeric with which the bride is bathed prior to the wedding, or pots
such as the spouted *wari* that are used by some castes to serve special
foods to the couple. By far the most extensive *warad* is that taken by the
shepherd caste which consists of the following pots: 6 *gagra*, 4 large and
4 small *divaniya*, 4 *mamatla*, 3 *patya*, 3 *katwa*, 3 *tolro*, 3 *wariya*, 3 spouted *wari*,
3 *kundali*, 3 *brahman dohni*, 3 *karela*, 3 *dhatri*, 1 *kalash*, 1 *bujhara* and 1 *kunda*,
a total of 51 vessels of 16 varieties.

A more typical *warad*, that of the *gujar*, may be related to the uses to
which those pots placed in front of the *mai mata* are put. These include 5
mamatla containing 2.5 kg of wheat, 2.5 kg of rice, fried *puri*, *ladu* sweets
and *jigri* (boiled sugar cane) respectively. A quantity of rice is placed in

Fig. 42. *Mamatla* in front of *mai mata* (mother goddess) at wedding

each of 16 *dhakni* which are later distributed to relatives. In a *kunda* is placed a *ladu* and 8 *puri*. In contrast, some castes only take a small *warad*, such as a *kunda*, a *kalash* and a *bujhara*, although most castes take at least some *mamatla* in addition to these. No systematic relationship could be found between caste hierarchy and the pottery taken.

The *mai mata* is a painted representation of the goddess on the inside walls of the houses of both the bride and the groom. An example of the paintings used to represent this image in the house of the bride is shown in Fig. 42. The pottery consisted of 4 *mamatla* for each couple, and a single group of a *kunda* set with a *kalash/bujhara*. There were also some *divaniya* set on each pair of *mamatla*, and others with wheat. In the potter's house, in front of the *mai mata*, for each couple to be married there was placed a *mamatla* containing boiled sugar cane extract set on coarse wheat, and next to it an empty *kunda* with an empty *kalash*, on which was set a *bujhara*. In front of these was a large *divaniya*, containing newly sprung wheat shoots.

The major group of pottery used at weddings in addition to the *warad* is the *cauri*. This consists of twenty vessels which are used to demarcate physically the space within which one of the most important of the wedding rituals takes place. This is formed by placing four piles of five pots at each corner of a square (Fig. 43). The *cauri* includes certain vessels

Fig. 43. Bride and bridegroom seated within *cauri*

unique to it. The basal pot of the pile is a *goli*. The next three pots are made in decreasing sizes, equivalent to a *matka,*a *gagra* and a *kalash*, but with a *goli*-style rim. On the top is placed a *bujhara*. The *cauri* was identical for the poor leatherworker and the rich *jat*. The only exception is the local Malwi sub-caste of the potters, who have only a *kalash* and a *bujhara* at the four corners. The potters explain this discrepancy with a legend, which tells how they once had to give up their own *cauri* to an important *asami*, when the *cauri* for the latter broke in firing. Fischer and Shah describe *cauri* for an area in Gujerat where thirty-six pots are used (1970: 210).

A sacrificial table (*yagna*) is placed (for most castes) in the centre of the area formed by the *cauri*. On this are placed various ritual paraphernalia, including a metal *lota-kalash* (i.e. a *lota* which stands for a *kalash*). The couple must walk seven times around this table, which is crowned by a sacred flame, having had their clothes tied together in front of the *mai mata* (Fig. 43). In the case of the leatherworker's wedding, where there was no central table, the top of the *cauri* was joined with white string and two *divaniya*, placed mouth-to-mouth and containing some money, were circulated in the opposite direction to the couple. This pattern of circumambulation within and around a square is typical of the use of space in Hindu ritual. It was mentioned earlier (pp. 118–19 above) as the structural principle underlying the *pan* design, and is related to the *mandala*.

Fig. 44. Carrying *kalash* containing Ganges water

A final example of the extensive use of pottery is provided by a ceremony performed only by the *jat*, out of those observed. This is probably because of the cost of the main constituent, the holy water of the river Ganges. The ceremony is known as *gangajal* and is mentioned also by Gupta (1974) as one of the wedding ceremonies. Thirteen women each take a *kalash* and carry water from one of the village wells (Fig. 44), which is then mixed with a quantity of Ganges water. A grid is then painted on the floor of the bride's house and the squares are filled with piles of nine kinds of grain and pulse in a pattern related to the taking of horoscopes, which is a major feature of the Hindu wedding. The perimeter is marked by two concentric squares on grain between which are placed the *kalash*, each topped by a coconut. A pair of *kalash* are set within the grid, one topped by a *bujhara* and draped with a woman's silver waist-ornament. A sacrifice is then performed, the groom placing ritual substances, such as clarified butter, into a sacred flame, and prayers are said (Fig. 45).

During the course of the ceremonies, pottery is also used for minor rituals, of which the most common is the claiming of *neg*. This is a kind of extra payment for services received during a ceremony, in addition to the normal remuneration. It is claimed by the presenter of a *kalash*, the money being placed in the *kalash* and then returned to the helper. In one case the potter added an extra *kalash* to the *cauri* in the hope of obtaining *neg*. A potter's daughter attempted to claim *neg* after the ceremony in

Fig. 45. Worship at the *gangajal* ceremony

which his kin and friends gave gifts of money to the spouse in their village (in this case they obtained 902 r from 70 individuals). The potter's sister's son's new bride claimed *neg* from me after she arrived in Dangwara.

The adopted father of one of the potters died at nine o'clock in the morning. By 11 a.m. he was cremated. A black *dohni*, having been broken at the rim, was first used for bathing the corpse and then fully broken outside the village. After three days, two *kulhri* were said to be taken to the place of cremation, one containing milk and the other cow urine. The ashes from the cremation ground were removed and the place replastered and purified. During the period up to the *ganta*, a funerary ceremony that takes place eleven days after the cremation, the potter did not lie on a bed or sit on a mat, and took only simple food, staying in his house accompanied by a growing number of relatives.

For the *ganta* the potter went to Ujjain, and undertook several ceremonies culminating in the throwing of the cremated remains into the sacred river Sipra. On returning to his house in Dangwara, thirteen red and buff *wariya* were placed in two lines, half-filled with water. The *brahman* then tied white string around each, and placed a *divaniya* on top of each of them, to contain various substances. Then, in turn, the potter, his brother and his children sacrificed clarified butter, sugar, boiled sugar cane extract and rice into a small fire in front of the pots (Fig. 46). The *wariya* were then taken and placed on the edge of a dung-collecting pit not far from the house, kicked into it and broken.

On the following day, the *pagri* ceremony was held, the climax of which was the ceremonial tying of turbans to the potter's head, marking the acknowledgement by the onlookers of his succession to the deceased. This was followed by the *nukta* feast, to which large numbers of the village and relatives were invited. After this ceremony, the son of the deceased is expected to present a *kalash* to the *brahman* every month, for eleven months. In the case of the death of a woman, an additional ceremony known as *gorni* takes place at the parental household, for which the pot known as the *gorni ki kundi* (funeral *kundi*) is made.

As in the case of the wedding, the details of funeral ceremonies vary in relation to caste. The *jat* and drummer use *kalash* instead of *wariya* for the *ganta* ceremony, but do not present a *kalash* to the *brahman* for the year. The *gujar* have an elaborate series of ceremonies, including the breaking of a *karela* and the kicking of the hearth. Dangwara village is comparatively less orthodox than many north Indian villages. In most areas, it appears that all earthenware pots are broken and have to be replaced after a death in the household. For example, Babb notes: 'the unglazed pots should be thrown away and new ones purchased' (1975: 96), but in Dangwara only the *brahman* removes his pots into his backyard after a death, and uses them thereafter only for washing. A detailed description of the ceremony for the full replacement of pottery, equivalent to the *ganta*, is described by Fischer and Shah (1970: 121–4), who provide more exegesis than could be found in Dangwara.

This description of the use of pots at weddings and funerals includes only those ritual usages which are established by precedence and should not be changed. It contrast to these, there is the *ad hoc* use of pottery, which depends entirely upon the wealth of the family involved and the number of people to be feasted. Here pottery is used mainly for the presentation of water and food. *Maman* is particularly used on such occasions, mainly by the potters themselves in serving water, as is a special pot known as the *nukta ka gagra*. One potter claimed to be making a hundred of these for the funeral feast of an important *asami* and certainly the numbers seen were not much short of that.

The use of pottery in annual ceremonies

The two annual festivals of *divali* and *akhartij* have already received some mention, since they represent occasions for the distribution of pottery to the *asami* and for payments for all services between castes. On *divali*, the *divali matka* are not themselves worshipped, but the *divaniya* (oil lamps) are much in evidence, lighting up the houses. On the following day of

Fig. 46. Sacrifice as part of a funeral ceremony

gobhardhan puja, which is dedicated to the worship of cattle, the landowner will take the *kulhri* to the fields and boil milk inside one. This is, in part, a worship of the fields, and the spilling of the milk, as it boils over, is said to promote fertility. The farmer may also watch to see which side of the *kulhri* the milk boils over, as a guide to which parts of the field will be most productive in the coming season. The *chhapa* is dipped in paint and used to decorate the cows and other animals, and the *kulhri* may also be used for this purpose, stamping a single circle with the rim as against the concentric circles of the *chhapa*.

At *akhartij* the pottery is still more central to the festival, since pottery-worship is itself a major *puja* (prayer) of the day. The new *goli* is placed on the ground next to an *akhartij gagra*, the area having been purified with cowdung plastering, and the vessels are then filled with water. On the *goli* is placed the *dhakan*, convex face downwards, and in this is placed a coconut and other fruit. A *divaniya*, containing a mango, is placed on the *akhartij gagra*, which rests on a bed of sorghum, and a *swastik* of rice is made on the ground near the pots. Coloured thread is put around the necks of the two pots and a *tilak* (a small red mark used to anoint married women and those who have attended a ceremony) placed on them (Fig. 47). A sacrifice is then performed with clarified butter and sugar, and a *mantra* spoken asking for wealth from Ganesh. The family then waits to

Fig. 47. Worship of pottery at *akhartij puja*

see the first drops of water form on the outside of the porous *goli*. This takes about a quarter of an hour and is thought to signify a prosperous year. The farmers are said to watch on which side of the *goli* these drops form, as a predictor of what season will be unusually wet. Going in an anticlockwise direction, if the drops form on the north it will rain more in *asarh* month, if on the west then *savan*, and so on. The potters did not know of this forecasting element in the worship. If a person has died that year, then a second *goli* is also worshipped. A *brahman* is called to flick water on to it from a *lota*, and the *goli* is then given to the *brahman*.

These occasions are also used by the potters for the worship of their instruments. The wheel is worshipped at *divali*, while at the *akhartij puja* the paddles and anvils are placed next to the *goli*, with a coloured thread tied around their necks and a *tilak* mark. Once again, other castes may have slightly different ceremonies. The *gujar*, for example, who take a different range of pottery at *divali*, have ceremonies which involve filling the *brahman dohni* with *khir* (rice boiled in milk) and other foods. There are a number of other pots taken during the year, often by only a few of the castes. The paint-makers and weavers take a *karela* two days before *dashera* festival and a *divaniya* before *garbah puja*. At a festival in memory of the lord Krishna, who is well known for the games he used to play, the villagers string up a *matka* from a tree and have a competition to break it. The *keliya puja* consists entirely of the worship of that particular vessel by certain castes.

Interpretation

Two major questions arise from this description of the very elaborate use of pottery at ceremonies. Firstly, how may the data assist in our understanding of the nature of the pottery corpus and in which ways may pottery forms be said to have meaning as categories? This is a central theme of the book, and will be discussed in the next chapter and further analysed in Chapter 9. There is, however, a second question, which is about the particular use of pottery at the ceremonies themselves. While there is good evidence that the elaborate use of pottery is both an ancient and extensive tradition in India, there is some disjuncture between the visual and verbal accounts relating to it, which may provide some clues as to interpretations of the use of pottery different from those commonly employed in anthropological analyses.

The ancient texts on domestic ritual (unlike more recent ones; see below) suggest an equally extensive use of pottery in the past. In a selection of the *grhya-sutra*, published by Müller (1886 and 1892), which are dated to *c.* 400 B.C. but may refer to a still earlier period, descriptions are given of the major domestic rites of the Vedic period, including weddings and funerals. In these, I counted forty-two specific references to pottery and many other references to sacrificial foods which would have required some such container. There are at least three cases where the use of a previously unused pot is called for. The spatial positions and even the direction in which the contents are to be stirred are described as part of a more general pattern of spatial concepts relating to the division between the world of the living and the world of the dead (analysed by Das 1977, chapter four). Most of the content and structure of these ceremonies has since disappeared, although there are certain superficial resemblances to modern ceremonies, such as the circumambulation of the fire. Clear historical evidence of the *cauri* can be found in a miniature painting from the Prince of Wales Museum in Bombay. This shows an episode from the Ramayana legend depicting the marriage of Rishyasringa, and was painted by Manohar in Rajasthan in 1649.

An equally extensive use of pottery at ceremonies is documented in modern practice for areas as far from this village as Orissa, on the east coast (Behura 1978: 213–16), and in Sri Lanka (Seneviratne 1978) in traditional temple ceremonies. A poignant indication of the importance of the festival pottery is provided by a contemporary story by Ramamirtham, published in the Penguin book of Indian short stories, *New Writings in India*. This is set in south India and tells of how a potter couple bore a grudge against the village in which they worked; having prepared the pots for distribution at the south Indian festival of *pongol*, the couple then destroyed them in front of the whole village, leaving the villagers no time to find replacements. The story indicates that the failure to celebrate the festival with the appropriate pottery was the cause of the downfall and destruction of the village thereafter (Ramamirtham 1974).

Some of the instances of pottery use at weddings appear to have direct symbolic or referential meaning. An example is the *kalash*, which stands in the centre of the sacred symbols drawn for the *gangajal* ceremony. This particular ceremony, which is also conducted by pilgrims who have returned from a visit to the river Ganges (usually to cast the bones of a deceased relative upon the river), has been analysed in detail by Gold (MS.), although there are some differences between her description and that observed in Dangwara. The deity of the Ganges is a goddess, and the decoration of the central *kalash* with a silver waist-girdle, worn normally by women, is suggestive of the representation of a female. In the context, it seems likely that it stands directly for the goddess of the Ganges.

Another example is the *cauri* itself. This is used to constitute a square within which the major rite of the wedding takes place. The *cauri* transforms the space into a sacred area, appropriate to the occasion, through two of its aspects: its square arrangement and the prominent use of the *kalash*. A representation of the *kalash* is almost ubiquitous as the pinnacle for Hindu temples. The temple itself is the representation of a complex system of symbolism, in such a way that its central axis, which passes through the *kalash*, may be taken to represent the axis of the universe (Kramrisch 1946). One of the most common features of Hindu worship is the use of symbolic drawings to mediate relations with the divine. These are the *mandala*, mentioned in the last chapter (p. 118 above) in relation to the painted designs. It was suggested there that the use of concentric squares and circles was of particular significance. The temple is itself built on the basis of *mandala* plans, as has recently been demonstrated through the analysis of some medieval Orissan temples (Boner and Sharma 1972), and worship often takes the form of circumambulation within and around the temple (Piper 1980). It seems reasonable, therefore, to take the *cauri* as a form of temporary temple within which the wedding is consecrated.

Pottery is not just an integral and prominent part of the wedding; it may of itself stand for the whole event. An illustration of this comes not from evidence within the village, but from wedding cards on sale in the London borough of Southall. One card (Fig. 48) is composed of a photograph of important wedding symbols, including the coconut, mango leaves and *cauri*. In the second (Fig. 49) the representation of the wedding is reduced merely to a schematic rendering of the *cauri* itself.

All of this evidence suggests that pottery is not only extremely common in ceremonies but is also of some significance. It may represent major figures in the rites, it may constitute the space in which the rites take place, its absence may be regarded as a failure to have carried out the festival in the proper manner, and it may even come to stand for the wedding itself. It has clearly maintained this prominence for a considerable period. There are problems, however, in understanding this use of pottery. A direct representational role for the pot form can only be ascertained in a small minority of cases. Symbolism of this kind seems most likely when the pottery is directly linked to an element of formal Hindu iconography, in rites that are consistent throughout the village. More common and problematic are instances, such as the pottery placed before the *mai mata*, where a great variety of ritual practices may be observed amongst the thirty castes of the village. For most of the ritual uses of pottery no local exegesis is discoverable. The villagers were always reluctant to discuss pottery, and they clearly felt some embarrassment at the attention being paid to these objects, which seemed to them to be missing the point of the ceremonies. With the exception of the interpretation of *kalash* as standing for the goddess of the Ganges, which was supported by some informants, any representational status for pottery was denied, and general descriptions of weddings, even when they mentioned such minutiae as particular grains and threads, tended not to mention pottery. There thus seems to be a considerable disjuncture between representations suggesting the extreme visibility and importance of pottery at ceremonies, and the apparent invisibility and unimportance of pottery in other representations of the ceremonies.

That this is not merely a result of my particular interaction with the villagers is suggested by the still more marked lacunae to be found in written texts. There are a number of books which describe both modern and historical weddings and set out the rules for their enactment (e.g. Apte 1978, Bandyopadhyay 1973, Kane 1930–62). Although these books pay considerable attention to the minutiae of ritual action – for example, the number of times people should walk in a certain direction, and the

Fig. 48. Wedding invitation from Southall, London

manner in which a variety of objects should be placed – there is again an almost complete lack of reference to pottery. I have not yet found a single mention, let alone a discussion, of *cauri* in such texts. Clearly, then, the main use of pottery is quite different from that of the class of what might be termed direct ritual symbols, such as are found in some Hindu rites, in the Christian Eucharist or the Jewish Passover, and in many puberty ceremonies described in ethnographies (Biebuyck 1973, Lewis 1980), where the objects themselves are subject to direct exegesis and can be analysed as expressing certain ideals and values to be inculcated as part of the ceremony.

This is hardly a unique case, since anthropological studies often stress

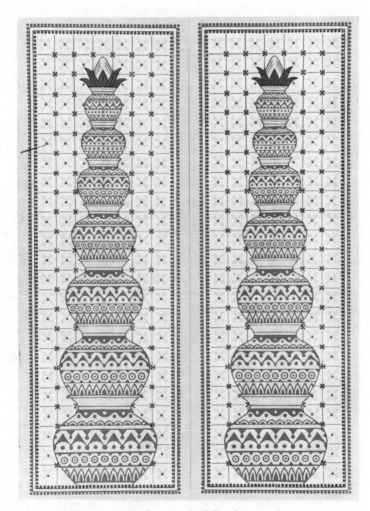

Fig. 49. Wedding invitation from Southall, London

the relative indépendence of visual categories from those of language. Commonly in such cases a different approach is used in the analysis of the material. Here, the anthropologist, rather than using local verbal interpretation, analyses the underlying structure of the events to elucidate consistent patterns in the employment of the objects. In South Asian ritual, examples might include the work of Good and others on ceremonial journeys (1980), Ortner's analysis of Dough figures used in Sherpa rituals (1978) and Sharma's analysis of domestic worship (1970). For such an analysis, a pattern in the use of the material with respect to the ceremonies must be demonstrable, so that the use of the object in one case builds upon and is consistent with its use in other cases. Such an analysis is quite possible for a range of other objects and actions which have been mentioned in the description of wedding and other rites. These would include the use of mango leaves and sweet basil, the application of a red mark to the forehead of a person or to an object, and the use of *mandala*-related symbols. These seem to have a relatively consistent meaning, and by their use signify the religious nature of the rite. Gold suggests, for example, that the tying of the coloured string (*laccha*) can be seen as an indication of the binding of an object or person within the subject of the ritual. Thus, we find the *laccha* tied around the wrist of the potter on the occasion of the worship of the wheel and around the pots and paddles worshipped at *akhartij* and *divali*.

This approach does not, however, prove any more viable than direct symbolic analysis in coming to an understanding of the use of pottery in ceremonies. There are two kinds of consistency that might be expected in connection with these ceremonies. That the suitability of particular vessels for use in ceremonies may be determined from the order of the pottery corpus as a whole will be shown in the next chapter. The other pattern that would have to be demonstrated in order to argue for the kind of analysis developed in the above examples is for pottery to be used systematically in relation to what it represents or to the castes that employ it. With one exception, the pots do not appear to have a consistent meaning or role. A *matka* in one case may stand for a person (see p. 145 below), in another case may be a receptacle for an offering, and in a third instance may be an augury. This is not merely the polysemic quality often pointed out in symbolic studies, since these pots may perform different roles for different castes, and most often they are used to carry or contain rather than to signify. The variation between castes is not systematic with respect to caste hierarchy. The *gujar* are often distinctive, and the untouchable drummers are often similar to the high-caste *jat*, whose particular clients they claim to be. Out of the pottery corpus, only the *kalash* may be considered comparable with other objects that might be used in such a structural analysis of the ceremonies. This pot is only constituted by its inclusion in ritual events (see pp. 180–1 below), and its link with the ceremonies is therefore much more direct. Although multivalency does not preclude symbolic analysis, the unsystematic microvariation between castes would be difficult to subsume and is often ignored (see Good 1983 for an exception here).

There have been occasional attempts to interpret the use of pottery in ceremonies in general terms. The most common assumption is that pottery in some way stands for fertility. This analysis is especially common for the use of pottery at weddings. A number of examples may be found in Freed and Freed (1980) and Crooke (1926). None of these authors provides sustained evidence, either in the form of local exegesis or through analogy, for such an interpretation, which seems to be based on the assumed universal significance of such rounded forms. On the other hand such evidence is provided in examples given by Kolenda (1983: 109) and Good (1983: 264–5), who see the pots as wombs.

A final approach might be to investigate the implications of the ceremonies for various social relations in order to determine if the pottery is directly implicated in these. Selwyn (1979) has shown how the wedding ceremony may involve a number of social conflicts, including the importance of strategy and alliance in choosing the spouse, and the asymmetrical relationship between males and females, wife-givers and wife-takers. Once again, however, there is no evidence that the pottery contributes directly to the development of these social relations.

The evidence for the extensive use of pottery in a highly flexible manner has been set against several approaches to the interpretation of objects used in rituals. Pottery (with the exception of the *kalash*) does not seem to accord with the expectations of these approaches. Rather, the general use of pottery may be characterised in relation to a recent work by Gombrich (1979), the art historian, with reference to a familiar ceremony, that of Christmas. It was suggested earlier that a focus on pottery may be a cause of embarrassment, and yet it is something that can stand for the wedding itself. Equally with Christmas, the associated objects – the use of trees, gifts, Santa Claus, cards, turkeys and other objects – may be more essential to the actual carrying out of the festivities to the English family than attendance at a church service, and yet if a naïve observer, who claimed an interest in understanding the basis of the performance, concentrated attention on these objects, these same families might well consider they had missed the point and might be reluctant (and in most cases unable) to provide any explanation of the use of the particular objects. Indeed, while some of these attributes, such as gift-giving and the use of bird symbolism, may have equivalents in other festivals and be part of the structure of festive celebrations, most are not central to the religious legitimation of the event, and are simply a part of the elaborate nature and idiosyncratic flavour of Christmas, serving to differentiate and particularise.

A model for this kind of paraphernalia may be found in Gombrich's book, *A Sense of Order* (1979), which is an analysis of ornament (that is, ornament as opposed to art, the subject of most of Gombrich's publications). One of the major differences he emphasises early in the volume is that art is intended as a focus of attention, whereas ornament is something which should be on the margins of perception, and is rarely an appropriate object of direct attention. It represents a kind of 'framing', quite literally in the case of the picture frame. This is not to say that it is unimportant; it should be appropriate to its context, but in a sense the more appropriate it is, the more it is mere background. We usually notice it when it is inappropriate, a discontinuity (or, as in the short story mentioned above, absent). Equally, ornamentation such as wallpaper is often pattern, not direct symbol (although it may sometimes be symbolic), and is thus differentiated from the more overtly representational which holds the attention.

This model appears to hold for the pottery. Ornament does not demand either direct representational significance or consistency of use. The potential ideological nature of an 'appropriate' background, which obviously naturalises and clarifies the symbolic and communicative aspect of the ceremony, will be discussed in Chapter 9. The pots are not irrelevant to the message of, say, wife-takers' superiority over wife-givers, but they are not themselves symbols of this relationship. Rather, they frame those symbols. They are part of a massive spread of paraphernalia, selected from the auspicious end of the spectrum of their respective domains. Thus, pots are used in conjunction with clarified butter, the most auspicious of foods, and also with sacred plants. All these elements are appropriate to the building up of the auspicious context of the major rites.

This interpretation and the social interests that may generate the observed microvariation in these ceremonies will be returned to in Chapter 9. At this stage, it should be clear that the pottery exhibits a plasticity and flexibility that does not end with the sheer number of categories created from the clay itself but is subject to complex manipulation thereafter.

8
A symbolic framework for the interpretation of variability

In this chapter the pottery assemblage will be reorganised in order to examine it as a symbolic framework. Much of the evidence has already been presented, but it is here collated and used to represent the pottery in a new form. The idea of a 'symbolic framework' refers not to debates over the degree of iconicity, or to elegant demonstrations of inversion and subtle metaphor, as in structural analysis. The intention is, in more prosaic terms, to demonstrate the nature of pottery in Dangwara as a dimension which is structured by the conventions which permit meaning. There are two stages in such an analysis: the first is to present evidence for the discovery of any pattern within the variability of pottery which appears to lend coherence and act as an organisational principle underlying the assemblage, and the second is to present evidence for any systematic relationship between this pattern and other such dimensions by which Dangwara society appears to be differentiated. Potential meaning is held to derive from the consistency and intelligibility of these relationships.

Such an approach comes close to Geertz's description of the analysis of a symbolic system: 'by isolating its elements, specifying the internal relations among those elements, and then characterising the whole system in some general way – according to the core symbols around which it is organised, the underlying structure of which it is a surface expression, or the ideological principles upon which it is based' (1973: 17, quoted in Turner 1975: 147). Turner expresses reservations about such an approach, which is clearly normative and abstracted and fails to deal with 'the informal logic of everyday life' (p. 147). This chapter is not, therefore, intended as the outcome of analysis, but rather as a reorganisation and systematisation of the material, acting as a bridge to the next chapter, where greater consideration is given to what such a formal presentation might represent in terms of analysis.

Variations on this approach are quite common in ethnographic studies of Indian society. In a number of recent works, the analysis has attempted to locate one particular dimension which is held to act as a kind of base-line from which other aspects of categorisation may be studied. In effect, many of these analyses attempt to 'privilege' such dimensions, upon which the entire presentation rests. The most widely-quoted example of this is Dumont's analysis of caste (1972), resting on the dimension of purity and pollution. Other writers have given prominence to dimensions such as heat or colour (Babb 1975, Beck 1969). An example of this is Babb's suggestion (1975: 235) that 'the opposition between hot and cold appears to be an ordering conception operative in an extensive domain of human concerns which includes such unrelated matters as the classification of foods and mankind's experience of divinity'. Such an ordering principle may be held to articulate with almost any given dimension, as is found in the following quotation from Sharma (1970: 20): 'Within almost any category the Hindu will rank some items as more pure than others. Thus among animals the cow is most pure; among trees the *pipal* and the *por* are pure and the *lasura* is impure – a "musulman" tree, too polluted to be used for timber. Among vegetables carrots and turnips are less pure than pumpkin and potatoes, which is why it is permissible to eat the latter on fast days but not the former. Of beverages, milk and clean water (especially Ganges water) are pure, and alcoholic drinks are impure.'

In some of the above works the selection of one dimension, such as heat, is held to imply a special status for that dimension. In this chapter, no such implication is to be derived from the discussion. Pottery is a trivial and unexceptional medium; if it appears to act in a similar fashion, as a 'privileged' base-line, it is only because it is the subject of the chapter. That it can be made to play a similar role in symbolic analysis gives cause for some scepticism over the claims made in the above examples for other particular dimensions. The implication which may be drawn here is that the creation of a meaningful dimension, a set of categories, from clay is a process of objectification by which the medium is turned by its makers and users into an instrument for potential representations of the nature of the world and society.

The pottery code: colour

The most striking distinction within the whole assemblage of pottery is that produced in the final stage of manufacture, the red and black created in the oxidised and reduced firings. While black may be taken as a homogeneous class, red must be further divided into the painted pottery class and the red and buff class. It was established in Chapter 4 that these classes could not be explained directly by reduction to pottery function. The association of the black clay with the use of the vessel on the hearth only accounts for a minority of the black vessels, while the distinction within the red pottery, that of the presence or absence of painting, seems by virtue of its decorative nature unlikely to be indicative of any such utilitarian relation. An attempt to establish the connotations of these attributes of the pottery may begin with a consideration of their use in other contexts. This may provide clues for their expected significance when these same attributes are found applied to pottery.

The attributes 'red' and 'painted' are found in a number of contexts from which their significance becomes apparent. The red applied to pottery is similar to the *sindhu* colour applied to all village shrines. The mere application of *sindhu* is sufficient to change a mundane form into an object of veneration, a rounded pebble into a symbol of the sacred *lingam* of Siva. Many of the village shrines consist of just such a *sindhu*-anointed natural object. As used in the *tilak* mark, applied to the forehead, it formally establishes the presence of an individual at a sacred occasion and is the usual sign of such attendance. Red, in the form of *sindhu*, is thus the colour most closely associated with the transformation of the secular into the sacred. Red has other symbolic effects – for example, the red at the parting of a woman's hair signifies her married status. Red is quite common as a colour for clothing. In the past it often had more specific associations, as for example with the red turban that indicated member-ship of the *bairagi* caste, or the red *sari* that indicated the married state of a woman, but today it is in more general use. It is not a common colour, however, within the house, being mainly found on the pottery. Accounts of religion at the village level commonly associate red with worship and weddings (e.g. Crooke 1926: 295), and Stevenson, in her account of Brahmanical worship has many references to what she terms 'red, the most auspicious of all colours' (1920: 190).

Whereas red is closely associated with religion but is also put to secular use, paintings are exclusively associated in the village with the realm of the sacred. There are no secular paintings in Dangwara (apart from those on the pottery). Paintings are found in two sets of circum-stances, either on the walls of the temples and shrines, or on the walls of ordinary houses when they are being used for ceremonial activities. The *mai mata*, described at p. 127 above, would be an example of the latter. The application of painting to the house appears to transfer it tempor-arily into a sacred space, appropriate for the carrying out of ceremonies. The act of painting and decorating is itself auspicious, helping to create the appropriate frame for a celebration. In Hindu aesthetic thought, artistic practice has clear religious implications, as a medium for the apprehension of transcendent unity (Coomaraswamy 1934). This associ-ation with religion is clear in the pattern of its use in the ordinary village.

That the class of red-painted pottery also has associations with religious ceremonies is abundantly clear from the material presented in the last chapter, in which virtually all the forms used in the ceremonies came from this class. This association is mediated through the relationship between the *kalash* and other pottery types of this class. The *kalash* may be said to stand for the entire class of red-painted pottery, as the quintessential form, embodying the properties of the class and providing them with a more abstracted and wider field of legitimation. The spatial and temporal referents of the *kalash* are immense. Literary references to the *kalash* go back to the earliest sources. In the Vedic period, the central ceremony of many rites was that of *soma* (probably the hemp that is still an integral feature of most Dangwara ceremonies), and the *kalash* was the term for the vessel that held the *soma* (Singh 1969: 304, Vira 1934: 283–305). Roy (1969: 261–74) mentions the *kalash* as used both for carrying water and in religious ceremonies, in texts dating from between the sixth and the second centuries B.C. There are many references to the *kalash* in the Deccan College Sanskritic dictionary project (inspected in 1980), including mentions of versions in gold, brass and earthenware. Today the *kalash* is no less important, as is indicated by its ubiquitous presence on the pinnacle of every Hindu temple. Kramrisch, in her classic study of the Hindu temple, notes: 'In the vase (*kalasha, kumbha*) of the finial (*stupika*) are collected (from the root *stup* "to collect") all the properties of all the objects and their potencies and merged in *amrta*, the deathless' (1946: 350).

Babb, in his analysis of village Hinduism in Chattisgarh (in the same state of Madhya Pradesh), has much to say of the *kalash*, there often found in a metal form. Describing the ordinary *puja* (prayer), he notes that 'attention directed towards the goddess centered on a rather insignificant looking object just to the base of the pictures, this was the *kalash* which in this case consisted of a small brass pot containing water, curds and *ghi*. Five mango leaves had been placed around the top and a coconut was set on top of the whole. The *kalash* is the most important item amongst the physical paraphernalia of ritual. It represents, a priest explained, the "finite in the infinite", that is the tangible form of the deity during ritual. In the present instance the *kalash* constituted the principal object of worship in the ceremonies that followed' (1975: 42). The *kalash* was a constant feature in the rituals described in the last chapter; it carried the wedding invitation, was used for *neg* supplication, and surmounted the *cauri* piles. In the *gangajal* the ability of the *kalash* to stand for the deity (the goddess of the Ganges) was clear, sitting within the auspicious piles of grain, draped with a silver waist-girdle. This is not unusual, as Good notes (1983: 234): 'The quintessential Tamil ritual of *Ponkal* cooking is but one example of a very general Indian phenomenon, namely the representation, containment and embodiment of divinity with a pot of some kind.'

The *kalash* may be used to fix one pole of the pottery code, and establishes the sacred nature of the red-painted class of pottery, in a set of elaborate linkages, both temporal, with traditions extending over three millennia, and spatial, with reference to the whole of Hindu South Asia. Even without the evidence of this vessel, the associations of other pottery forms in the red-painted group would be evident from their role in ceremonies. As the *kalash* can undergo theomorphic transformations, so other vessels of this group can undergo anthropomorphic transformations. An example is the setting up of two pairs of pots before the *mai mata* representation: these appear to stand for the bride and groom in supplication before the image throughout the wedding ceremonies, a position held by the actual couple for only a short part of those rites. Although I did not observe this, informants claimed that, for some castes, the pots on one side are decorated with a woman's silver waist-ornament, which would strengthen such an interpretation. All the vessels of this class undergo some direct transformation when used during ceremonies. For the *matka* and the *gagra*, there is the direct morphological transformation, which links them with the sacred, in the form of the festival pots *divali matka* and *akhartij gagra*. The *chuklya* undergoes its own transformation, when it becomes the *kalash* (see pp. 180–1 below). The *goli* does not undergo any morphological transformation, but it is directly worshipped in the *akhartij* prayers, and is the basis for the *cauri* piles of pots. Thus, both individually and as a group, this class is concerned with the transformation of the secular into the sacred. Only the *batloi*, which is occasionally painted, though more commonly plain red, has no such ritual associations and appears to be a direct skeuomorph of the metal water vessel of the same name. All of these pots are associated with the area of the *pirendi* water-table, one of the areas of the house most protected from outsiders.

In contrast to the red-painted class is the black class. Again, analysis can begin by an examination of the more general associations of black. This presents its own difficulties. Black can often be represented by the mere absence of colour, such as in night, or the dark interior of a low-caste home. Essentially, where red is auspicious and favoured, black is inauspicious and avoided. It is not found on the clothes of the village Hindu, and in the house is mainly represented by the pottery. The one circumstance in which it is directly applied is in the avoidance of the 'evil eye' (Malone 1974: 174–5). A beautiful girl will have a small black spot put on her face, a large expensive house will have a broken *dohni* vessel hung from one of its eaves. Crooke gives several such examples of the use of black marks or objects in confronting the evil eye (1926: 294). These are thought to distract malicious thoughts or evil intent that might form against a thing of beauty. Black skin is the misfortune of a young girl as the most significant factor in arranging her marriage. Skin colour is also assumed by villagers to be directly associated with caste position, given the significance of the lighter-skinned Aryan in the mythology of Hinduism. These associations suggest a significance for black pottery that is in direct contrast to the red-painted pottery. In the last chapter, references to black pottery were rare, limited to the broken *dohni* used to bathe the corpse. The black pottery is mainly noticeable for its absence on ritual occasions. It is therefore to be associated with the secular realm. This distinction becomes still more pronounced in the area of exchange and sale.

In Chapter 5, the *asami* system was described in detail, and a marked contrast was noted between the form of exchange for red-painted pots, which constitutes part of this system, and that of black pots, which does not. One is given in fixed quantities on fixed occasions and exchanged only for services and payment in kind; the other is given on an *ad hoc* basis on any occasion and may be paid for in cash. The ordinary *asami* is only expected to purchase the painted red pottery from one particular potter, but in the stronger form of relationship known as the *ayath* the black pottery is also included. This may also be related to the potters' own conception of their rights in the area. The potters view Dangwara as part of their 'territory' with semi-jural rights known as *hak*. The potters say they would stop, by force if necessary, any other potter who attempted to sell red pots within this area, but they say they would not have any such claim against a potter who attempted to sell black pottery. Potters sell only black pottery in a market with which they have no formal ties.

The distinction between red-painted and black pottery is equally pronounced in their differential use. Red-painted pottery is essentially used for the carrying and storage of water. This may be seen as an odd statement, given that there were many examples in the last chapter of this same pottery being used for the presentation of food. The two are not contradictory. Water-carrying is the task of these pots in relation to human beings and daily tasks, but, for the deities, this pottery is suitable for the presentation of food. It is common in Hindu practice for the action appropriate to humans to be stepped up by one 'stage' in purity when applied to the deities (Gardener 1978). An example is found in *prasad*; food is first presented to the deities and then distributed to people. The food, having been offered to the deity, is regarded as the leftovers' of the meal, and ritually polluting in relation to the deity, but it is now acceptable food for human consumption. All the examples described in the last chapter, where red-painted pottery was used to carry food, represented sacrificial offerings placed before the deity. In contrast, in the field of human relations, it is the black pottery that is deemed fit for the preparation, storage and presentation of food in daily circumstances. Ordinary food is considered by villagers to be one stage less pure than water and this further marks the distinction between the two classes of red-painted and black pottery in terms of ritual purity.

The dichotomy so far presented appears to be quite straightforward, but in practice it is complicated by several factors, some of which lead to a further elaboration of the pottery code. Firstly, two of the principles outlined may clash in some situations. For example, there are cases when pottery, which is normally used for food, will be given as part of a *warad* wedding-pot group, which is a ceremonial presentation. In these cases the presentation seems to be more important than the use, and so a pot such as *dhatri*, which is normally black, will on this occasion be fired red, and the red *dhatri* given in the *warad*. When a *karela* is given (for example, to the *gujar* caste at *divali*), then an alternative strategy is adopted, and the *karela* is given by the potter in an unfired state. There are, however, other ambiguous situations which seem to be resolved by the creation of a third class of pottery, the red and buff ware.

Red and buff is not found as a colour combination in any other circumstance, but once the poles of the pottery code have been established with reference to external associations, it can be examined internally to explain the appearance of these vessels. In the context of the pottery code, the red and buff ware may be expected to represent some intermediate position between the two classes of red-painted and black pottery. As an intermediate group, it may be related to ambiguities that would be posed by a simple dichotomy. These ambiguities take various forms. It has been noted that food presented to human beings ought to be in a black vessel but that presented to the deity in a red-painted vessel, and that food presented at ceremonies ought to be red, as opposed to that presented on secular occasions, which should be black. What happens, then, when food is presented to human beings on ceremonial occasions? The *brahman dohni* is morphologically similar to the ordinary black *dohni* (though it sometimes has a different rim), but it is fired red and buff and may be used to present food at feasts – for example, at weddings. In this case, the name of the form itself is expressive of the ambiguous position suggested in its decoration. Also in this group are the *katwa* and *patya* of the *warad*, which are also used to present food at weddings. The *wariya* is normally used for keeping salt or chillies, in which case it is black, but when used for ceremonial purposes, such as holding turmeric to bathe the bride, or in the funerary *pagri* ceremony, it is red and buff. The *kunda* is a water pot, which means that it ought to be red and painted, but both its main uses signify a polluting variant of this association with water. It may be placed under the *pirendi* water-table to catch the waste water dripping from the porous pots, which can then be used for washing hands. In this case, it may be susceptible to some of the low and unclean associations of waste products. The other main use is in the unclean activity of giving water to animals for drinking. In all of these examples, therefore, the 'half and half' decoration constituted by the red and buff appears to be apt. It is both generated by, and, in turn, helps to confirm the order and consistency of, the dimension.

There is a significant exception to the associations of colour so far described. This is the *keliya*, a pot which is used only for water, is given only on ceremonial occasions, and is always black. The explanation for this anomaly lies in the details of the nature of the *keliya puja*, the particular ritual when the *keliya* is always presented. This rite is carried out mainly by the *rajput* and washerman castes. It always takes place on a dark night, by a river bank. No explanation of the nature or intention of this rite could be obtained from any of those who carry it out, the mere following of precedent being the justification given for this, as for many other ritual activities. It seems likely, however, that the immediate association with night may dominate the more general symbolic significance of the vessel, and the inversion of normal time may be echoed in the inversion of normal appearance. I could find no reason, however, for the black colour of the *maman*, the only other exception encountered.

A pattern is therefore established, relating to the three main decorative classes of pottery. Potters and other villagers do not themselves suggest, or agree with the suggestion, that pottery is ordered in the manner here outlined. They do, however, differentiate the red-painted pottery as appropriate to particular contexts, and it is the observation of their activities that permits this construction. They may articulate these relationships in a general sense, and indeed most of the above account could be generated from the implications of a single statement of one of the potters that 'Red pottery is the pottery of *dharma*, black pottery is not the pottery of *dharma*.' *Dharma* is that innate knowledge of what constitutes correct action.

Morphology

The implications of morphological features are more difficult to ascertain than those of decoration. That this should be so is predictable, on the grounds that while attributes such as colour may be found in a variety of other media with which consistency might be expected, and their symbolic effects are mediated by those relations, the major morphological features of pottery elaborated in their creation as categories are unique to container vessels. Elaborate rim forms occur only on these vessels and there is therefore nothing for these forms to be consistent with. This is not to say that the use of rims and other morphological features is arbitrary, since they may be used systematically, as in the creation of gradation. The discussion of morphology will be based on three elements of the pot form: the rim, the *parti* and the degree of closure.

Morphological distinctions may be expected to be at least partly redundant with respect to the major decorative groupings, given the latter's wider symbolic framework. Their main significance is more likely to be in the creation of a further level of differentiation within these larger classes. A confirmation of this expectation is found in the distribution of rim forms. Pottery that is otherwise distinctive in shape, such as the *dhupana, chhapa* and *harawla,* do not show any elaboration of the rim. Rim elaboration only occurs on pots which are otherwise not easily distinguished – in particular, within the range of round-bodied, narrow-necked, basic container forms. There is a general association between the painted red ware and the use of the split rim. This is most pronounced on the *matka* and the *surahi* (where it is the basis for the common alternative name of this vessel, *badak,* meaning 'duck'). It is also found on the *gagra, dhakan, maman, keliya, goli* and *kunda,* and is sometimes applied to the otherwise vertical rim of the *batloi.* No split rim is found on a black pot except the *keliya* (which is, of course, a water pot) and the *kundi,* while no sloping rim is found on a red-painted pot.

Although the rim form may at first appear to be a redundant criterion with respect to decoration, the actual type of split rim varies greatly from the subtle break made with the finger nail in the *goli* and *kunda,* to the broad depression of the *matka.* The split rim also acts as a point for differentiation when creating direct contrasts, as, for example, between the *matka* with its split rim and the *divali matka* with its flat rim, or the *akhartij gagra* with its split rim and the ordinary *gagra* with its round rim. A similar situation is found with the range of black cooking vessels, which will be explored in more detail below. These show a general association with the sloping rim, which then acts as the basis for further differentiation. The single food vessel with a split rim, the *kundi,* may be a response to another ambiguity, in that, although it is used for the storage of flour, informants noted that in the past it had been included as part of the *asami* distribution, but I was unable to determine what colour it had been at that point. The rim form seems to be closely related to the division between the two major functional classes of pottery, that is, pots used for water and pots used for food. Of the red and buff pots, the *kunda,* used for water, has a split rim, while the *wariya* and most *brahman dohni,* used for food, have a sloping rim, although the *pawanda,* used for paint but with a sloping rim, may contradict this. In summary, the rim form in part duplicates, in part cross-cuts, but generally expands into much finer discriminations, the classes presented by decoration.

The second major contrastive dimension to be found in pottery is the form and number of body facets, created in the beating stage of manufacture. Again, this is peculiar to container vessels. Commonly it merely reinforces distinctions also found in the rim differentiation. The 'two *parti*' flat facet is only found on water vessels. It may also be used for differentiation within those classes: the *matka* has no *parti* while the *divali matka* has two, and the *gagra* has no *parti* while the *akhartij gagra* has one. The *keliya* has one *parti* and, apart from colour, is almost identical with the *akhartij gagra.* The pots with a skeumorphic relation to metal vessels follow their prototypes; the earthenware *batloi,* for example, has two *parti.*

In general, then, these distinctions both reinforce and extend each other, creating categories which are then 'available' for signifying differences in association, but doing so within a framework of recognised dimensions that makes them appropriate to that association.

The third morphological criterion is the degree of closure. A gradation might be expected in the direction of closed vessels being more pure, following general principles of aesthetics in which the closing of form is related to an approach towards the unity which is the goal of all religious and artistic practice (Coomaraswamy 1934). As with colour, there are therefore external contexts which have relevance to this specific case. Such an association seems to hold for the general class of red pottery, since all pots that are painted in the manner described in Chapter 6 are closed forms with small mouths, while a number of the red and buff pots such as the *wariya*, *pawanda* and the various forms of *kunda* tend to be more open, with wide mouths. In Chapter 4 it was shown that degree of closure was not a response to efficiency of use; the relation to purity, by contrast, can account for the specificity of variability in this dimension. To understand how this, and other associations between morphological dimensions, may occur, however, we need to examine in more detail the connotations of some of the other codes with which pottery is associated. The three codes to be discussed in detail – food, gender and caste – all have been mentioned previously, but their relationship to pottery will be examined here to uncover any systematic relationship.

Pottery and some related codes: food

If pottery has not been a subject of any great concern to most ethnographers in South Asia, the study of food is established as a key area. The acceptance or rejection of various foods by different social groups is a common basis for the characterisation of caste hierarchy in ethnographies (see Marriot 1968 and 1976); the subject achieves a separate chapter in Dumont (1972); and there are two complete books on food preparation among a group of *brahmans* by Khare (1976a, 1976b). Babb describes the kitchen as the 'heart of the sacred geography of the household' (1975: 106) and Kane calls *bhojana* (rules concerned with food) one of the most important topics of the *dharmasastra* (Hindu law) (1930–62 4: 757–806). The functional links between food preparation and pottery were described on pp. 57–60 above. A major symbolic association was also noted, represented by the absence of earthenware plates or dishes (with the exception of the *harawla*), food consumption being the domain of metal forms.

Khare's two books illustrate the complexity of food symbolism. The books are premised on the assumption that cooking is intended to 'conjoin the cultural properties of the food with the cultural properties of the eater' (1976a: 12); it is regarded as a moral placement of food. Khare's method of analysis is similar to that used here in the analysis of paintings (see pp. 98–106 above), based on the Saussurian principles of paradigmatic and syntagmatic rules. This has already been loosely applied to English meals by Douglas (1975: 249–75). Khare divides food preparation into six fields: (1) food area, (2) cook, (3) utensils, (4) cooking ingredients, (5) cooking technique and (6) food type. Each of these fields is presented as a string of symbols representing alternatives, and these are then combined to form 'sentences' giving the requisite food preparation for a given occasion. In Dangwara an ordinary meal observed for a potter's household might read: (1) household hearth, (2) painter, (3) *chayra dohni*, (4) lentils, (5) boiling and (6) *kaccha* (cooked in water). In contrast to this, the same household preparing for a funeral feast might be read as: (1) special firing pit, (2) hired *brahman* cooks, (3) metal vessels, (4) various 'feast' foods such as rice and sweets, (5) frying and (6) *pakka* (cooked in clarified butter).

Khare gives similar sequences for sixty different food 'cycles', including eleven appropriate for different parts of the wedding ceremony alone. This degree of elaboration, written on the basis of ethnographic study amongst an orthodox *brahman* community, could not be matched in Dangwara. Khare does not discuss pottery in detail, since *brahman* have little use for it, but what he says of the more general class of utensils may be generalised: 'Utensils produce a highly complex system of symbolism, organised on the basis of their material, shape and contextual use . . . If cooks handle foods by being properly ranked, the utensils likewise "contain" foods during the cooking process by the virtue of their ritual rank and purity' (1976a: 53).

If Khare's approach is over-detailed for the Dangwara material, there are three basic divisions that assume importance in understanding Dangwara vessel variability. The division between *kaccha* (cooking in water, literally 'raw') and *pakka* (cooking in *ghi* – clarified butter or a vegetable oil substitute, and literally meaning 'cooked'), although not as crucial a distinction as it appears to be in many other areas, is used to divide off certain ceremonial or special feasts. These terms, as used here, refer to the relative resistance to pollution of the *ghi*, but the same terms may be applied to a variety of semantic domains. A *kaccha*, untarmac'd road is opposed to a *pakka*, tarmac'd road. A pot prior to firing may be said to be in a *kaccha* state; after firing it becomes *pakka*. This is significant, since it means that, while the fired pot is stored in the potter's house, other villagers, including low castes, can inspect the pot, which is resistant to pollution. Once the pot has been taken, and is filled with water, it then reverts to a *kaccha* state and is highly susceptible to pollution, so that it is forbidden for most outsiders to approach the water-table area. For this reason also, some families who have pots from their daughter's wedding, which, strictly speaking, belong to the family of the groom but which often the latter family do not bother to remove, will only use the pots for dry storage, which leaves open the (again largely theoretical) possibility that the pottery could eventually be claimed.

A second distinction is between wheat and sorghum. While the first distinction relates to purity, this relates to wealth. Sorghum is a less costly grain than wheat and the use of the two grains is associated with caste and wealth. In pottery, this relates not only to the *karela/kareli* distinction; the metal *parat* tray seems to be more commonly used for making wheat dough, while the earthenware *dhatri* is most often used for the preparation of sorghum dough. This association has the effect of transforming a distinction which would otherwise represent only a difference in wealth into one that has connotations of a distinction in purity.

The third and most important distinctions arise from the general associations of the various food categories. These may be divided into three main classes: foods associated with the milk products of the cow, and having, therefore, sacred and pure associations; foods, such as grains and pulses, which are comparatively neutral in their associations; and foods associated with meat or alcohol, which are considered polluting or 'marked'. The pots in immediate association with this clear gradation in the food code are the black vessels, which are used mainly for food preparation. It is likely therefore that the variability of the black pottery may have been generated by the need for compatibility with these distinctions. In this case, the three aspects of morphological variation discussed above can be related, in some detail, to their role in the creation of further divisions within the main classes established by decoration.

The red-painted pots have been shown to have one associated rim variety, the split rim, which was then varied and opposed. All these vessels were associated with water. In the case of the black pottery, however, it is a gradation of food qualities that has to be expressed, and therefore the morphology must be varied more systematically. A graded series (Fig. 50) starts with the *bhartiya*, an earthenware vessel identical with a metal form of the same name, having a completely rounded body, and an unusual rim with a rounded top. This pot is unambiguously associated with the heating of milk products. The second vessel is the *dohni*, which has one *parti* at the shoulder, although this is comparatively unpronounced, and a rim that is also essentially a *gol* form, but more angular. The *dohni* has been associated with milk since Vedic times (Vira 1934). Evidence that this association is no longer as clear as it once was will be presented in the next chapter. The third pot in the series is the *chayra dohni*, which means merely 'sloping *dohni*'; the pot has a more angular shoulder and a pronounced sloping rim with straight sides. This pot is associated with the cooking of pulses and grains. The fourth pot in the series is the *jhawaliya*, which has a distinctive squat appearance with a sharp shoulder and a rim which is an elongated exaggeration of the sloping rim. The *jhawaliya* is specifically designated for the cooking of meat. We have here, then, four pots which form a distinct morphological series, drawing out the expressive associations of the food they contain. This is consistent with the earlier suggestion of a dominant rim form in the two major functional classes: the sloping rim, which occupies the centre of this sequence, with a rounder rim associated with the more pure (and liquid) milk. This cross-cutting extension would be associated also with the round rim of the *kalash*, the *kulheri* and some other pots used for ritual purposes. The sequence is found equally in all three morphological variables, the extension of the rim, the angular *parti* and the decrease in closure. This last attribute confirms the earlier suggestion that closure indicates degree of purity, which may be related to its wider reference.

There is also a candidate for a fifth pot in this sequence. This pot is made in two versions, both called *tapeli*. One form with straight vertical sides is a faithful representation of the metal *tapeli* used as a cooking vessel, but an alternative form is a pot, still more squat and angular than the *jhawaliya*. The associations of the *tapeli* are less clear; its metal prototype is a common cooking vessel and is used for making tea. The fact that the pot bifurcates morphologically and that one version appears at the extreme end of this sequence may, however, be related to one use mentioned for the earthenware version, which was that older women,

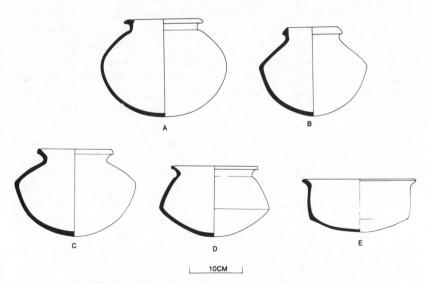

Fig. 50. Morphological gradation associated with relative purity of cooking vessels

who prefer not to go out to the fields, use these vessels to urinate in. This, obviously, could not be observed, but, if it is the case, it is certainly suggestive of a still more polluting association than the cooking of meat.

Caste

The association between food and pottery cannot be viewed in isolation; in effect, there are complex networks relating the many dimensions of variability. Food may be connected with social hierarchy either directly, through the principles of purity and pollution, or indirectly. For example, many foods have connotations of being 'hot' or 'cool'. Milk products are cool, and therefore curds are generally not eaten in the village during the winter season. Indirectly, however, this connotation also associates food with the social hierarchy, within which high castes are known as 'cool', as against the 'hot' low castes. These terms carry semantic associations similar to the English 'hot tempered' as against 'cool' or 'placid'. The meat and alcohol combination is a marked hot category, which may either be avoided by vegetarians, or used on marked occasions by others. One of the six potter households is vegetarian, and does not consume either substance, while the others will mark a major occasion such as the visit of potential in-laws by a feast with meat and alcohol.

Dumont's 'structuralism' has strong Durkheimian overtones (Durkheim and Mauss 1963), with the social gradation of caste representing the privileged base from which a plethora of other symbolic dimensions emerge, such as relationships between the sexes, relationships with the divine, and the gradation in foods. His principle of hierarchy is echoed in everyday village discourse in which castes and people are referred to as *umca* (high) and *nica* (low). It is elaborated in many everyday expressions – for example, in the variety of greetings used for individuals of higher and lower status than oneself (as analysed by Levinson 1982, for a village in South India). These relations are associated with the pottery, both through the general hierarchy represented in the pottery code, as in the three decorative classes, and through the two main forms of pollution perceived in Dangwara, that is *jhuta* and *aprana*. *Jhuta* is pollution based on the touch of the saliva or other excretion of another individual. Once having put food into the mouth with the hand, other food which is then touched with the same hand is *jhuta* and should not be eaten by others. This notion is of importance in relation to the deities, since *prasad* (see p. 146 above) is accepted by human beings, despite its status as a leftover (i.e. *jhuta*), thereby indicating the humility of the human with respect to the divine. In turn, the lowest castes are expected to accept leftover foods from the highest caste, and in accepting the pollution involved, to reproduce their ascribed lowness. The higher castes therefore become an intermediate group between the deity at the top and the untouchable at the base. It may be that the sacred cow complex is a logical extension of the fact of accepting milk, an excretion from the cow. This is also the main legitimation for the distinction between pottery and metal vessels, since it is the ability of metal to resist *jhuta* pollution, needing only to be washed, that makes them preferable to the earthenware that would have to be broken after each meal.

Aprana is simply the pollution based on touch or association with an 'untouchable' low caste. It is in the fear of this *aprana* pollution that untouchability finds its most common expression in the village. One obvious example of this is the separate 'hamlet' of the leatherworker and weaver castes, away from the main old village. That the untouchable should not touch the earthenware vessel of the higher caste is a basic rule of daily life. A *brahman* related how he had to put a pot outside in the yard after a weaver woman had accidentally brushed past it, when his own wife was taking it to the well to fetch water. A potter had recently broken a vessel that had been touched by an untouchable while at a funeral feast. A *jat* woman commented that she would either return a pot that had been touched by an untouchable to the potter to use as sherds for the firings, or hand it over with abuse to the low-caste person responsible. Most villagers, when asked, could recall a similar incident within the previous year. Metal vessels are also more resistant to *aprana* pollution, and only have to be cleaned.

There were two wells in the area near where I was staying. One was said to be clean water fit for drinking, the other dirty water only to be used for washing clothes. The terms used – *saf* (clean) and *ganda* (dirty) – were, however, found to have further connotations than those first mentioned (Mathur 1964: 98). The well described as dirty was in fact built by the government to supply clean water, but being government-constructed there could be no caste restrictions on its use, and the Muslim castes who lived nearby were major users. The other well was privately dug and the owner had imposed strict rules on its use. There was a complete ban on castes such as the leatherworkers, weavers, basket-makers and mat-makers; castes such as *musulman* and blanket-weavers were permitted to draw water provided they used metal vessels, although other high or middle-ranking castes were free to draw water using earthenware vessels.

These associations are demonstrable primarily in the creation of pot forms as categories, but they are also observable in the distribution of pottery. The *chayra dohni* and *jhawaliya* are not only associated with low castes, but were also more often noted in use by them, compared to the *dohni* and *bhartiya* favoured by the higher castes. The relationship between distribution and social hierarchy is more pronounced in the differential distribution in metal vessels as shown in Table 8 (p. 73 above). All Dangwara villagers agreed that food cooked in an earthenware container tasted better than that cooked in metal: the *roti* bread cooked on a *karela* or *kareli* had a superior taste to that cooked on a metal *tawa*; the vegetables from a *chayra dohni* tasted better than those from an aluminium *bhandia*, or a poorly-tinned brass *tapeli*. Equally the water from the porous earthenware vessel was far cooler and fresher-tasting than the water from copper and brass metal containers. Despite this, the figures show a strong association between the number of metal vessels and the caste and wealth of the household. Most *brahman* and other castes with pretensions to orthodoxy will tend to abjure the use of earthenware cooking vessels, so that the proscription long accepted for consumption is now being extended to preparation. During the caste-based census, the wineseller, who is in a somewhat ambiguous position in relation to other castes, claimed to be higher in purity than the *brahman*, since he used no earthenware vessels for cooking, while the *brahman* used such vessels.

The distribution of pottery within the house is also significant. Pottery is concentrated, while in use, in two main areas (see Table 7, p. 71 above), the water pots on the water-table and the black pots in the area of the hearth. These two areas are thought to be particularly susceptible to pollution. While I was able to wander freely around most high-caste homes, some families would not allow me to approach either of these two areas, and the measuring of the pottery had to be undertaken by my *brahman* research assistant.

Gender

The division of space is also important in relating pottery to the distinction of gender, as the house is differentiated into areas associated with each sex (Jacobsen 1973: 42). There is a considerable variety of house types in the village, but these tend to divide into two main forms. In higher castes, which have some pretensions towards *purdah*, the house may be surrounded by four walls, and contain a large open courtyard area. More commonly, however, the house itself may be represented as a kind of gradation, being composed of a series of rooms in a linear sequence. Men are associated with the front of the house, and artisans often work on their front veranda, which is also the area for male conversation, and the area in which men sleep in the summer. Women, by contrast, are associated with the back of the house and in particular the area of the hearth. This association is, of course, more than metaphorical, given the extensive time taken to prepare the bread for the two daily meals (Jacobsen 1973: 228).

Although it can be said that women are low with respect to men (it is a common village cliché that the husband is 'god' to the wife), they are not low in the same sense that untouchable castes are low. On the one hand, both are associated with the black ware, the untouchables for the reasons already outlined, and the women by reason of their close association with the hearth and food preparation. But this in some ways represents an opposite association: whilst the women are expected to spend a considerable time by the hearth, except during menstruation, when they are forbidden to approach either the water-table or the hearth, untouchables, by contrast, would normally be rigorously excluded from approaching the hearth. Women are thereby regarded more as comparable with the hearth itself, in that both are seen as susceptible to pollution. The act of eating and the act of sexual intercourse both render a person unclean. The gender relations also cross-cut hierarchy in that women, in their marital relationship to men, are also associated with red, and it is the women who usually carry the red-painted pots. Women wear a red streak in the centre of their forehead to signify their married status. A red *sari* is also commonly a sign of marriage. This may parallel the relationship between pottery and exchange, in that the proprietorial role assumed by the potters in relation to red pottery may be echoed in the way marriage is viewed locally in terms of exclusivity of rights.

Conclusion

The above evidence establishes the manner in which the variability of pottery can be comprehended by viewing it as a meaningful dimension, that is, as a semiotic code. It also establishes a relationship between pottery and some of its referents. For example, certain social groups, regarded as low, appear to be associated with the black colour of a class of pottery and also with the 'low' foods with which some of these pots are in turn associated. This helps to fix one end of the pole represented by the pottery as a dimension. At the beginning of this chapter, a general relationship was posited between the class of red-painted pots and that which was high and auspicious. The final relationship necessary to 'tie up' these associations is, therefore, to relate the high pole of the pottery code specifically with the high pole of the social code, which in effect means demonstrating a link between the red-painted pots represented by the ritually high *kalash* and the high castes represented by the ritually high *brahman*. Indirect connections through the mutual associations with religion are evident. A more direct association was suggested by one of the priests of the village. He claimed that the two are mutually essential for worship: 'It is a tradition that without a *brahman* and without a *kalash* there cannot be worship.' He proceeded to relate a long tale about the god Siva and goddess Parvati which explained why the *rudra kalash* (*rudra* being an aspect of Siva) was vital for the act of worship along with the *brahman*: both mediate in prayer to the deity. The *kalash*, the *brahman* and the particular association of the potters with Ganesh may all be connected as symbols of transformation from the secular to the sacred (J. Parry, pers. comm.). Although I was unable to observe a *brahman* wedding, my *brahman* research assistant claimed that an extra *kalash* is normally set out for this, as opposed to all other weddings. A *kalash* is also used for the sacred-thread ceremony which establishes the 'twice born' high ritual status of the wearer. In Dangwara, this is worn only by the *brahman* and the *bairagi*.

The aim of this chapter has been to demonstrate that the pottery could be shown to relate systematically both to an internal organisation and to other meaningful dimensions. In particular, it has tried to illustrate how this approach could account for the specificity of the variability represented by the corpus of pottery. Associations have been posited for the precise orientation of the rim, the presence or absence of a particular form of description, the degree of closure – that is, for the very minutiae that constitute the variety of forms. This is precisely what the process of production, described in Chapter 3, created but could not account for, what function and efficiency, discussed in Chapter 4, could only articulate with at the level of wide and generalised parameters. The approach represented by this chapter not only accounts for the richness of the material, but does so in a manner that relates it directly to the full social context – in other words, the people who create and use these forms.

The results of the ideas discussed in this chapter can be presented in the form of an abstract chart (Fig. 51), in which the extent of parallel alignment is suggested for a variety of dimensions. This form of presentation is clearly simplistic; a multidimensional table, which did not demand absolute parallels and would not therefore equate, for example, women directly with low castes, would be preferable. The figure highlights not only what can be achieved by the analysis of the pottery as a symbolic system, but also what is sacrificed in order to obtain the clarity of a systematic set of relationships. Firstly, such a presentation is clearly normative and assumes that these meanings and relationships are the same for all members of the village. Secondly, it represents a simplification of the actual relationships, which may vary depending on the context with which one is concerned. Thirdly, it suggests a relatively passive role for the pottery, fitting into existing distinctions and reflecting them. Fourthly, it is synchronically conceived and leaves no room for change. Fifthly, it renders the individual members of society equally passive as mere reproducers of cultural patterns, and does not indicate how they work as agents in the reproduction or alteration of these relationships.

Pottery is an artificial creation, whose acknowledgement as an active material intervention requires a more positive 'constructivist' model of the members of the society which are its context. It will be the aim of the next chapter to break open the evident rigidity of such a structure and

POT	STATUS	GENDER	COLOUR	CASTE	CONNOTATION	CONTENT	EXCHANGE	HEAT	RIGHTS
Kalash Dhupana Divali matka Akhartij gagra Mamatla	Divine Ritual	Male	Red painted	Brahman	Auspicious		Jajman system		Contractual
Goli Matka Gagra Chuklya Batloi				High castes		Water	Embedded exchange	Cold	Proprietorial
Brahman dohni Patya Wariya Kunda	Human		Red and Buff	Middle castes		Milk			
Neutral pots									
Bhartiya Karela Dohni Kareli Dhatri		Female	Black	Low castes	Inauspicious	Wheat	Market system		Non-contractual
Chayra dohni Jhawadiya Harawla	Polluted			Untouchables		Sorghum Pulse	Monetary economy	Hot	Non-proprietorial

Fig. 51. Association between pottery and major social variables

reveal the actual variability which it conceals and the kinds of social forms which must be postulated to account for it. This diagram does not reveal an objective 'reality'; rather, it represents a heuristically necessary stage in the elucidation and understanding of variability.

9
Pottery as categories

The intension of this chapter is to address the material presented in Chapters 2 to 8 in terms of the ideas discussed in Chapter 1, with the aim of gaining a further understanding of the factors which generate the variability of the Dangwara pottery as a set of material categories. The dominant theme will be the relationship between those processes which may be conceived as creating a 'formal' order or normative structure and the contextual practices which result in the observed variability, in which state any formal order is always realised. This basic tension is evident in all the preceding chapters.

In Chapter 1, it was suggested that contemporary social theory has shifted in recent years away from a structuralist emphasis on formal order, which concerned itself with the relationship between relatively autonomous categories and the cognitive processes which might be postulated, on analogy with linguistics, as giving rise to structure. Today, there is an increasing interest in the problematic informality of observed 'everyday' practices, with such an approach neglected. In so far as the process of understanding this variability still presumes the existence of underlying generative patterns (in the mode of neo-realist epistemology, Bhaskar 1978: 45–62), these are now examined for their production within historically contingent contexts and in terms of their 'specificity'. In Chapter 1, the influence of approaches providing a more flexible mode of representation of categories was noted. These approaches range from the work of the psychologist Rosch on the 'fuzzy' logic of categories to Bourdieu's notion of 'habitus', which interposed time and strategy between a structure of dispositions and their specific articulation in practice.

Some of these ideas are paralleled by recent representations of the major principles of South Asian social organisation, discussed in Chapter 2. These have shifted from Dumont's analysis of caste as a formal structure of concepts generating specific categories, whose meaning lies in their relationship to the whole and in their abstracted principles of legitimation, to more recent work (e.g. McGilvray Ed. 1982), which emphasises a relativist and particularist approach to the workings of caste interaction and the variable definition of caste and other basic social categories, in given contexts. Both these approaches were employed to model Dangwara society – the formal normative demands of caste, such as *jati dharma*, and the observable variations from such norms in everyday village life. When the village was characterised in terms of the relationship between major variables, such as wealth, caste and family size, as much emphasis was given to the generalised parallels and associations between these variables, as to evidence for variation arising because households chose to emphasise different goals, or have achieved wealth and status beyond what is customary for their given structural position.

In Chapter 3, the notion of style was introduced. This was addressed to a similar set of questions but in a very different sphere, the examination of the manufacture of the pottery. It was shown how style may be created by the selection of particular dimensions, such as rim form and body profile, to create variability, and it is these conventional foci for difference, as well as redundant similarities, which constitute the pottery as a familiar series, recognisably the product of a particular area. Style is derived from the exploitation of particular parts of the manufacturing process, such as beating the base, and a tendency towards repetitive technical sequences in constructing the majority of forms. While much of the observed variability may be subsumed within such a pattern, there are individual pot forms, such as *dhatri* and *surahi*, which were found not only to have a more individual morphology, but to involve more idiosyncratic methods of manufacture.

In Chapter 4, which was concerned with the relationship between form and function, pottery was found to group around two areas of utility. The painted red pots were all associated with the same function of carrying and storing water, in such a way that their morphological variability was in no way associated with their use. The other major functional class, that of black cooking pots, exhibited a close association between individual form and the cooking of particular produce; but this was an association of convention rather than efficiency. There were, however, certain pottery forms which were understandable primarily in terms of this particular contextual relationship – the musical instruments, for example, and other forms constrained by a highly specific purpose.

In Chapter 5, it was found that the mechanism for the distribution of pottery revealed a particularly clear division between formal and informal modes of organisation. The red-painted pottery was associated with the local variation of the *jajmani* system, a formal mode with fixed principles and expectations centred around two festivals. This was contrasted to the market system in which black pottery was sold according to the practical considerations of supply and demand. Each mode could be studied for its articulation with contextual factors as it was realised in practice; for example, the influence of wealth and political affiliation were noted. The informal mode was found to support rather than oppose the formal mode by providing it with a necessary flexibility.

In Chapter 6, a formal order was constructed which appeared to subsume the observed variability of painted designs within relatively few rules and procedures. It was shown that this 'structure' related to the order of painting and the steps by which painting was learnt. Again, this relatively simple order was found to break down, as designs tended towards a closer articulation with their context. In this case, it was the more representational designs, with particular referents, which were difficult to describe in terms of the analysis which had been developed.

In Chapter 7, a further example of formal order was identified in the ritual practices, in which pots are used in life-cycle and annual ceremonies. Here the fixed selection of particular pots to be employed in a prescribed manner could be contrasted with the more flexible use of pottery in the secular domain.

Finally, in Chapter 8, a systematic attempt was made to subsume all observed variability within a consistent order, using the methods of symbolic analysis. Here, pottery was presented as an abstracted code, whose internal coherence generated particular rim forms in relation to a gradation of other rim forms, or particular decorative modes such as 'red and buff', exploiting the interstices and thereby the ambiguity between the two major decorative classes. An equal consistency was assumed between this code and the major dimensions of social order in the village; in particular, caste. In this case the informal order was not considered, but will be a major concern of the present chapter.

In each chapter, the presentation has attempted to reduce variability as far as possible to some order, norm or rule, and then to consider that which it is difficult to subsume within this order. Variability was found to be concentrated in particular areas, such as rim morphology, cooking as function, exchanges at a set time, the shoulder field in painting and so forth. This reflects in part the nature of academic discourse. It is a convenient form of analysis to reduce as much of the observed variability as possible to a set of rule-like actions and concentrate on their description. The linearity of academic discourse thereby imposes closures which in turn have to be reopened.

In each chapter there are factors peculiar to the concerns addressed, which may, in part, also account for the formalist tendencies exhibited in the material and thereby permit this form of presentation. Manufacture and painting may tend to repeated basic sequences for reasons of efficiency of effort. Distribution may be easier if certain conventions develop which are not subject to the transitory status and means of particular exchange-partners. These factors, as has been shown (for example in Chapter 4), are limited, however, and do not address the overall consistency between these fields, such as the use of black pottery in a number of the more informal or contextual modes, which emerged in Chapter 8.

As a first attempt towards an understanding of the formal aspects of pottery variability, ideas developed in cognitive psychology and structural anthropology will be employed to identify the nature of pottery as a 'code', in which the specifics of form in a given material category are understood in relation to all others within that code. This will be expanded into a consideration of the relationship between pottery as a code and all other elements of the social and material order with which it interacts, using the concept of a 'grid'. This consideration of the processes behind tendencies to the formal will then be complemented by a consideration of the more intractable nature of the informal variability of observed practices. This variability will be located in the pottery itself, in the heterogeneity of village social organisation and in the variety of contexts in which the pottery is used. The relationship of form to context will be analysed under the term 'pragmatics'.

Variability is not only found in form and context, but also in the differential interpretation of the same form by the same persons. As an interpretation which emphasises cognitive processes is developed into a more general consideration of relevant social forces, this variability will be found to be understandable only in terms of the variety of interests and modes of representation in the village. These modes and their pervasive or limited nature are related to questions of power and control, a procedure which leads to a more dynamic model of the construction and continual re-formation of the pots as material categories. Finally an attempt will be made to expand from the question of representation and symbolism towards a perspective based on the circularity inherent in the interpretation of the objects as constructions by subjects, and, in turn, on the construction of these same subjects in terms of a material world that situates them as subjects. This sequence leads to a far more complex model of the factors involved in understanding the variability in material categories, but one which may encompass a degree of variability that the kinds of approaches used so far in this study have been unable to address.

Pottery as code

The formal aspects of the Dangwara pottery, studied as material categories, divide into those pertaining to the internal organisation of the pottery and those relating it to potential external referents. Throughout this study, the pottery has been conceived as a set, in which the precise form of any one pot is understood firstly in relation to all others. This is on analogy with the concept of 'field' in semantics and 'code' in semiotics (Lehrer 1974: 1, Lyons 1977: 268). In linguistics, the study of internal organisation is usually based on the dual principles of hierarchy and contrast.

The concept of style, with its equivalent assumptions of internal order, depends on the manner in which the pottery is characterised. No attempt has been made to define the overall set of pots. The core subject of the earlier chapters has been the thirty rounded container vessels along with twenty further forms made by the potters, with the assumption that the more specific the vessels are to some contextual feature, such as function, the higher the probability that they will be difficult to subsume within any overall characterisation. Certain more particular products of the potters, such as tiles and figurines, have not been included, and their form would not be subsumed under a discussion of style.

The main features emphasised have been the rim and the degree of angularity in the body profile, as areas where variability is 'concentrated'. Other dimensions of variability, such as the presence or absence of a flat base, could equally well have been considered. There are numerous alternative methods for characterising the pottery as a style. An example also using morphology considers the degree of curvature of the body as it 'grows' out of the base. Most of the container shapes consist of approximations to segments of circles. Some of these are only short segments, as in the case of *divaniya, tolro* and *harawla*; others, such as *dhakan*, build an elaborate rim or neck on to this. The next class takes the segment a little higher from the ground, as in *wariya, jhawaliya* or *pawanda*. A further set of forms takes the segment almost two-thirds to closure; these include the *kunda* and the *dohni*. Finally, there are pots which take the circle almost to closure, such as the *goli, chuklya* and *bhartiya*. On this basal segment may attach other segments of circles, at a tangent to the first, or straight sections, as in *chayra dohni*.

This characterisation, which again situates the individual forms as positions within a series, employs elements of shape ignored in the previous attempt, but in turn excludes rim form. A given assemblage may be considered to exhibit 'formal' order, to the extent that the total variability can be subsumed in such attempts at an overall characterisation. The Dangwara pottery, with an almost complete absence of lugs, handles and other asymmetrical attributes, is easier to contain within a given characterisation than many other comparable earthenware assemblages. The value of a characterisation from this perspective is precisely the degree to which it reduces the assemblage to an economy of synthesis.

Synthesis is vital to the notion of a category, which always implies equivalence. In the ordering of the external world, categorisation has as its first principle 'the almost common sense notion that, as an organism, what one wishes to gain from one's categories is a great deal of information about the environment while conserving finite resources as much as possible' (Rosch 1978: 28). It might be expected that the principles which refer to the organisation of our perception of the external world would carry over into the creation of the artefactual world. Thus, style implies an economy of logic found also in perception (Boas 1955: chapter two, Gombrich 1979: chapter two).

The resultant pattern is, however, polythetic and may not be reduced to a single classificatory principle. Rosch has recently developed a 'prototype' model of categories, which contrasts with the earlier logical contrast approach, and refers back to the earlier work on the polythetic nature of linguistic categories in use by Wittgenstein (1958: passages 66–71). A classification depends upon the criteria by which it is generated, as is found in the following three attempts to classify the Dangwara assemblage (Fig. 52a–c). In Fig. 52a the basis for classification is the major decorative groupings that have proved of significance in the organisation of several of the previous chapters. There are two major classes, the black and the red-painted, with a smaller class of red and buff, the whole being complicated by pots that may use these as alternatives or which may employ additional possibilities, such as solid red decoration.

The second classification (Fig. 52b) is based on semantic labels. It was obtained by asking informants the dual questions: 'What kinds of A are there?' and 'What is A a kind of?' The specific names of pots may derive from morphology (*goli* means 'round'), function (*jhar ka kunda* means '*kunda* for tree') or metaphor (*badak* means 'duck'). There may be alternative labels for the same vessel, which vary according to caste (*badak* for low caste, *surahi* for high caste) or region (the alternative use of *matka* or *mayna* for the same vessel seems to imply area of origin). The superordinate terms may also refer to morphology (the *kunda* seems to subsume an open-mouthed series) or function (the *dohni* refers to most pots used on the hearth).

The third classification (Fig. 52c) is based on function. There are two major classes, and a number of smaller groupings, which are cross-cut by a dimension indicating the degree of secular or ritual association. This is one of the most significant classifications, and one of the most immediate connotations of the semantic label.

It is semantic classification that has been the subject of most of the debate concerning categorisation. Rosch's notion of prototype, also called type-token, is defined by Tyler as:

A congeries in which several disjunct focal concepts serve to order central tokens into exclusive classes and peripheral tokens into partly overlapping classes by a variety of non-intersecting features or relationships. It is by far the commonest form of classification because it permits us to use a variety of information and, because it does not require a monolithic and internally consistent structure, can be quite flexible, responding readily to our different purposes and motives for classifying. (1978: 278–9)

This seems to represent a better description of the organisation observable in the three parts of Fig. 52 than that suggested by the older tradition, exemplified in componential analysis, for which categories are 'logical bounded entities, membership in which is defined by an item's possession of a simple set of criterial features, in which all instances possessing the criterial attribute have a full and equal degree of membership' (Rosch 1976: 21). In Dangwara there were disagreements as to

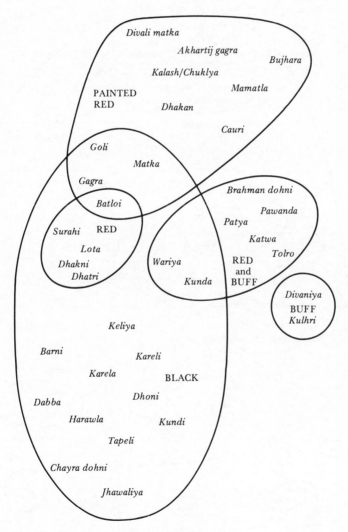

Fig. 52a. Classification of pottery by colour

whether lids are really a type of pot (*bartan* or *thamra*), and what is really a type of *dohni*, indicating the peripheral position of the respective hyponymic forms. In Chapter 3 gradation in category membership was also reflected in the quantitative characterisation of the pottery morphology (Figs. 12–14, pp. 46 and 47 above), and was still more pronounced in the relationship between painting and pottery examined in Chapter 6, in which the kind of painting used on a pot seemed to extend the differences

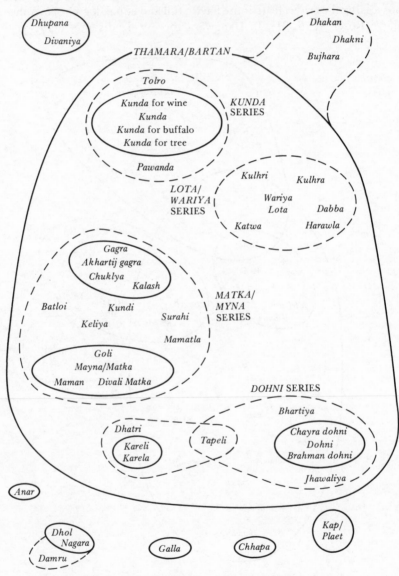

Fig. 52b. Classification of pottery by semantic label

between the larger and smaller examples of a given category (Fig. 38, p. 114 above).

Attempts have been made to use logical contrast in pottery classification. A recent study of Mexican pottery (Kaplan and Levine 1981) attempted to relate quantitative modelling and informants' views on discriminant variables. This approach adopts formal expressions of difference, such as the presence–absence of ninety-four features identified by acknowledged 'master' potters. The search is for formal exemplary knowledge rather than everyday understanding. Dangwara potters, by contrast, rarely articulate such discriminant features and ordinary users of pottery still less so, but this does not make the complexity of the corpus and the 'reality' of its structure any less 'real' or informative.

Although the three forms of classification presented in Fig. 52 clearly exhibit overall parallels, there are also major inconsistencies between

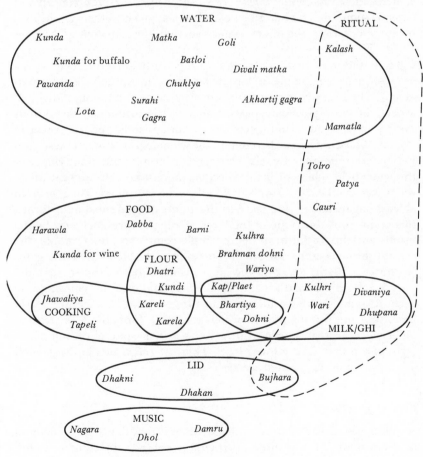

Fig. 52c. Classification of pottery by function

them, and there are no grounds for privileging any particular one (for example, as 'emic'). The pots are material categories and possess therefore an order, if a variable one, which is intrinsic to them as cultural forms. As pointed out in Chapter 1 they are not merely the product of the abstracted 'hypotheses' of the academic (Hill and Evans 1972).

These three classifications represent only examples of those possible. One important additional factor in characterising the process of categorisation observed in material forms, which tends to be ignored in a psychological literature with an Aristotelian base, is that classes may be influenced by predominant local views (in this case Hindu) on the actual structure of classification and the properties of superordinate terms. On occasion, references have been made to pots that 'stood for' more general groupings of pottery, without specifying the nature of this relationship; for example, the *kalash* stands for the painted red ware, or, as here, the *dohni* for the *dohni* series. According to Hindu concepts of classification, the higher the position of a given category within a taxonomic series, the more transcendental the category (Gardener 1978). This is true also for the production of form (Coomaraswamy 1934). In the classification of pottery, a superordinate term, such as *dohni* or *kunda*, is often used as a 'base level' term (in Rosch's 1976 terminology). The lower categories are conceived of as containing individual aspects of the higher categories, rather in the manner of the various avatars of the god Vishnu. Krishna is both Vishnu and an aspect of Vishnu. *Dohni* and *kunda* also contain the wider legitimation of these pan-Indian terms,and thereby relate the specific forms found in the village to this wider field. These principles become important in the present study, when they can be shown actively to affect the morphology of a form. In at least one instance – the *kalash* as the quintessential subsuming form – this seems probable. One of the signs of a higher presence may be the insubstantiality of form; in many temple complexes, for example, the central shrine is crude and small compared to the elaborate outer gates (Kramrisch 1946). *Kalash* is the most insubstantial of the red-painted pots; it is both the smallest and has the most rudimentary paintings. As such, it stands for that which it almost transcends. This feature is also important for the manner in which the more formalised, abstracted higher-level category can, through its wider sphere of reference, legitimise practices at a lower level. Thus the *kalash* aids in the general sacralisation of the painted red series.

Pottery as grid

A common criticism of structuralist writings is that they tend to focus on a formal analysis of the internal articulation of the subject material and thereby, in their opposition to empiricist accounts of meaning, fail to deal adequately with external relationships (e.g. Gellner 1982). It became evident in the last section that internal classifications may vary on the basis of selected criteria, which, as in the case of function, may be referential. A relatively crude presentation of external reference as part of formal order is its representation as a grid, in which the internal order of the code is simplified into a rigid linear form and laid out as a construct in multidimensional space, where its potential articulation with all other such codes is made evident. This is the underlying assumption behind Fig. 51. The individual pot is fixed into a set of conventional relations by its place within the code. Thus a *dhatri*, coming low in its position within the pottery code, might be expected to refer to items at the 'low' end of other codes, although this may manifest itself through various transformations.

The logic generated by such a grid is the same as that discussed by Gombrich (1969) in his account of a game he played as a child, in which a missing person was selected and the participants asked: 'If he/she were a flower/car/colour/etc., which would he/she be?' The consistency of equivalence between apparently absurd connections was the lesson of the game. Theories of metaphors often make similar assumptions. Basso (1976) suggests that cross-code equivalence is particularly powerful where it exploits lexical 'gaps' in particular codes, as in the Apache statement 'Butterflies are like girls' (see also Fernandez 1974). Psychologists working in the same area have suggested a domains-interaction model (Tourangeau and Sternberg 1982), which attempts to measure the extent to which the meaning of categories within a given domain (code) are influenced by their use as referents to equivalent positions in other domains. It would attempt to determine, for example, how far the meaning of the *dohni*, as pot, is affected by its use in the avoidance of the evil eye. The place of the pottery as a code in the grid is thus affected by its use.

The emphasis on the dialectical nature of the metaphor is paralleled by the more sophisticated work in post-structuralist studies, one of the main points of which has been to formulate a critique of the simple relationship of sign to referent assumed in some symbolic studies. This reveals not only the power of the referential system itself to control the nature of the signified but also the implications for relations of power (e.g. Coward and Ellis 1977: chapter four). Sperber (1980), taking an approach based on presumed cognitive processes, also attacks the semiological view of signs, and suggests a rather more general structure of the homologies and their variable evocation. He argues for the primacy of 'rational' processing, which then gives way to secondary evocative or symbolic operations (a view qualified by Toren 1983). This approach is critical of ideas developed by psychologists emphasising linguistic models, such as semantic networks (Boden 1977: 1253, Corton and Klanzsky Eds. 1978), spreading association theory (Collins and Loftus 1975), engrams (Hunt 1978) and conceptual cores (Miller and Johnson-Laird 1976: 690–707). Some recent work has used as a central part of these models Rosch's notion of prototypes in categories, in such a way that processing proceeds from the core elements of a category and then proceeds to the periphery, but allowing for schemata of expectations and 'fuzzy' rather than grammar-like associations. This has been taken up, in particular, by some of the recent Artificial Intelligence programmes (e.g. *KRL* Bobrow and Winograd 1977, 1979). This last example (as also Sperber) emphasises how evocation is controlled by context rather than simple abstracted association (the subject of the section on pragmatics, below).

It is the nature of such a grid, which permits the kind of 'privileging' by anthropologists of particular base-lines, such as caste and heat, which was criticised in Chapter 8. What is implied here is that even the most trivial code, such a pottery, can be articulated with almost any other aspect of conceptualisation, both by the villager, if a reason should arise, and also by the anthropologist. This may be briefly illustrated with two relatively 'extreme' examples. The first shows how pottery appears as consistent with major Hindu principles and the second how it could be made to relate to a set of structural transformations.

In previous chapters, it has been shown how pottery may be related to fundamental legitimatory principles, such as *dharma* (in the importance of *jati dharma* for the *jajmani* system in Chapter 5). A further major principle held to underlie the nature of human existence is *asrama*, which refers to the temporal properties of life. This establishes the ideal that a (male) human being passes through several life stages. As child, and then as an apprentice, he is established as a member of society by passing through a series of rituals from birth to marriage and learning the behaviour that pertains to his position. In a sense, in this phase, he represents less an individual responsible for his actions, than the subject of rites and instruction, exemplifying his social position without initiating action. In the next phase of life, the individual takes on practical responsibilities for the upkeep of his household, performing that task ideally related to his caste position, that is, his *dharma*. In the third stage, the individual may become an ascetic, renouncing the order of this world in preparation for the next. In this phase, caste position and the rules of pollution are dissolved, as is individuality, while worldly position gives way to a transcendental state. Here, the individual becomes a store for the collective wisdom of experience, which is used to help release him from this world.

Pottery in Dangwara may also be represented as a trajectory through three contextual moments. The first is the context of presentation, described in Chapters 5 and 7. This applies to all pots that have ritual connotations – to all, that is, except the black pottery. This is the phase at which they acquire these associations; through their use in theomorphic and anthropomorphic transformations, they are the subject of prayer, and in almost all cases receive a *tilak* mark. At this stage, they do not stand for themselves as *goli* or *gagra*, but rather they are used as part of ritual performances, in which they undergo some transformation, as is the case with the child.

It is in the second stage that each pot assumes the character which pertains to it as a conventional category. Here, they are all most closely associated with their secular practical function. They serve some particular designated purpose appropriate to them (their *'dharma'*), and have their greatest degree of individuality as pot forms. In the third phase, any pot type may be taken from its normal functional context and used for general storage purposes. At this stage it is of no consequence what the form of the pot has previously been; black, red, *kalash* and *harawla* are all used for the same purpose, in the same place. These stages are irreversible; a pot should not be taken from storage and used for practical purposes, and a ceremony requires the purchase of a new pot, not the use of one already employed in domestic duties. Clearly, a strong parallel can be drawn between the ideal stages of human life and those of the pot. Although no villager was ever heard to express such a relationship or interpret the cycle of pots in this way, the possibility for a more philosophically-minded individual to muse on the nature of life, using the pot as metaphor or parable, is therefore present.

A second example is the use of pottery to construct a model of oppositions and transformations, typical of derivative symbolic analysis. The possibilities of such an analysis are evident in the presentation of the contents of the previous chapters, with which this chapter began. Each chapter included at some point a duality. These dualities could then be treated as oppositions, homologous or transformational with respect to each other. If they were laid out systematically, they might appear as follows:

Manufacture	Beating	Wheel
Decoration	Black	Red
Function	Food	Water
Distribution	Akhartij	Divali
Ceremony	Funeral	Wedding
Symbolism	Low	High

The next stage would be to privilege one particular duality and use this as the base line for examining the others. For example, it could be argued that the opposition between wedding and funeral, as reflecting that between life and death, is fundamental. During the occasion of the wedding ceremonies, actions could be interpreted as referring to the other oppositions. The wedding starts with the worship of the potter's wheel (*chak puja*), it includes a number of uses of red, and indeed the married state of the woman is symbolised by a red streak on her head. There are several uses of water, as in the *gangajal* ceremony, and references to wealth, whose goddess, Lakshmi, is the subject of *divali*. Weddings are usually hypergamous and the ceremony which is held in the bride's village has been analysed as the symbolic representation of the asymmetry between the two families (Selwyn 1979) which thus signifies an advance in status. Thus, all the right-hand sides of the pairs may be linked. The next stage would be to locate a series of oppositions related to the funeral service which revealed how the dichotomies, previously understood only in terms of pottery, such as red against black, were best understood from the perspective of their coherence with these more 'fundamental' oppositions of life against death: for example, the feeding of the ancestors at funerals, as against the use of water at the wedding. If these oppositions could not be adequately documented in village practice then the abundant textual material on Hindu ritual symbolism could be brought in to complete the coherence of this pattern.

Structural analysis tends to formalise such oppositions to reveal, not only the polysemic nature of the symbolism, but also how certain transformations occurred in their realisation. They do so, however, often at the expense of an analysis of the diversity of forms in their context. An example is the comparison between the richness of the Stratherns' analysis of Mount Hagen body painting (1971) and the formalist (semiotic) version concocted by Neich (1982). There is certainly some value in this exercise; it would provide a much more convincing understanding of the *chak puja* than the general references to 'fertility' that were noted in Chapter 8, and may even provide clues to the developmental sequence of objects as categories (e.g. Lévi-Strauss 1982). It seems more valuable, however, to interpret the cross-cutting references of Chapter 8 in more general terms as evidence of a structure of wide potential, and then to concentrate on the social conditions for its particular realisations. Evidence for structure is not itself evidence that the resultant pattern of potential evocations are in practice employed; only a portion of them ever could be, and there is no reason to expect that this would be the same portion for all.

These two examples indicate the interpretative possibilities contained in the concept of a grid. They are far more complex than that which is suggested by the common use of this term, but assume the same principles of equivalence. The result is effectively that described by Bourdieu (1977), which works 'through the magic of a world of objects which is the product of the application of these same schemes to the most diverse domains, a world in which each thing speaks metaphorically of all others' (91). While the generative potential of such a grid is now clear, its epistemological status is less sure. When presented as Fig. 51, it appears as a form of objectivism, a given structure for all villagers at all times.

Some psychologists, who have employed the term grid most widely, have, however, used it in a very different fashion. The most common form is the 'repertory grid technique' developed by Kelly (Fransella and Bannister 1977). His intention was not to characterise normative conventions, but, in contrast, to understand how, on the basis of such conventions, individuals construct their own view of the world; how for example they recreate social stereotypes such as 'alcoholics are bad' or 'the status of women's work is low', and yet simultaneously differentiate themselves, if they happen to be alcoholics or female workers (Bannister Ed. 1977). For Kelly, a given grid is a transient and individual construction for a specific time and purpose. Such a grid is more an interpretation than a representation of the formal order of Fig. 51. It allows for a much more active model of people interpreting their world than the structuralist presentation, and places Kelly alongside Piaget as the leading exponents of a constructivist model of persons, opposed to the passive models of behaviourism.

The structured set of alignments represented in Fig. 51 cannot be held to have any existence except as the objectified postulation of the author, necessary for the understanding of observed patterns, as in neo-realist epistemology. Rather, there is a set of individual and transient realisations in particular contexts and strategies, which treats these alignments as generalised potentials rather than rules of meaning. Chapter 8 and its concluding model can then be understood in Bourdieu's terms as a 'methodological objectivism', which as 'a necessary moment in all research, by the break with primary experience and the construction of objective relations which it accomplishes, demands its own supersession' (1977: 72).

The informal mode

The attempt to understand processes tending to the formal and abstract may be represented as occurring at three levels: firstly, that of a pot as category, a category being defined by equivalence, which relates individual examples of the same form; secondly, that of pots as a code, which relates different pot categories as internally articulated within a series; and, thirdly, that of pots within a grid, which relates the pottery series to its potential external evocations. In each case, the formal is constantly qualified by breaking down as category (to the different actual pots of the same form), code (to the variety of classifications) and grid (to the variety of 'evocations') into the informal and realised, which produces an array of different and sometimes inconsistent patterns. Although the mechanism of distribution of pottery, outlined in Chapter 5, accorded closely with a set of formal ideals, the resultant distribution of pottery, outlined in Chapter 4, was only loosely connected with them. Even in the act of distribution there is flexibility; a potter will give out a pot which may not have the appropriate decoration, if that is what happens to be available in his store, and there is no firing of the relevant pot planned. An exception here is vessels intended for ceremonial use, where the term 'rule' would be appropriate.

The opposition of formal and informal is not restricted to that of process and realisation, as implied here. It can apply to a large number of contrasts: between ritual performance and secular practice, or between the authoritarian possibilities of relatively autonomous formal order and practical action which is more susceptible to challenge (Bloch 1977). There are a number of approaches which might assist in characterising the informal modes. In Chapter 3 this was attempted in terms of the actual quantitative variability of the pottery, while in Chapter 2 the variability in the village society was noted as a factor potentially creating differences in the way in which the same category would be interpreted. A third approach is to examine how far interpretation is context-dependent. This represents an important stage in showing how highly variable and inconsistent practices are made compatible with formal order, through an aspect of pragmatics which will be termed 'framing'.

In much symbolic analysis, one of the major problems is the highly normative nature of the presentation. Studies are commonly presented as though 'A means this' or 'B evokes that' in a given society. Yet what would a 'society' represent in the case of Dangwara? Is a female leather-worker a member of the same society as a female *brahman*, when, although living in the same village, they may never have met? These two persons are more likely to constitute, in themselves, a bi-polar construct, a dimension representing systematic differences in their conception of what a given category actually 'is'. This would imply that a member of the village, whose structural position lies somewhere between these two individuals, would also have a conception of a given material category that lay between theirs. These differences, as characterised by the dimensions of wealth, caste and family type, have been presented in Chapter 2. A similar point would arise from the analysis of ideology in which society is taken not as a coherent whole but in terms of the conflicts and contradictions which arise between interests and perspectives.

A recent research project by Kempton (1981) was designed to demonstrate and measure how the heterogeneity of a society is expressed in the diversity of its conception of categories. Using ideas from Rosch, Lakoff and Labov described in Chapter 1, he devised a technique for showing how the boundaries of a given category varied systematically according to several social dimensions, such as gender, occupation and rural as against urban residence. The technique was to make a series of drawings

Table 13. *Average use of the terms* surahi *and* badak *in response to pottery shapes*

Castes	Number of informants	Use of *surahi*	Use of *badak*
High	11	5.6	2.2
Middle (except potters)	19	1.1	4.3
Low	15	0.4	6.0
Potters	10	3.8	1.9

of common Mexican pots, varying them impressionistically, and showing them lined up in horizontal and vertical rows. These were presented to informants, who were asked to draw boundaries around those shapes which would be acceptable representations of a given semantic label. This experiment is limited to the relationship between words and objects but provides a clear demonstration of the influence of divisions by gender, town as against rural occupancy, age and expertise.

The factors which are being used to signify social differences are cultural and therefore arbitrary. The process of emulation, which will be examined in the next chapter, results in a homogenisation of elements which at one point were discriminable. It was shown earlier that in the distribution of pottery only certain categories were sensitive to any particular social division under investigation. This conclusion may also be drawn for the use of words as a classification of the pottery categories. In an experiment in which 165 computer-drawn shapes simulating the village pottery were shown to informants, an attempt was made to locate differences which were relevant to caste. A multi-dimensional scaling showed that if responses to these questions were taken as a mass, no significant pattern, or at best, a slight tendency for the highest and lowest castes to separate, was found. This suggests that the use of most labels for pottery categories has become universal, many of these terms having been in use for centuries.

Underneath this apparent homogeneity, however, certain terms may be isolated which are direct signifiers of caste differentiation. As might be expected, it was the relatively recent introductions which were most usable in this respect. In Table 13 the use of the terms *surahi* and *badak* are given for 55 Hindu informants, chosen as part of the census of pottery. The recognised 'proper' term is used by the higher castes, while the metaphorical term *badak* (which means a duck and refers to the split rim) is used by most low castes. As might be expected, the potters themselves, having a particular knowledge of this area, are much closer to the high castes than to their own middle castes.

The effects of the heterogeneity of the village may also be adduced from other evidence. As was found in Chapter 7 the ritual requirements are specific to the sub-caste level: for example, the pottery required by the *gujar* and the basket-maker at most annual and life-cycle ceremonies is quite different. Ritual differentiation may provide the most pronounced and the most clearly articulated variation. More subtle but equally important are the differences found in everyday utilisation of the pottery, which are probably more rarely noticed by the villagers and represent differences in normative models. It was found, for example, that while higher castes usually call the *dohni* a pot for boiling milk, middle and low castes tended to describe it as a pot equally for this purpose or for cooking vegetables and pulses. The degree of rigidity of convention may also vary by caste: the *brahman* who work as priests may be relatively observant of convention, as was found in their choice of vessels for cooking in the pottery census, while the *jat* may be relatively lax.

Pragmatics

Variability may be illustrated quantitatively in terms of the measurement of the pottery, and the differential interpretation of the same forms by different people may be hinted at by the use of different words or in ritual and secular utilisation of the forms. The implications of the informal mode can, however, be considerably extended, if the variability in the interpretation of the same pot by the same individual is also taken into account. This variability is dependent upon the particular context in which the interpretation takes place. The effect of context upon understanding has been the concern of an area of linguistics called 'pragmatics' (Levinson 1983). Pragmatics is the study of utterances and speech acts, and goes beyond the literal semantics of a statement and its presuppositions to the question of its contextual entailments. Much of the current debate centres on the nature of communication and the kind of assumptions about mutual knowledge which are necessary for understanding to be possible (Smith Ed. 1982). For Sperber and Wilson, 'a contextual implication of an utterance is a non-trivial logical implication derivable not from the content of the utterance alone, not from the context alone, but only from the context and content combined' (1982: 73). In linguistics, the consideration of pragmatics tends to be addressed to the highly specific nature of language (e.g. Smith and Wilson 1979: 172–89), and is not directly usable in other forms of analysis.

I propose to adopt the term 'pragmatics', but to use it in a broader manner than that implied in linguistics. Here, it is used to subsume all aspects of the relationship between conceptualisation and context, and is thus closer to the treatment of meaning in current work in Artificial Intelligence (e.g. Boden 1977). As applied to the problem of material categories, it may then include the implications expressed in the colloquial phrase 'pragmatic considerations' which emphasises practical constraints on desired actions. This is important since utility as context is of obvious significance in understanding artefacts.

A central question in the application of pragmatics to this material is why, in certain circumstances, difference in context appears to result in actual differences in pottery morphology or decoration, whereas in other instances contextual discrimination is dealt with at the level of differences in the use or interpretation of the same pot form. One of the main conclusions of previous chapters has been precisely that the actual variability of pot form – that is, the production of over fifty different types – may be largely accounted for by the tendency of these types to remain compatible with variability in the social context.

The painted pottery seemed most subject to differentiation by ritual context, with the *divali matka* being divided from the *matka* as ritual from secular, and with the wide variety of pots used in ceremonies. The black pots seemed most subject to differentiation with respect to conventional usage, with the cooking pots differing in relation to the foods which they normally contained. There is also a clear example of discrimination based on differential utility in the red and buff *kunda* series. The link between the *kunda* from which animals drink, that used for the planting of mango trees, that used for making wine, that used to collect water for washing hands from under the water-table and the *pawanda* is in the first instance morphological: all these pots are used for purposes which demand relatively open mouths. There are ambiguities with respect to some of these uses which account for the red and buff decoration (as shown at p. 147 above) but these do not account for the morphological connection. Rather, it appears that functional considerations (as in the colloquial term 'pragmatics') have in this instance encouraged assimilation within an overall series. *Kunda* is the superordinate term, being a pan-Indian word for a vessel with historical and contemporary connotations which rival those of the *kalash*. In this case, function, rather than being privileged as a prior causative agency as in some of the approaches discussed in Chapter 4, may be treated rather as a secondary pragmatic entailment that generates actual variability.

A contrast may be drawn between the *kunda* and the *goli*, a painted pot, which is only represented by a single morphological type, although there is a functional basis for similar differentiation. In conversation, a distinction is sometimes drawn between the *goli* and the *goli* for *chach* (whey). This is because the use of a *goli* for this alternative function (see Fig. 22, p. 69 above) results in a hardening of the inner surface and an elimination of any porosity, so that the pot can no longer be used for water-storage purposes. The *goli*, purchased at the local market, has a slightly different rim from those made in Dangwara and at least one household has exploited this difference to create its own particular *goli* for whey. This *goli* has a sloping rim and is referred to by one potter as the *chayra goli*, thereby evoking the *chayra* rim of the food vessels and thus implying an association, whey as 'food' being opposed to water. In general, however, this division is not made, and is not reproduced as a separate pot form by the Dangwara potters.

Why should functional differentiation result in a morphological distinction in one case, but not in the other? The *goli* is used to make whey and butter, which, in its clarified form of *ghi*, is one of the most sacred substances for the villager. By not dividing the vessel, the villagers have indicated a preference for a link between these substances and the ritually cleansing water, rather than with the category of food. This contrasts also with the black cooking pots in which milk is boiled. It has already been noted (see p. 147 above) that the waste water collected in the standard *kunda* from under the water-table is considered impure and ambiguous, and it is with respect to this that differentiation may be occurring with the *pawanda*, used in pot manufacture, and the *kunda* for growing trees in. Morphological divisions are more often generated by a desire to maintain difference (fundamental to any notions of purity and pollution) than for reasons of efficiency, although the latter also has its consequences, as in the creation of the *kunda* series as a semantic set (linking the wide mouths). The 'fuzzy' nature of these conceptual distinctions permits flexibility in the creation of these configurations.

These distinctions pertain to a constant relationship between particular categories and different contexts. There are, however, also distinctions which apply to the same pots at different 'moments'. It was suggested earlier that pots may be seen to have a trajectory analogous to the human life cycle. Each stage is marked by different requirements as to the specificity of the pot. In the first stage, that of the various ritual uses and transformations described in Chapter 7, it is of undoubted significance that the particular prescribed pot is used, and no alternative is countenanced. This accounts for many of the rarer pot forms such as *patya, tolro, mamatla, katwa* and the spouted *wari*. In the second, functional, phase, pots have their specific uses, but some flexibility was observed, as where a *dhatri* was used as a lid for a metal *tapeli* (see p. 68 above). By the third phase, discriminations are not made between the pots and any form will serve for storage purposes. Clearly, the conceptualisation of what the pot represents differs radically in each phase.

It is the *kalash* which most clearly demonstrates the implications of pragmatics in the interpretation of pottery. This pot is unique in being defined solely in terms of its context. There is no morphological or decorative distinction between the vessel sometimes called the *kalash* and that sometimes called *chuklya*. It is only the fact that the former appears in a ritual context, closed by either a coconut or a *bujhara* lid, while the latter appears in the ordinary domestic context, which tells villagers what category is implied. This, of course, enhances the transcendental qualities of the *kalash*, noted earlier on in terms of the overall pottery classifications, since it has therefore no permanent earthly form.

Examples have been cited elsewhere in this study where this same vessel form was shown to represent: a small water vessel carried by young girls, a deity, a gift to the *brahman* in the months following a funeral feast, the apex of the Hindu temple or a representation of a temple, a pot for keeping vegetables in storage and an auspicious gift to a guest. Despite this multivalency, the villager has no difficulty in knowing which particular form is represented at a given time. The cues may be physical, as with the silver waist-girdle, *bujhara* and *tilak* mark used in the *gangajal* ceremony (Fig. 45, p. 129 above), or they may be derived merely from contextual knowledge.

The notion of 'cues' is parallel to that of 'frames', introduced in Chapter 6 and an important element of pragmatics. If the same pot can signify in an entirely different manner, both to different people and to the same people at different times, this results in a polysemic quality with the potential to develop into inconsistency and extreme variability. Yet, paradoxically, these same forms were earlier analysed as exhibiting formal modes in their organisation. The importance of frames is that they make possible the articulation between the formal and informal modes, by dividing off the various contexts in which interpretation occurs and thereby maintaining coherence in each. In Chapter 7 it was suggested that pottery itself acted as a framing device – that is, it provided cues which had the effect of establishing the ritual significance of the events taking place. It was suggested there that this accorded with Gombrich's study (1979) of the frame as appropriate background, establishing the setting for the actual symbolic display or behaviour, but not of itself representational. In Chapter 7, pots were found to act both as framing devices and, on occasion, directly as symbols.

Other writers who have used the term 'frame' include Goffman (1974), who examines frames as a means by which people are cued into appropriate behaviour (for example, theatre and ritual), so that they do not have expectations inappropriate to the interpretation of these events, but which is intended ultimately as a means of showing how a notion of reality is constructed. As developed in Artificial Intelligence (Minsky 1977), frames have become the key to simulated human reactions. They are used to separate different spheres of behaviour, in each of which a certain relatively predictable sequence is suggested, as for example going into a restaurant or taking an examination. Frames therefore control spheres of evocation: for example, the term black may evoke fear, night and evil, but it is more appropriate that it does so with respect to a Victorian melodrama than in relation to a sheet of carbon paper. Frames, then, extend the earlier models of cognitive processing and relate them systematically to the context in which they take place.

It is the use of frames which accounts for villagers' being highly concerned as to whether they have the correct pot when constructing a *cauri* for a wedding, but not at all concerned when using the same pots for storage. Equally they allow the same pot to be used for a variety of purposes and evocations, without necessitating the generation of different morphological types in each instance. Framed behaviour is particularly important in public performance. The number of *matka* used at a feast, or *divaniya* placed around a house at *divali*, may attest to the wealth of the participants. Yet these same individuals may be much less concerned with their behaviour outside the village. Thus the *harawla*, the only pot made specifically for the purpose of eating food, is much more likely to be encountered in the fields, where people take a midday meal, than in the village, where such behaviour is likely to be 'recognised' (Gilsenan 1976, 1983).

Frames also determine which attributes of the pots have significance in particular circumstances. The paintings are important in the distribution at *divali* and *akhartij*, where their quality may be compared with that of the pots received by one's neighbour, but they are of no importance when the pots are used for drawing water later on. Indeed, the ochre paint is highly fugitive and the outlines of the paintings are hard to identify in use. Frames allow people to select when contradiction in meanings may be ignored and when brought into direct confrontation. They thereby contribute to the enactment of strategy which is the subject of the next chapter.

An important conclusion to be drawn from this discussion is that, although models have been derived from two branches of linguistics – semantics and pragmatics – it may be that their relative importance in the interpretation of material forms is the inverse of that in linguistics, where pragmatics still represents a relatively minor field of study. Pots, by and large, rarely figure directly as signs or symbols; they can rarely be said to 'mean', in the empiricist sense of direct reference. If they 'denote', it is merely the category of which they are an individual example, while what they evoke is dependent largely on contextual discrimination. Pots as physical forms are usually less remarked upon than that which they contain. They are therefore frames in the physical as well as the literal sense. Equally, they serve more often as conceptual frames for interpretation than as the direct subject of comment.

It has been suggested in this section that frames can permit an impressive multivalency in the pottery itself and, through the use of pottery in turn as a framing device, in other categories. This contributes to the overall complexity of interaction developed in the village. Pragmatic analysis, as outlined here, in which the variability of form is related both to the variability in the interpreter and the variability in the context in which interpretation takes place, is therefore able to encompass a far greater degree of variability than the kind of approach exemplified in Chapter 8, in which both of these factors were ignored.

10
Pottery and social strategy

Although at several stages in this study critical comments have been made about unwarranted attempts to privilege certain elements in analysis, there are clear grounds for doing just this with respect to one factor in the generation of observed variability, and this is human interest. Pottery as an artefact is not reproduced either by itself or by some abstract structures, cognitive or political, but through the active intervention of human agency, which at any given time must be credited with a rationalisation of its interests with respect to its actions, even though these may not be conscious or articulated in language. There are theoretical problems in privileging human agency as 'subject' as opposed to pottery as 'object'; the inherent circularity will be noted in Chapter 11. While the study of material categories has tended so far to be synchronic, a discussion of agency and interest in the construction of category variability demands a more dynamic model of the development of these categories.

Characterising human interest itself raises major problems. Interest, in an anthropological enquiry, cannot be reduced to individual motivation or desire, as in some psychological approaches. Interest is taken rather as conventional, the individual seeking that which is socially desirable, according to the position which he/she holds in relation to society. The interests of women are likely to differ from those of men, and the interests of members of high castes from those of members of low castes. This creates what may be termed 'social strategy'. Individuals are not, however, determined by their structural position; a measure of 'discursive penetration' (Giddens 1979: 5) must be ascribed to them – that is, an understanding which enables them to rationalise their interests as strategy; and they must be credited, too, with some flexibility in the determination of the particular nature of that strategy. Interest in some studies has tended to be reduced to material advantage, but a more flexible approach for a village that exhibits ascetic as well as profit-orientated goals might follow Harre, who suggests that 'the pursuit of reputation in the eyes of others is the overriding preoccupation of human life, although the means by which reputation is to be achieved are extraordinarily various' (1979: 3). This approach may encompass symbolic as well as material capital (Bourdieu 1977: 171–83). Strategy most often consists of steering a course between the respect sought and the contempt feared in the attitudes of others. This may be particularly felt in the relatively closed environment of a village.

Strategy may work through individuals or through a group. The latter is more common in Dangwara, since, if an individual *gujar* wishes to raise his/her reputation in the eyes of only the other members of the caste, then individual behaviour may suffice, but if it is the opinion of members of other castes that is of concern, then the attempt must be made to raise the status of the whole caste as represented in the village, since the individual is held as an exemplar of caste stereotypes. In recent years, this caste has made a group decision to become vegetarian, a social strategy aiming to appropriate the high status of this practice which symbolises the following of the brahmanical model of behaviour. This represents an example of a phenomenon commonly observed in South Asian ethnography and termed by Srinivas 'Sanskritisation'. It is the process

by which a 'low' Hindu caste, or tribal or other group, changes its customs, ritual, ideology, and way of life in the direction of a high, and frequently 'twice-born' caste. Generally such changes are followed by a claim to a higher position in the caste hierarchy than that traditionally conceded to the claimant caste by the local community. (Srinivas 1966: 6)

What has been exemplified in this case is the process of emulation. This is of particular importance here for methodological reasons. In developing a more dynamic model of the construction of material categories, there is often a dearth of relevant evidence. The particular material being investigated is of such a trivial nature that it is hard to obtain information relating to previous periods. Little conscious attention is given to pottery, and questions about changes in pottery received only vague and unclear answers. The pots themselves do not last long; most break within a year or two, and no records of them are kept.

In a parallel situation, the sociolinguist Labov (1972) has shown how processes such as emulation allow for a diachronic analysis based upon synchronically derived material. The actual process of emulation occurs when hierarchy has developed as a fundamental principle of social organisation. Words and objects may become symbolic of persons or groups within such a hierarchy, in the most formal cases as insignia of rank. In this situation, when an individual or group wishes to raise its relative position within the hierarchy, it may seek to copy the group above by adopting some of the products or styles associated with that group. If the higher group wishes to maintain the previous contrast, it must seek either to prevent this or to promote new differentiating symbols in order to maintain the distinction. Fig. 53 illustrates the effect of emulation upon pottery, where pottery has become associated with social status. If higher groups adopt new forms (a pot with a handle, for example), as a result of emulatory pressures, this will result in a dynamic force continually producing change in the material forms, but having no significant effect upon the social structure itself. Labov has pointed out that one effect of this is that, at any given time, certain words (or objects) will be in the process of moving along this sequence, and for the period,

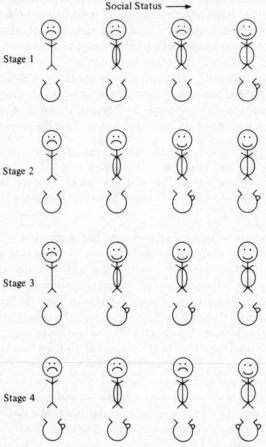

Fig. 53. The process of emulation. While the social hierarchy remains constant, the process of emulation provides a dynamic force producing continual change in material items. Stage 1: highest status group adopts a change in conventional pottery form. Stage 2: second highest status group adopts innovation. Stage 3: third highest status group adopts innovation. Stage 4: lowest status group adopts innovation, but by this time highest status group has adopted another change and thereby maintained the contrast.

until they become universally adopted, will be symbolic of social differentiation. He states of New York, where he worked: 'In every context, members of the speech community are differentiated by their use of (ing), so that higher and lower scores for this variable are directly correlated with higher or lower positions on socioeconomic indices' (1972: 239). Thus a dynamic sequence may be inferred from synchronic material.

The effects of such strategies may be discernible in the pottery of Dangwara. Firstly, as was found in the previous chapter, differentiation may occur in the interpretation or use of pottery. Secondly, there may be differentiation in the distribution of types of pottery through the village. It was found in Chapter 4 that, whereas most pottery did not show any association with the differences in caste, a few forms did appear to be significantly associated. Where these distinctions are linked to some external factor, such as the association of *kareli* to sorghum and *karela* to wheat, they are likely to remain discriminant, in this case because of the difference in the cost of the two kinds of grain. By contrast, a decline in the use of the *harawla* is likely to continue throughout the community, since the polluting implications of eating from earthenware holds for all.

In terms of the subject of this study the most interesting case occurs where the process appears to be responsible for actual changes in the material forms themselves. Again the synchronically observable differentiation may allow the postulation of a dynamic sequence. The clearest example is found in the range of cooking pots. This series is based around the *dohni* form, which is also the superordinate term, being often used by villagers to refer to any of the members of the series. *Dohni*, like *kunda* and *kalash*, is a term with a considerable history and is used today over a wide area. The term is closely associated with the preparation of milk products, but, as previously noted, it is also used for cooking vegetables and pulses. In this case, emulation works in a slightly different manner from that shown in Fig. 53. The problem for high castes is not that lower castes are using these pots, but that they tend to use them for purposes which are 'lower' than that with which the pot had previously been associated, so leading to a 'contamination' of that pot as a category. This may be followed in turn by further differentiation, creating a new pot category, a clear parallel being the construction of new castes from divisions in the relative purity of sections of a given caste (Dumont 1972: 243–6).

There are four pots which can be understood as extensions from the *dohni*, which acts as the prototypical form in Rosch's sense (1976). The series starts with the *dohni*, as a form traditionally associated with milk, but sometimes used for cooking other substances. The *chayra dohni* divides from the *dohni*, taking over a function which threatened its purity, and is now the 'proper' pot for cooking vegetables and pulses. The *jhawaliya* goes further in this direction by its association with the cooking of meat. In the opposite direction is the *bhartiya*, which uses its metal skeuomorph to establish itself as the pot with the clearest and most exclusive association with milk, while the *brahman dohni* is established as a red and buff form on the basis of the ambiguity between an association with a ritual context and also with food. The implications of these differences for the morphology and decoration of the pots concerned was demonstrated in Chapter 8. The most recent of these extensions is the *bhartiya*, which seems to have been promoted in recent years by one potter in particular, who regards it as his most successful innovation to date.

This example illustrates how a strategy (emulation), applicable to all castes, can result in the typical homology of structure between pottery as a code and other associated codes. Pottery lends itself to emulation because of the ease with which new forms of earthenware can be created and changed. It is, however, only one of several strategies that act towards the maintenance of the social hierarchy. An alternative is simple coercion, where lower groups are forbidden to adopt the traits of higher groups. In one recorded example, a district regulation asserted that untouchables 'should not use other than earthenware vessels in their houses' (Srinivas 1966: 16). Further, it may not always be reasonable to assume that a strategy will work in the same way for all individuals and groups, and the heterogeneity of the village again imposes itself upon the analysis. Even within a single strategy, such as emulation, there may be contradictions between the various interests involved. The *gujar* adoption of vegetarianism does not imply that all high castes are vegetarian; the higher caste of *rajput* are quintessentially meat-eaters, employing a strategy based around a martial stereotype, which contrasts with the brahmanical model (see Marriot 1976 for a formal analysis of caste strategy). A more sophisticated model than simple emulation may be developed if consideration is given not only to the differences in interest between groups, but also to the differences in the ability of these same groups to pursue and to represent their interests.

For purposes of presentation, four major classes of interest and strategy may be defined in the village: the *jat*, representing practical interest and material advantage; the *brahman*, representing religious authority and symbolic capital; the potters, representing a particular perspective in relation to the material under consideration; and the remaining castes, which are concerned with micro-differentiation between themselves.

The *jat*, although the dominant caste, have been noted as somewhat maverick in South Asian ethnography on account of their lack of orthodoxy. They are best known for their martial and more especially for their practical abilities, both stressed in the modern Sikh population, which consists, in large measure, of *jat*. In Dangwara they are most closely associated with the highly successful, recent improvements in farming and agricultural productivity. They tend to sell most of the village surplus produce, and are responsible for the importation of most commodities. They gain power, therefore, by their ability to control forces external to the village. In a particularly clear example, several *jat* obtained money from banks and institutions at only 0.75% interest per month, and then lent this in turn to other villagers at the rate of 2% per month.

The direct use of pottery is not particularly developed in such enterprise, so that the importance of the *jat* 'interest' with respect to pottery is not commensurate with their dominance in the village. An exception here is the recent increase in the use of the *kunda* for tree growing. This appears to be a copy of the *gumla*, or flower pot, common in the towns. This vessel exploits the increasingly systematic planting of young fruit trees, especially mango, and one potter claims to have sold 250 of these to a *jat* and to two *brahman*. Several ritual uses of pottery also have strong associations with agricultural practices, including the placing of a new *matka* on the fields of landowners at the beginning of the new farming season, as part of the *jajman* system. This will be used to keep water cool during the year's labour. The *kulhri* is used as an agricultural augury at the festival of *gobhardan puja*, in which it predicts the differential fertility of the fields, and the use of the *goli* in a similar predictive function at *akhartij*, in relation to the year's rain, is particularly associated with the *jat*.

Although the *brahman* are representing here a more expressive form of interest, the actual members of the caste present in the village are divided between those who follow a priestly profession as clients for all middle and high-caste villagers, and the landowners who are amongst the wealthiest in the whole village. There are, however, other groups with an equivalent emphasis on religious practices, in particular the *bairagi* mendicants. As with the *jat*, the *brahman* (priests) gain their power from their manipulation of forces external to the village. They are able to interpret the wider religious and moral values held by the Hindu-dominated society. They interpret these abstract values in terms of their specific significance for villagers. In short, if the *jat* are important for bringing in commodities, the *brahman* are significant for their influence over what those commodities come to represent.

Certain pots have become more imbued with ritual associations than others, and it is noticeable that of these two forms of function, the practical and the ritual, it is the latter which is most effective in preserving the particular category over time. In recent times, several pot forms have fallen out of use, including the *chillum* used for smoking tobacco (ousted mainly by cigarettes), the *kundi*, which has declined with the rise of electric flour mills, and even the *matka*, which is much less common as a result of the widespread use of metal buckets to draw water from the wells. Pots having a ritual significance, however, will be retained even when their ritual 'function' has not only lost any exegetical significance, but even, as in the case of the *katwa* taken in the shepherd's *warad*, when no one can suggest any use, ritual or functional.

The potters' peculiar importance with respect to this particular material domain lies in the fact that they both produce and distribute the forms, although this is not to say they can control what these forms come to represent. The potters' interest lies in establishing a higher status for earthenware as a whole, and in establishing the need, either practical or otherwise, for new forms of pot, thus expanding their work and significance. As was shown in Chapter 5, there are already far more pots produced than can possibly be used by the villagers, and at least one cause of this may be the perseverance of the potters in insisting that individuals 'need' given forms. They may attempt to introduce new forms on the basis of importation of types established elsewhere, such as the *surahi*, which has been coming into fashion in north Indian villages in recent years. They may copy forms in other materials; copies of metal vessels include the *batloi* and *bhartiya*, while copies of china vessels include the *barni* and the *kap/plaet*.

The easiest way for the potter to introduce a new form is through the *asami* system. If the potter merely kept a new pot in his courtyard, the middle and low castes, who buy directly from him, would be unlikely to adopt a new form, without knowing its associations. Rather, the potter will take some of these forms and present them, without expecting payment, at the houses of some of his wealthier and more influential patrons. During the census, cases were found of households claiming to have discarded pots that had been given to them because they had no real idea what to do with them. An example was a form of frying vessel which could have competed with the metal *karai* and was well suited to this proposed purpose, but, as a black pot with elaborate decoration, did not fit within the general code. In contrast, the pot which has been most successful in recent years, the *bhartiya*, although totally redundant in practical terms, fitted well into the code as described above. This is one of the few forms whose recent history is reflected directly in the distribution of pots, since it is more common, at present, in the households of higher castes. The potters are one of the groups who most strongly support a strategy of 'ritualisation', ensuring, for example, that the shepherds accept the *katwa*. The ritual status of pottery not only ensures the continued massive production of pottery beyond the demands of utility, but also acts to further the overall status of earthenware as a suitable medium for sacralisation, and vicariously to raise the potters' own status.

The final perspective is that of the majority of castes, whose main concern is the kind of micro-variation and jostling for status which was assumed to generate the pattern of emulation described in Fig. 53. This kind of behaviour is centred on the high and especially the low castes, of whom a recent study noted: 'Structurally it is here shown that where untouchables are excluded they replicate. They recreate amongst themselves the entire set of institutions from which they have been excluded by reason of their extreme lowness' (Moffatt 1979: 5). The practices may be weakest amongst the middle-ranking castes, especially where they form 'allied' groupings (see p. 24 above and Mayer 1960). A further consideration of this mechanism points to some of the wider implications of differential power in the enactment of these strategies. This example refers not to a pot form but to a piece of heavy silver jewellery called the *kariya*, which is worn around the ankle. According to a wealthy *jat* landowner of Dangwara:

Only the high castes used to wear *kariya* on their legs, but now low castes have copied it and are so fond of it that they are ready to sell their land for it, so now the opinion of the high castes is that because of their weight, the number being worn are decreasing day by day. Whether it is in the field of eating or wearing, the low caste is copying the high caste, so for the *brahman* it is the high castes, we *jat*, *gujar* and *rajput* that are copying them, while in turn these untouchables are copying us.

This statement is rare both for its explicit acknowledgement of the emulation process, and also for the way it exemplifies a particular form of rationalisation. Although the pattern of change is clearly emulatory, it is legitimated in terms of the weight of the anklet. In effect, as the anklets have become socially less desirable, they have become heavier to wear. This is an example of the process of naturalisation.

Naturalisation describes the process by which that which is created by human artifice takes on the appearance of the natural properties of the artefact. As such, it is perhaps the most significant factor in interpreting the relationship between the social and material worlds. As a process, it can be described in a number of ways. Barthes attempted a semiotic analysis in his book *Mythologies* (1973) by describing naturalisation as the relationship between the denotation – that is, the literal symbolism of the form (which tends to include its 'natural' qualities, such as functionality) – and its connotation – that is, the secondary implications of the form (which tend to include its social symbolism). Naturalisation inverts this relationship, and makes the artificial representation of a society, a representation which may favour the interests of a particular group, appear as the natural order of things. More recently, Barthes has repudiated the privileged base suggested by the idea of denotation, and has come to regard the problem in terms of a general plurality of meanings and perspectives (Barthes 1977: 169); indeed, his earlier semiotic perspective seems rather narrow as an instrument for the analysis of material culture. More developed is Bourdieu's analysis of the relationship between practical and expressive modes. In so far as pottery translates its articulation with a certain representation of the social order into a given 'functional' form, it may be seen to exemplify the process described by Bourdieu whereby 'Practical taxonomies, which are a transformed, misrecognisable form of the real divisions of social order, contribute to the reproduction of that order by producing objectively orchestrated practices adjusted to those divisions' (1977: 163). In critical studies, naturalisation is associated with the more general tradition of the *ideologiekritik* which developed from Marx's analysis of the illusory nature of representations of 'value', and, more specifically, from his analysis of the 'fetishism of commodities' (Larrain 1979, 1982).

The significance of this for the present study is that the analysis has throughout assumed a relationship between pottery and society which is denied by the villagers, for whom the pottery is noted only as a trivial, practical medium, with some additional ritual 'functions'. Essentially, for the villager, pottery is constituted by and 'is' its function. The material world, as an established environment for social action, always tends towards naturalisation, not because of some deliberate exercise of reification, but because of its very materiality, which, given an asymmetrical distribution of power, means that the manner in which the material world acts to objectify a particular representation of society tends to favour that representation which reflects the perspective, and therefore also the interests, of particular social groups. The process of naturalisation often takes the form of a simple dovetailing between two forms of legitimation: for example, the 'core' of the black pottery might be considered as that used on the hearth, and the use of black might be explained by the discoloration resulting from use, but this 'natural' link is extended into the more general corpus of black pottery, the majority of which is not used on the hearth. It follows that the manner in which black, as opposed to other forms of decoration, reproduces asymmetries in the social hierarchy through its associations, as described in Chapter 8, is the more likely to remain unconscious and unquestioned.

Mundane material culture, such as pottery, therefore, achieves its cultural significance, ironically, because its two major attributes are (a) its functionality and (b) its triviality. In the first case, the arbitrary cultural divisions are superimposed on 'natural' (i.e. functional) associations, and in the second case, pottery as trivia contributes to the process of cultural reproduction, because, being very rarely the focus of attention, it is well suited to framing, in Gombrich's sense (1979: chapter two). Thus, the significance of pottery is best appreciated in combination with many other elements of the material environment, such as clothing, field systems, houses and the spatial organisation of the village itself. These taken individually may be trivial, in that, for example, emulation in a single instance would not in itself raise the comparative status of the caste concerned to any significant degree, but together they constitute a highly significant aspect of what Bourdieu calls 'doxa', a representation of the given order of the world that constitutes an environment for living (1977: 164–71).

As practised in the village, this is clearly not a simple case of dominant and dominated groups: there is a whole series of different interests represented, and, equally, a multitude of different interpretations of the same objectives. These interests depend on the structural position and personal inclination of the individual, and may vary for the same individual according to the particular context within which interpretation and action take place. Thus, control over interpretation may often reside in control over the frames that situate it, rather than in control over morphology. For example, the influence of religious authority works through the establishment of ritual frames, within which pottery is interpreted in a highly particular manner, while the impact of the interests exemplified by the *jat* is exerted through their influence over interpretation as to practical utility. This allows two major forms of perspective, which might otherwise tend to contradiction, to co-exist without necessarily confronting each other, except when, as part of a strategy, an individual decides to 'break frame' and expose the basis for conflict. Occasionally, the resultant inconsistencies between action and legitimation become particularly evident, as in the example given at p. 117 above, when the potters simultaneously painted peacocks on the pottery and told stories about how they were forbidden to do so.

Nevertheless, there are parameters to this flexibility. The pottery itself, while subject to differential interpretation, embodies a structure as a material code, and fundamental social change may demand a corresponding change in the pottery itself as the 'text' which is being interpreted. Thus, objectification in concrete form is a constraint, if a loose one, with which frames must have some alignment, and through which they obtain their coherence. It is therefore highly significant that the *brahman* can 'capture' the highest end of the codes, in almost all cases, and gain a direct association with them. It has been shown in Chapter 8 that the *kalash* is closely identified with the *brahman*, just as the *brahman* is identified closely with the cow, the killing of either being regarded as an equal sin. The cow and the *kalash* represent the apex of their respective codes (Dumont 1972: 195).

The dynamic qualities of these relationships and the manner in which they act upon the changing material categories in the village may be explored through a consideration of the relationship between earthenware and metal container vessels. The use of metal vessels, as against earthenware, has been increasing throughout modern India, and it is probably the case that the Malwa area is relatively conservative in its extensive use of earthenware forms, whereas in, for example, Maharashtra, metal is far more prominent. The process of replacement can be observed in Dangwara today and within it the effective articulation between the various interests may be discerned.

The census in Chapter 4 indicated the positive association of metal vessels with caste and in particular with wealth. The major political change in recent times has been the increasing importance of the *jat* in the village, as against the *brahman*. An anticipated effect of this change might be an increase in the importance of objects symbolising discrepancies in wealth, as against those signifying differentiation in ritual status. Metal, because of its comparative cost, is clearly a more likely vehicle for such differentiation than pottery: metal vessels are closely associated with dowry, which is the most important single expression of wealth in village life. With this change of emphasis from earthenware to metal, it would appear that the medium of discrimination is changing its nature. Earthenware is constructed from common materials, so that 'difference' has to be created symbolically from the play of the code, and this lends itself to the ritual authority of the *brahman*. Metals such as copper are, however, comparatively rare, so that 'difference' tends to be expressive of differential access to commodities, which lends itself to the practical authority of the *jat*.

The interests of the majority of castes result in an emulatory pressure on the adoption of metal vessels. The exception here is the potters, whose interests are naturally conservative in respect to this shift. Until recently, the metals used for container forms were mainly brass and copper, which have always been comparatively expensive; today, however, aluminium has become very common, and traders in aluminium pots are often found passing through the village. As a result, metal vessels have rapidly increased in numbers and now virtually all households possess a quantity of these vessels, as shown in Table 8 (see p. 73 above).

Such a change might be thought to threaten the interests of the *jat*, who would otherwise have favoured a simple shift from earthenware to metal; the ownership of metal vessels would now no longer be so clearly discriminating. There is, however, another major perspective and source of interest, exemplified by those who follow the goal of religious orthodoxy. When the progression from earthenware to metal is examined more closely, the paramount importance of their interest becomes clear. Firstly, there is the determination of the appropriate contexts for using metal as opposed to earthenware. The general emulation of the principle that earthenware should not be used for eating has, as shown above, almost completed its trajectory across the village, so that the use of earthenware in this context has been virtually eliminated as a significant discriminatory feature. This is a very long-term shift, which has occurred over approximately two millennia (Miller 1981b: 96–7). It appears that the elimination of earthenware for cooking may be the next phase in this process, and one that, in contrast, has only just begun. The census showed that orthodox *brahman* had virtually given up all earthenware cooking vessels, although these are still freely used by almost all other castes. Thus, the very logic which produced the extensive range of earthenware cooking pots will, in the presence of metal vessels, probably eliminate them.

The influence of this particular interest is also evident in the use of particular metals for different vessels. The metal vessels which are skeuomorphic with the painted red pottery, such as *batloi* and *gagra*, are all of copper or brass (a 'red' metal), while those skeuomorphic with the black pottery vessels are composed of a number of metals. A griddle of steel competes with the *karela/kareli*. The *bhartiya* and *parat* are always brass or copper. The *tapeli* may be copper, brass or aluminium, the *katora* may be steel or aluminium and, finally, the *bhandia* is always aluminium. No functional basis could be found for the differential use of these metals. These patterns, however, can clearly be accounted for in the light of the symbolism of particular pot forms. The positive associations of the painted red forms are reproduced in the selection of the more expensive metal. The *dhatri* and *bhartiya*, although black in colour because of their association with food, are not used for any impure purposes, and their skeuomorphs are therefore of copper and brass. The metal *tapeli* is morphologically distinct from that version of the earthenware *tapeli* which has impure associations, the former having completely straight sides and a short rim. In contrast, there are two metal forms which reproduce the low status of their earthenware skeuomorphs: one is the *katora* which is equivalent to the *harawla*, and the other is the *bhandia*, which, with its squat form and splayed rim, is the equivalent of the *chayra dohni/ jhawaliya*. Recently, one of the potters has begun to model his *chayra dohni* exactly on the *bhandia*. In as much as these two forms are of the more inexpensive metal, the difference in value appears to reproduce that in status. There is also evidence that the ritual implications of the earthenware have also accrued to the metal.

Within the village, aluminium is known as a 'musulman' metal. In the eyes of the dominant Hindu community, 'musulman' is a term commonly used to indicate that a substance is impure (as in the quotation from Sharma (1970: 20) at p. 142 above). The nature of any supposed connection between aluminium and Muslims remained obscure, but the connotations of this term were sufficient to create a divison in terms of purity between aluminium and all other metals. A brass or copper vessel is usually first received as dowry, and is commonly given in ritual contexts. The aluminium vessels, however, are purchased on an *ad hoc* basis from passing traders and are not used in ceremonial contexts.

This example illustrates how a transformation which is not only a change in medium, but also in that which is being represented (i.e. wealth as well as ritual status), has been mediated by a pre-existing structure of differences. This is not to say that no change has occurred. Rather, the metal pots act to synthesise distinctions in the two dimensions of purity and wealth. This presents a contrast with the pottery, which exhibits no intrinsic articulation with wealth, but the change is not as profound as at first appears. As yet these associations are of a general form, and no doubt they are currently the subject of unconscious but effective 'negotiations'.

11
Conclusion:
archaeology and society

One of the basic capacities of the spirit is to separate itself from
itself – to create forms, ideas, values that oppose it, and only in this
form to gain consciousness of itself. This capacity has reached its
widest extent in the process of culture.

Simmel 1968: 45 (1911)

This study has had as its primary aim the exemplification of an approach
to material culture by which the variability of artefacts is interpreted
through their analysis as categories. The majority of the theoretical
models and methodological problems discussed in this study have
derived from archaeology. It is archaeology which has provided the most
sustained attempt at comparable studies of artefactual variability and
which would be a major beneficiary from any advances in material culture studies. It has often been assumed in archaeology – for example, in
the continued debates over artefact typology (e.g. Whallon and Brown
Eds. 1982) – that archaeologists are searching in their classifications for
something which is self-evident to the anthropologist or student of contemporary material culture. In deciding whether nominal or continuous
variables can more accurately detect 'actual' classes, or whether variables selected accord with 'real' cultural dimensions, it is assumed that
there are relatively unproblematic cultural categories in the living population to which the archaeologist is attempting to approximate. It follows
that the problems faced are peculiar to archaeology and the nature of the
archaeological record, and therefore that the approaches to be developed
are also unique to the discipline.

One of the major implications for archaeology of the present work is its
demonstration of the fallacious nature of these assumptions. This study
has deliberately selected data commonly used in archaeology, both in
terms of its material and the parameters by which that material is represented. The emphasis has been on areas of ceramic variability such as
rim shape, painted decorations and general pot morphology. It should be
evident that what might constitute a 'type', 'class' or 'category', what
demonstrates the 'cultural significance' of such dimensions, represents
a problem for the study of contemporary ceramics which is very similar
to the problem encountered in the field of ancient ceramics. It is an
illusion to think that in most cases there are informants who can provide
an 'emic' representation of these material phenomena that gives

197

immediate access to their cultural implications – in short, that you need only ask your informants.

In Dangwara it was found that, while there was a complex and varied range of vessels which exhibited consistent patterns of form and use, these were only discernible from the investigation of the material itself. Although semantic labels exist for all pot forms, they almost exhaust the information that can be directly obtained. None of the villagers is concerned with the minutiae of rim form or pottery decoration; indeed, one of the major analytic classes, that of the red and buff decoration, has no special term of description. Not even the potters are concerned to articulate the micro-differentiation of their products. While there is at least a little information on the technical properties of form and style, the assertions made as to the cultural 'logic' of the pottery, the manner in which it relates to major social dimensions, cannot be elicited from direct enquiry and are denied if presented. Pottery is by no means unique in this respect. In Dangwara the massive variability of most of the material world and even of ritual practices is rarely the subject of exegesis and comment. Nor is this true merely of the area studied in this research. It is the common finding of anthropology, and in particular of the analysis of complex symbolic and ritual practices (e.g. Gell 1975: 211), where the richness of practice is contrasted with the absence of articulation in language.

The implication of this finding is that the kind of translation in which archaeology is constantly engaged, between the material and the social, demands a conception of material culture which is not readily available in contemporary studies. The attempt by the archaeologist to employ systematic association between the object of study and the context in which it is found is comparable with the common modes of enquiry in studies of contemporary materials. This is not to deny the particular problems of archaeology – the static nature of its context, and the discovery of the material usually only in its final 'moment', and often as broken forms. However, in the present work it is the complex categorisation represented by the pots themselves that has formed the central part of the evidence, and this is often equally available to the archaeologist. The intention of this analysis was not to demonstrate the limitations of archaeology with respect to ethnographic enquiry, as a kind of extended 'cautionary tale', but, on the contrary, to demonstrate that the kind of micro-scale analysis of objects, which is the staple of archaeological enquiry, is dealing with material which provides enormously rich evidence for social relations, yet is often neglected in ethnographic enquiry, precisely because of the existence of other, more easily available, sources of evidence. A society studied through its material rather than its linguistic manifestations is in no sense less immediate or less real.

A dichotomy between formal and informal order has run throughout this study, and has important implications for the use of these ideas in archaeological investigations. Formal order relates to the relatively autonomous construction of artefactual order as categorisation, whereas informal order is directed, in the main, to the manner in which the forms related to external contexts. In archaeology, studies which are directed towards the formal order of a range of artefacts may be identified with what has been termed here stylistic analysis. Style is identified with the extent to which a range of forms is subsumable into some model of its variability. In some instances, this is all that is possible for the archaeologist, when, for example, there is virtually no contextual information about a range of pottery being studied. Normally, however, the archaeologist wishes not merely to characterise, but also to interpret, and this must be done with reference to the available contextual information. In effect, this may often become reduced to a comparison between one range of artefacts and others found in association, or it may include information about economic practices, burial remains, and the dimensions of time and space. In this case, the elements which have been analysed here as informal order become more important.

The degree of formal order, or style, is itself significant precisely because it is relative, and may change over time. The village of Dangwara lies next to an archaeological site where remains dating to some three and four millennia earlier have been uncovered. These chalcolithic potteries are conveniently divided into an earlier series, termed Malwa, and a later series, termed Jorwe, and have been labelled 'cultures', thereby acting as normative signifiers for all the other remains associated with them. Previously it had been thought that the two series represented a mainly spatial division, with Malwa named after the present area in which Dangwara is situated and Jorwe associated with sites to the south (e.g. Dhavalikar 1979), but, since further evidence showed both pottery series to be found in a roughly coterminous area, the temporal distinction must be seen as of greater significance. The main difference between these two is that, whereas the Malwa pottery, as found, for example, at the excavations at Navdatoli (Sankalia *et al.* 1971), includes a very varied set of forms and decorations and requires a large inventory which is difficult to subsume under any simple order, the Jorwe (e.g. Sankalia and Deo 1955), which is clearly a continuation of the same ceramic tradition, shows a much greater degree of formal order.

At least some Jorwe material has been shown through statistical analysis to be highly consistent between different sites (Dhavalikar and Marathe 1979). All the vessels, apart from a few simple bowls, consist of a shallow base joined abruptly to a concave section. The difference between what are termed 'carinated bowls' and vessels termed 'long-necked vessels with globular body' is actually the height of this concave section. Another common transformation occurs when this concavity is reduced to two straight sections meeting at an angle. The decorations painted on the upper part of the vessel are equally reducible to the trans-formations of two variables, one a series of parallel lines and the other a squiggle (or zigzag). These may be transformed through a variety of means: by being placed in alternate directions, through superimpo-sition, by being filled in, made into rows and other such treatments. This is not to say that every vessel can be reduced to translations of these four elements, two of shape and two of decoration, but the exceptions are few. The Malwa ware by contrast, although recognisably related, could never be treated in this manner and a 'grammar' of description would be very complex indeed.

In this case, the prehistoric ceramics may be analysed as to the degree of style revealed. The contextual information presently available is not adequate, at this stage, to attempt an interpretation of the changes in the degree of formal order, but a further example illustrates what can be revealed when such contextual information is available. To the north-west of Dangwara, stretching over almost the whole of modern Pakistan and much of north-west India at the slightly earlier period of 2600–1000 B.C., is found the material evidence for the most extensive of all the ancient civilisations, known as the Harappan or Indus civilisation (Wheeler 1968, Possehl Ed. 1983). Analysis of the material evidence demonstrates a unique degree of homogenisation, considering the spatial and temporal parameters. Although a number of local wares are found, the best-known black and red ware consists of a limited range of decorative motifs and forms, which enables it to be recognised as a style over this vast area and period (Manchanda 1972). In this case the homogeneity of the material may be set against a number of sources of contextual information which allow it to be interpreted in terms of its contribution to societal reproduction. These additional sources include the settlement plans, the lack of imported manufactures, the lack of social differentiation in burials, the uses made of fire and water in rituals and the evidence for the final decline. Taken together, these illustrate how material taxonomies, such as pottery, may be used as part of a severe curtailment upon the forms of representation which reinforced a homogenisation of social forms comparable to monastic and ascetic-based societies of later times, but with a number of individual features (Miller Forthcoming a).

This represents a strong contrast with present-day South Asian societies, which seem to generate differentiation along a variety of dimensions, as illustrated by Dumont (1972), who emphasises in par-ticular the dimension of purity and pollution as a primary principle relating these differences to social hierarchy. David (1977) provides an analysis linking individual castes to the society through variable forms, mediated by normative models, in an analysis similar to the notion of style used here. This is not to suggest that the degree of variability informs us directly as to the nature of the social formations. Its implications will differ according to the material analysed, and its interpretation is relative to the other contextual information available.

The point of a contextual analysis is that it relates apparently disparate sources of evidence to make each, in turn, the context for the others (e.g. Hodder 1984). Similarly, in the present study, it has been shown how approaches normally analysed separately actually have implications for one another. Often approaches derived from technology are used to analyse manufacture, those from utility to analyse function, those from symbolic analysis to deal with ritual and religion and so forth. Using the central theme of artefacts as categories, it was shown in Chapter 3 that, rather than representing merely a description of the creation of a set of forms, technology could be analysed as the systematic exploitation of the range of methods used in order to produce patterned variation. The process of creating patterns, such as gradations in body angularity, or a variety of major rim types and their subvarieties, becomes clearer, once their analysis as a code has been constructed. Instead of presenting these attributes as the products of given dimensions, resulting from technology, the technology itself can be understood as a result of the complex structural nature of the relationship between artefactual codes and their social homologies.

In a similar fashion, function can be seen both as a causal constraint upon morphology and as a secondary pragmatic entailment of an association between categories. Again, the use of the dichotomy between formal and informal analysis, and the specific definition given to the concept of style, help to indicate how each perspective highlights an aspect of what is recognisably the same phenomenon. Thus, the perspectives can build upon each other, rather than tearing the object of study into discrete chunks to be separately consumed.

The central theme of this study has been the nature of artefacts as categories. To analyse artefacts as categories is to determine the conditions for the creation of difference and equivalence, and to recognise that distinct objects may be created as representations of identical concepts. It was suggested in Chapter 9 that pottery, as a set of categories, should be considered as a pattern with structure, which permitted convention and mutual understanding. This order was analysed on three levels: that of the individual pot as representative of a category, that of the pottery categories as constituent elements of a pottery code, and that of a grid in which pottery as code was related to all other codes. Although simplified in this representation, such structure can generate transformations and interpretations of enormous complexity. It was shown that such patterns could then be broken down into their contextual realisations, which were contingent upon the variability of the people interpreting and manipulating them. This in turn related to the various structural positions held by individuals in society, and the resultant differences in interests and strategies, and the different frames which organised the perspectives from which they viewed the material at a given time.

The particular approach to categorisation was influenced by recent work which indicates that the process of human categorisation uses properties of variation and 'fuzzy' logic rather than the previously assumed, discrete logical classes. This is closer than might at first appear to the procedures of the contemporary archaeologist, who tends to represent form as variability, even if only as statistical distributions. Variability should not be viewed as a mere side-effect of the inaccuracy of representation in material form, but as an essential property of categories. The notion of categories was extended in two further directions. Firstly, it was shown that the variability in forms, the production of over fifty different pots, represented only a part of the actual variability of pot categories, which also encompassed the heterogeneity of the social context (Chapter 2), and the variety of contexts in which interpretation occurs (Chapter 9). Thus change may sometimes result in shifts in actual morphology, but may also operate merely as shifts in interpretation or in contextual frames. The second development of the notion of categories was to show that this extended variability of everyday practice need not be opposed to the representation of pots as structured categories operating through codes and grids. On the contrary, variability was shown to represent a necessary property of categories, permitting the maintenance of structure in the face of the heterogeneity of context and practice. This was particularly clear in Chapter 5, where the informal mode of exchange was interpreted as the necessary complement of the *asami* system, and in Chapter 10, where the variety of social strategies employed was shown to produce sub-varieties of pottery which preserved the associations of certain forms.

The use which has been made of established classifications of society – in particular, caste – as a basic characterisation against which the variability in pottery has been analysed should not be construed as an intention to find a reflection, or representation, of caste in ceramics. Nor has it been demonstrated that an archaeologist may directly use material variability as a symbolic rendering of an equivalent social classification. On the contrary, the classes represented in pottery may be dualities between wealth and ritual status or between formal and informal action which are not emphasised in caste, and the normative categories of caste may be broken up (for example, the priestly *brahman* as against the landlord *brahman* of the last chapter), when related to pottery variability. Both caste and the material dimension are constructs which capture and in turn constitute elements of culture, but within an array of alternative, sometimes complementary and sometimes conflicting representations. There is no privileged real 'society' that is being represented; there is nothing else behind these mirrors. The term 'representation' refers to a circle of form and understanding, and culture is exhausted by the same constructs through which it is understood.

The implication of this for archaeology is that categorisation found in material form may be as fully constitutive of society as a normative articulated social categorisation, equivalent to caste. Different methodologies emphasise different constructs and representations; analysis proceeds through the study of variability in contexts, which in turn becomes the subject variability for other contexts. The set of relationships uncovered may include contradiction and the separation of spheres, not simply a coherent or consistent 'system'. One of the major results of contemporary studies of South Asian society has been to reveal the non-mutual reducibility of different social dimensions (Dumont 1972). Although Dumont emphasises caste, his analysis actually demonstrates that neither social nor material categories can provide privileged access to some coherent category to be reified as 'the society'.

This has important implications for archaeological analysis, because it implies that one set of material in contextual analysis cannot simply be reduced to another. Recent archaeological work has found that, in the same prehistoric society, buildings may suggest a strong degree of differentiation in wealth, burials may suggest a lack of social differentiation and the ritual structures may be interpreted in terms of competing representations of the 'proper' nature of society (see individual papers in Miller and Tilley Eds. 1984). Such 'discrepancies', rather than being seen as a source of confusion, represent a valuable source of evidence for relations of power, revealed through the differential ability to objectify interests. The concept of 'frames' as used here may be useful in analysing these aspects of ideology.

This in turn implies a major role for mundane artefacts as ideologically informed cultural traits. The ability of such objects to play this highly significant role in social reproduction has been a further theme of the present study, because of its stress on those very attributes which have tended to result in such material being dismissed, especially as possible evidence for social relations. The three properties of function, concreteness and apparent triviality are linked together in this regard. It is because objects such as pottery are usually held to be produced for specific functions which 'explain' their presence and shapes that they are therefore considered unworthy of direct contemplation, and unimportant in cultural life; and it is because their concrete nature again appears to imbue them with a fixed presence and meaning that they are not generally associated with the abstractions of thought and language in which real 'understanding' is achieved. The actual ability of such forms to affect all these areas is therefore at present underestimated.

It is these same three properties which may make pottery and other similar artefacts suited to a role of considerable significance in the construction of culture. Their part in understanding the construction of the individual's sense of self, of self in relation to society, and in the flow of interests, representations and understandings which make up cultural knowledge, has tended to be ignored. The very functionality of pottery – its place as container, transporter, framer of other substances – makes it suited to the role of 'framing'. Different forms of social action and interpretation demand different kinds of responses and interaction. Some are concerned with more practical effects, some with ritual action, some with status, and some with the exercise of power. Pottery does not often signify directly but more commonly acts as an 'appropriate' setting, for the exchange relationships that make up and define the *asami* system, for the ritual action of a wedding and for the display purposes of a major feast, as well as for the practical (but also the 'appropriate') transformation of foods in cooking.

In a similar way, the trivial nature of pottery means that, in so far as pottery acts as frame or its own significance is in turn determined by frames, it is not usually subject to conscious consideration or intention. Two pots, by their difference, may manifest some other difference between those who tend to use one form and those who prefer the other, whether in a funeral ceremony or for eating. If such homologies arise between sets of vessels and caste or gender divisions, this reproduction is not perceived as such and may be denied if asserted.

The effect of such relationships is determined by the third aspect of pottery, its concrete nature. Being material and embedded in practical life, it is not usually subject to the same kind of symbolic exegesis as those areas such as myth, art and ritual, which are formalised, or abstracted from society. Yet it is precisely the fact that pottery is so mundane that gives it its consequences for 'objectification'. This term denotes the process described by Simmel at the beginning of this chapter. The person, as an individual in relation to society, understands and constructs his or her notion of these two phenomena 'person' and 'society' occasionally in relation to some thought-out, articulated reference-point, such as law, religious exegesis or explicit social rules. However, underlying these are more fundamental constructions, socialised from early infancy, which relate to correct action, and the differences and equivalence between things. These are formed in the everyday world of direct experience and learning. Objects created by individuals of one generation become the given environment through which individuals of the succeeding generation are themselves constructed as subjects.

Mundane objects have often been studied as an external environment, to which attributes are ascribed as part of the process of understanding, whether as structural homologies (Lévi-Strauss), as the symbols of positive and negative attitudes (Freud), or as reified commodities signifying and reproducing social asymmetry (Marx). The concern of this study has been to illustrate how objects do not merely constitute a given world which can be thus manipulated, but that these same objectifying processes also have consequences for the creation of the artefactual world itself. There is therefore a continual dialectic in which mundane objects, such as pottery, are understood, not only as aiding in understanding the world, but as simultaneously constituting that world. This circularity, which is intrinsic to the process of meaning (Hobart 1983), as well as understanding (Taylor 1971), and the construction of the subject (Coward and Ellis 1977), may allow a more positive conception of the place of the mundane. Pottery may come to be seen more as an enabling structure, one of the many which contribute to the development of multivalency and complexity in cultural processes. Such a perspective views material forms as part of the central order of cultural construction, rather than as either so embedded in an 'immediate' relationship with the environment as to be virtually 'non-cultural', or analysed as 'art', and therefore as virtually autonomous.

The micro-analysis of the material world may in conjunction with archaeology provide important evidence for the manner in which culture and society are reproduced and transformed. Human subjects cannot be treated as pre-social and pre-cultural beings who enter into relationships with objects. The importance of material culture lies in the ineliminable relationship by which subjects and objects are mutually constituted. On analogy with archaeology, this study may be said to have attempted an excavation, an uncovering of the material foundations of apparent structures, by exposing that which underlies our basic assumptions as to what is 'important' in society. It thereby challenges the primacy of the articulate and the articulated from the perspective of the embedded and the silent.

Detailed description of pottery manufacture

The potter's equipment and the place of manufacture

The piece of equipment most readily associated with the potter is the wheel, which has both a ritual (see Chapter 7) and a functional significance for the villagers. The Dangwara potters use the socketed block wheel (Saraswati and Behura 1966: 10–13), set on a base consisting of a roughly-shaped stone disc, about 4 cm thick and 40 cm in diameter (Fig. 54). In the centre of the base is set a stake of hard wood. The base and wheel are usually placed in a shallow pit created in the working area, just larger than the diameter of the wheel.

The wheel itself is made of a mixture of clay with goat's hair, date-palm fibre, cotton, sand, coconut fibre and donkey dung. The actual process of manufacture was not observed in Dangwara, although a description was given which matches that of Saraswati and Behura (1966: 10–11) for north-west India. After considerable pounding and kneading, the mixture is left for about a fortnight, and the circle of the wheel is then excised using a kind of wooden compass. The example owned by one of the potters in Dangwara has several settings for wheels of different diameters. The Dangwara potters claimed that, after cutting, the wheel would have to be left to dry for about two months before it was ready for use. A small depression is made on the top surface to accommodate the stick for turning.

At the centre of the upper surface of the wheel may be set either a wooden disc or a coil of rope of about 40 cm diameter. At the centre point on the under surface is a stone, said to be brought from the Narmada river by peddlers, which measures about 8–10 cm in length and has a depression of around 0.8 cm diameter and 0.8 cm depth to receive the top of the wooden stake. This pivot is kept lubricated with peanut oil during throwing. The average diameter of ten wheels from Dangwara and a village to the south measured 90 cm, with a range of 85 to 101 cm diameter. At its outer circumference the wheel has a band 10 to 14 cm wide and 11 cm thick; within this is a depression about 6 cm thick, after which the wheel gradually thickens towards the centre. During throwing, the wheel may gyrate to a degree that makes centring quite difficult, but at no time was a wheel observed to leave its pivot during throwing.

For beating, the potters use a set of stone anvils, obtained either from itinerant castes or from Ujjain, and a set of wooden paddles made in the village. Each potter has a standard series of at least three anvils and three paddles (Fig. 55).

The anvils are of the knobbed form found throughout Madhya Pradesh, Maharasthra, Gujerat and southern Rajasthan (Saraswati and Behura 1966: 22). They cost from 15 r for ordinary stone to 25 r for the white quartz, which, although less durable, has the advantage of not sticking to the clay during beating and is usually used for the largest of the anvils. The paddles are commonly carved on both sides, so doubling the number of surfaces available for use. The main distinction between them, that of their degree of concavity, relates to the stage of the beating. The flat paddles are used first and the more concave later on.

The other tools used for pottery manufacture are of a fairly simple variety. They include the donkey bag made of rope, made on a light wooden frame by the potter, a wooden mallet to crush the clay and dung, and a stick to turn the wheel. One type of pot, called the *pawanda*, is made exclusively for the potter's own use to hold the water, slip or paint. Two of the potters have a small saddle quern set into their shared working area, which is employed to crush the schist used for

Fig. 54. Underside of wheel

decoration. Another has a small cogged wheel used in decoration. Such cogged rollers appear to be common in north India (Saraswati and Behura 1966: 32). Each potter has a string of glass beads or wild nuts for burnishing (Fig. 56). Other items are not exclusive to the potters and include cloth, cowrie shells and plastic ornaments for decorative purposes, twisted twine, a beating-base made from a metal *tagari* bowl filled with straw and covered with sacking. Finally, sherds are used for a variety of purposes – for example, providing a cover for the firing, and serving as tools for impressed decoration.

Fig. 57 is the plan of two of the potters' houses showing their work areas. There is some variety in the arrangement of work-spaces. The main potting area, which consists of the wheel, usually set in a pit, and a clay soaking pit, may be found in an enclosed courtyard, or on the front veranda, in a side extension to the veranda, or as a separate work area adjacent to the street. This means that, with one exception, the manufacture of pottery is a very public activity, fully visible in all its stages to any casual observer. This contrasts with many areas in South Asia, where potters are said to be secretive about their methods (e.g. Saraswati 1979: 33). The area for firing is usually located near the entrance to the house, often in the place where animals are kept. In one instance it is behind the house. In two cases the firing site is shared by two brothers. The location of firing is, however, the least fixed of all the potters' facilities. Large areas for the storage of fired or unfinished pottery may be found in all the houses. In two houses pottery is stored in a loft, reached by stairs.

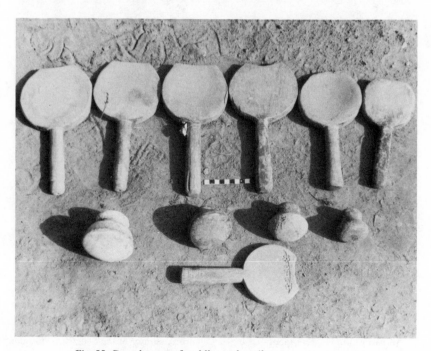

Fig. 55. Complete set of paddles and anvils

The selection of raw materials

Earth is taken from three deposits. These form a kind of gradation, exploiting the local distribution of soil types.[1] The first deposit lies next to the river Chambal, a kilometre from the present site of the village. The earth consists of a yellow, clay–silt mixture with calcarious inclusions. Clay is taken from directly below an archaeological site containing material of Malwa affinities dated to around 2000 B.C., identical to that found in the excavation by Wakankar further down the river (Wakankar 1982). The mound originally measured about 30 m by 6 m, but has been divided into three by stream channels. The potters collect clay about twice a month from an exposed face about 3.5 m high. The land is owned by a *gujar*, but the potters have traditional rights to extract clay without payment. The clay is dug with hoes and carried by a donkey in rope bags (Fig. 58). This deposit is known locally as *pilimitti* (yellow earth) or *lalmitti* (red earth).

The second deposit lies on the other side of the present village on a path some 200 m from the edge of the village and approximately 1.5 km from the river. This deposit is known as *dhamnemitti* (mixed earth), representing the border area between the alluvial earths and the main black earth deposits. The third source lies at a higher point, some 5 km from the river, and approaching the next river valley which runs parallel to the Chambal river. This deposit is viewed as a par-

Fig. 56. String of nuts used in burnishing

[1] All earth samples were identified by Dr C. Forbes, curator of the Sedgwick Museum, Cambridge.

ticularly good example of the *kalimitti* (black earth). It is a black clay with a high organic content, known as the 'black cotton' soil for its high fertility, and derived from the Deccan trap rocks. The deposit itself is a slight mound rising about 1 m above the surrounding area. While the first two deposits are exclusive to the Dangwara potters, this third deposit is also used by potters in Baleri, Ingoria and Gharsinga villages. Clay is extracted from this deposit much less frequently, once or twice a year, depending on the potter, who may use a donkey or buffalo cart for transport. The basic properties of these soils are well known to the dominant farming community. The old village (*puranagaon*) is located on yellow clay which was extracted from the site and used in the building of the new village (*nayagaon*). The latter lies on black earth, which is considered less suitable for building, being more inclined to crack. Despite this, the potters' own descriptions of the earth are limited and of a fairly general form. Attempts to reproduce Arnold's (1971) analysis of the relationship between 'etic' laboratory and 'emic' classification of earth were not successful. Arnold has himself, however, suggested that his example was exceptional (pers. comm.). I accompanied the potters to the main clay deposits and took samples of the soils extracted for pottery manufacture. The potters were then asked where the edge of suitable deposits lay, and a further sample was collected some distance beyond this point. In the case of the alluvial clay, the unsuitable sample had larger and more common calcarious concretions, many over 2 mm in size. The unsuitable black earth

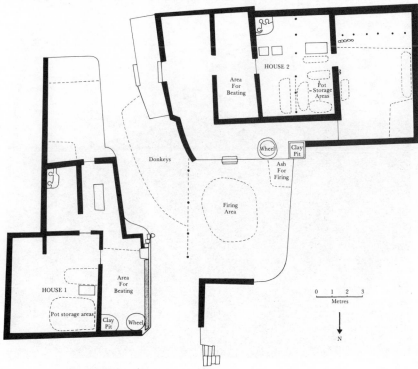

Fig. 57. Potters' houses

also had more coarse fragments, although this is not an obvious disadvantage, since sieved sand is added as an inclusion, but the inclusions in the rejected sample may have been too angular and variable in size.

A further division is represented by the use of two forms of inclusion. The commonest form is donkey dung, which is obtained either from the donkeys owned by the village potters or purchased from other villages. The dung is first beaten and then passed through a sieve of approximately 0.4 cm mesh. Less common is sieved sand, which used to be taken from the local stream beds, but is now collected from the road.

The earth is considered ready for use as soon as it is brought to the village. There is no souring, although the clay will be kept under sacking until the potter is ready to use it. The men collect the clay, but the women undertake the initial cleaning by smashing the clods with a wooden mallet and removing any stones or other inclusions. The clay is not usually sieved. The clay is covered with water and soaked overnight in a pit approximately a metre square. Shepard comments that 'the working quality of clay can be improved by very thorough soaking with water in order to wet all the particles completely' (1956: 52). From the clay of one pit, a potter was able to make nineteen medium-sized vessels. In the morning, some of the levigated fine fraction is scooped from the top for use as a slip. The clay mass is then taken from the pit and donkey dung is poured over it. There is no fixed ratio, the dung being added until the earth has reached the texture of turf, and can be rolled, but the mixture is approximately one part of dung to four parts of earth.

Fig. 58. Digging yellow clay

For the initial kneading the mixture is piled into a circle and then trodden out by foot several times (Fig. 59), the potter feeling also for any remaining stones. The adding of dung and kneading by foot takes around forty minutes. Hand kneading is carried out in a similar fashion to that used by British craft potters, with throwing, slapping and pressing with the palm to produce a cylindrical form called *pinda* (Fig. 60). An example of hand kneading consisted of forty-two 'rolls' taking two minutes.

It is not possible to distinguish from the appearance of a vessel either the kind of earth or the kind of inclusions which have been used. How far the materials directly affect the technological process is difficult to determine in any detail. The salts in the donkey dung may contribute in a significant manner to the properties of the earth, but it is quite possible that the dung merely represents a convenient source of chopped straw (London 1981), donkey dung being used because cow dung is in much demand for other purposes. In Gujerat, horse dung

Fig. 59. Kneading clay and donkey dung

is most commonly used (Bose 1980). The potters suggest that the correct proportion of dung aids in throwing, and it is assumed it helps provide the correct degree of plasticity. The black clay and sand combination is not thrown on the wheel, but is closely related to the intended function of the vessels, being used only for the base of those pots which will be used on the hearth. It might be expected that an inclusion chosen for the base of cooking pots would act to reduce differential thermal expansion, but experiments as to the suitability of a variety of materials have come to opposing conclusions. Rye's experiments on New Guinea earthenwares (1976) would appear to favour high porosity in reducing the likelihood of thermal-induced fracture, and therefore would make the donkey dung inclusion seem suitable, but Woods's findings on British material (forthcoming) are more supportive of the beneficial effects of sand, as found in this case. It is possible that the grainy texture of this combination makes it unsuitable for throwing.

Fig. 60. Making the *pinda*

Throwing on the wheel

Throwing on the wheel is one of the two stages in which variability in the final shape is produced. This stage is not as dominant as in most wheel-thrown pottery-making traditions, since most of the vessels obtain their final base and body shape in the later stage of beating. The clay to be beaten out, however, is first distributed during the throwing. The description here will emphasise the creation of different rims, since the rim and the neck are the only parts of the pots which retain in the finished vessel the shape they receive on the wheel. Some small forms, such as oil lamps and lids, are, however, entirely shaped by the throwing process.

Potters usually squat by their wheel in throwing, although they stand to pull up some of the larger forms, such as the *goli*. A small piece of wet clay is first smeared on the centre of the wheel to facilitate bonding with the clay cylinder. The number of vessels which can be made from a single cylinder varies from one for a *goli* or *dhatri* to a large number for *divaniya* or *dhakni* (see Table 14). The size of the cylinder also varies. When the wheel has been set in motion with the hand, a stick is placed in a depression on the top surface, near the edge of wheel (Fig. 61b). By turning this about thirty times in as many seconds, sufficient momentum is built up to make a single larger vessel or several smaller ones. The *goli* and *dhatri*, however, often need several turnings to complete a single vessel.

To describe the process of throwing, a generalised description of the making of a standard container will first be given, to be used as a basis for the examination of more particular techniques. A cylinder is set on to the wheel (Fig. 61b) (often the base of the last cylinder will not be used but left to receive and bond the next). Centring appears to require relatively little effort and may not be exact. There follow several stages common to most throwing traditions and illustrated in Fig. 61c–f. For a smaller vessel, the cylinder is narrowed at the top to a cone. Plunging is always done with the two thumbs, while the hands support the expanding cylinder. The left hand is then thrust in to deepen the depression. Dislodged clay is extracted from the centre at this stage (Fig. 61c), and some water added. The potter then places both hands on the exterior of the cone and presses upwards and inwards, making the hole narrower and deeper. Then the main shaping is carried out with the left hand inside the pot, pushing the clay out, and the right hand supporting the walls, the fingers pointing downwards (Fig. 61d–e). Often the pot is first brought up with cylindrical walls. Next, the wall is brought out and often, near the top, curved inwards again. Most container forms have a shoulder and a neck. The shoulder is made using either the thumb and side of the right hand (Fig. 61f), or the forefinger supported by the thumb of the left hand. The neck is remade several times during the moulding of the rim. Generally, the thumb is used first, then the forefinger, and, if a narrow neck is required, the little finger may also be used in the later stages.

It is the rim which distinguishes between all vessels at this stage. It may be formed in a variety of ways, creating a small number of general classes, each with its own specific variations. Generally, after the shape has been drawn out and the shoulder and neck formed, there is a slight accumulation of clay at the top, forming a bead. This is made more regular in appearance to create the simplest rim, used on some *chuklya* and *gagra*, known as the *gol* (round) rim (Fig. 62a). If the rim

Table 14. *Major technological variables for Dangwara pottery*

	Common pottery forms							
	1	2	3	4	5	6	7	8
Akhartij gagra	1	2 or 3	3	1	P	N	N	N
Bhartiya	2	2	3	0	B	N	Y	Y
Batloi	1	2	3	2	R or B	R or B	N	Y
Brahman dohni	1	2	3	1	H	N	N	N
Bujhara	1	M	0	–	P	N	N	N
Chayra dohni	2	2	3	1	B	N	Y	Y
Chuklya	1	4	2	0	P	N	N	N
Dhakan	1	12	1	–	P	N	N	N*
Dhatri	1	1	3	–	B	R†	N	N
Dhakni	1	M	0	–	R or B	R or B	Y	N
Divali matka	1	2	3	2	P	N	N	N
Divaniya	1	M	0	–	U	N	N	N
Dohni	2	2	3	1	B	N	Y	N
Gagra	1	2 or 3	3	0	P	B	N	Y
Goli	1	1	3	0	P	B	N	Y
Harawla	1	10	0	–	B	N	N	N
Karela	1	2 or 3	2 or 3	–	B	N	N	N
Kareli	2	2 or 3	2 or 3	–	B	N	N	N
Keliya	1	2 or 3	3	1	B	N	N	N
Kulhri	1	M	0	–	U	N	N	N
Kunda	1	1	3	0	H	B	N	N
Jhawaliya	2	2	3	1	B	N	Y	N
Mamatla	1	2	2 or 3	0	P	N	N	N
Matka	1	2	3	0	P	B	N	N
Surahi	1	1	–‡‡	0	R	Y	N	N
Tapeli	2	2	3	0	B	N	Y	Y
Wariya	1	4	1	1	H	B	N	N
	Less common pot forms							
Anar	1				–§	N	N	N
Barnai	2				B	N	Y	N
Barni	1				B	N	N	C
Chhapa	1				R	N	N	N
Kap-plaet	1				B	R	N	C
Dabba	1				B	N	Y	Y
Damru	1				P	N	N	N
Dhol	1				R	N	N	N
Dhupana	1				R	N	N	Y
Galla	1				B	N	N	N
Katwa	1				H	N	N	N
Kulhra	1				B	N	Y	N
Kunda (tree)	1				P	N	N	N
Kunda (wine)	1				R	N	N	N
Kundali	1				B	N	N	N
Kundi	1				B	N	Y	N
Kundi (funeral)	1				P	N	N	N
Lota	1				B	R	N	Y
Maman	1				B	P	N	N
Nagara	1				P	N	N	N
Patya	1				H	N	N	N
Pawanda	1				H	N	N	N
Tolro	1				B	N	N	N
Wari	1				B	N	N	N

Key to Table 14
Column 1: Materials used.
    1 = Yellow clay and donkey dung.
    2 = Mixed clay and donkey dung (top), Black clay and sand (base).
Column 2: Usual number of pots produced per cylinder (*pinda*).
    M = More than 15.
Column 3: Usual number of beatings.
Column 4: Number of *parti*.
Column 5: Usual form of decoration.
    P = Painted.
    R = Red.
    B = Black.
    H = Red and buff.
    U = Unpainted.
Column 6: Alternative form of decoration.
Column 7: Impressed, incised or applied decoration.
    Y = Present.
    N = Not present.
Column 8: Existence of metal skeuomorph.
    Y = Present.
    N = Not present.
    C = China skeuomorph.

* There is a metal *dhakan*, but the shape is different.
† This is very rare.
‡ There is a variety of ways of beating this vessel (see pp. 221–2)
§ The *anar* is not fired, and is grey.

is to contain or begin with a straight section, it will most often be held between the thumb and first finger of the left hand, the forefinger of the right being used to straighten it or smooth the lip. The rim held in this fashion, and bent over into the horizontal, creates the *chappa* (flat) rim of the *divali matka*; if bent to an angle, it creates the *chayra* (sloping) rim of the *chayra dohni* or *jhawaliya*. If the rim is left in a vertical position but straightened, this creates the *sidha* (vertical) rim of the *batloi*.

Often the rim is folded in upon itself, creating a thicker version of the round rim, while an additional slight angularity creates the *dohni* rim (Fig. 62b). If left thick, the rim can be 'split' using the forefinger of the right hand or the thumb of the left. A deep depression impressed here creates the *chrima* (split) rims of the *matka* (Fig. 62c–e), *maman* and *keliya*. Alternatively, a kind of 'pseudo-split' may be created, using just the fingernail, as is done with the *kunda* and the *goli* (Fig. 62f). The lip is usually formed with the forefinger of the right hand during these processes. The inner face of the rim may be straightened or eased over slightly to turn the whole rim outwards.

Although in the foregoing description the use of particular fingers in various operations has been noted, this reflects common or 'typical' usages, rather than fixed, invariant procedures. The forefinger of the right hand is the most important all-purpose 'tool', performing a great variety of functions, but it serves as a general tool, rather than part of a precise sequence of action. After the potter is satisfied with the effect he has produced, a wet cloth is placed lightly over the rim to smooth the features, and a cord of twisted cotton is used to cut the base of the pot from the remainder of the cylinder. The vessel is then lifted off, usually with both hands, and placed on a patch of ground previously prepared with ash.

The above account describes the manufacture of about half the total variety of

Fig. 61. Main stages in the production of container forms

Fig. 62. Production of individual rim forms

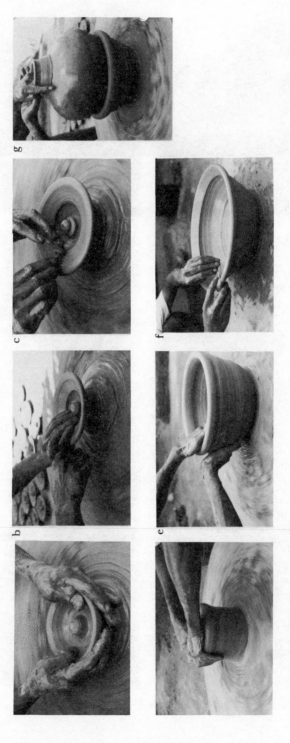

Fig. 63. Production of *dhakni*, *dhatri* and *surahi*

forms produced. It will be clear that significant distinctions in rim form are created with slight and simple alterations in the position of the fingers, used as templates. Rather than detailing all variants of the process of manufacture, the remainder of the account will focus on a few distinctive forms, providing details also of individual variations and the methods used in a newly introduced vessel.

Vessels such as *wariya*, *kunda* and *tapeli* introduce only minor variations into the general container production process. The *dhakan* lid is interesting, since its production consists mainly of those actions used in making the rim and neck of container forms, but without the attached body. The rim is bent between the thumb and first finger of the left hand, and the lip smoothed by the forefinger of the right. The *dhakni* lid is distinctive in that excess clay in the centre is left to form the basis of a knob (Fig. 63a–c). One hand is held below the vessel in plunging, to help draw it out, and then the sides are brought up with both hands, the two forefingers acting as templates to shape the inner portion. As with other small vessels, the lid is separated from the cylinder by squeezing the base between the forefingers, prior to cutting. The *dhakni* is one of the few forms to which decoration is occasionally applied during throwing, in this case with a cogged wheel. A further example of a particular technique is the creation of the *dhatri* (Fig. 63d–f). Here the plunging is exceptionally deep, on one occasion being carried out three times to force the clay on to the sides. If the weight of clay is not supported while the form is being raised, the vessel will collapse, an occurrence which was frequently observed. The rim is formed by the forefinger of the right hand, in a crooked position, and is bent over in relation to the main body. Both the *dhakan* and the *dhatri* are often cut with the string so as to leave an open base, which is closed during the beating.

So far, the descriptions have assumed a constant method of production. In practice, however, individual potters differ in their exact methods and are not always consistent themselves. This is exemplified in the manufacture of the *goli*, one of the largest forms, in which the cylinder has to be lifted to a height of about 35 cm. The first major difference is in the number of times the potters have to bring up the sides of the vessel. A strong potter can bring up the whole vessel, if it is not too large, in a single movement, while the oldest potter usually took three attempts. Half the potters use their right thumb to bring in the shoulder, and the other half their right forefinger. Only one of the six used his little finger to deepen the neck. Two potters merely expand the rim to make the round form, two turn it fully back on itself, while the remaining two use an intermediate action, tipping the edge rather than turning it. These differences are not evident in the final forms.

The variability between potters is further illustrated in their attempts to produce a relatively new pot form, the *surahi*, the number of which is increasing throughout India at present (Saraswati 1979: 39). So far, the paucity of tools and the limited nature of the techniques has been evident; there are no templates and only simple hand movements are used. That the potters are quite capable of much more elaborate methods is clearly demonstrated in the making of *surahi*. The problem with this vessel is that it requires the production of a narrow rim – so narrow that the hand cannot be inserted into the pot in order to beat the base. Of the three potters who make *surahi*, one makes an ordinary *chuklya* form, beats the base and then cuts off the rim and neck. The painter prepares a new disc of clay and the vessel is returned to the wheel, resting on a *dhatri*, and the potter then applies this disc and forms it into the new narrow neck (Fig. 63g). The rather inefficient way in which this was performed suggested that the technique has only recently been developed. A second potter made the rim during the initial throwing, but then broke a hole into the base and did his paddling from the underside, later repairing this hole with a patch of clay. The third potter used a method only seen once, in which, instead of beating the vessel, the base was made sufficiently round during the throwing process. The side was brought in at the top with the hand, and then the finger. When there was no further room, a small piece of wood was used to close the top. A narrow rim and neck were made separately on the wheel, rather in the manner of a spout, and when the pot was dry, the top of the main vessel was broken and the neck luted on to it. In another case, a groove was left around the circumference of a flattened example and two lugs were made around sticks, resulting in a form rather like a pilgrim flask which could be hung from string. The manufacture of *surahi*, then, clearly indicates an ability to use a variety of techniques which are not otherwise employed.

Drying and beating and pot

Most container pots, when they are removed from the wheel, have a flat base around 10 cm across and several centimetres thick, and thick walls. During beating they are transformed into round bodies with maximum diameters far in excess of the rim and reduced to a thickness of half a centimetre or less (Fig. 64).

Fig. 64. *Matka* before and after beating

Certain distinctions are also introduced by varying the angularity of the body. This transformation has to be carried out with care, since if the pot is too dry or too wet it will crack. Most pots are therefore beaten in several stages. The usual number of beatings for each of the common pottery forms is listed in Table 14. The drying period varies, depending upon pot size: the *goli* requires around eight hours before the first beating, three before the next and five before the third, but the equivalent intervals for a *dohni* are only three hours, two hours and half an hour. These intervals may be extended, and beating usually takes place the day after throwing. Some *gagra* were once seen being beaten entirely in one session. The potter explained that he had allowed them to dry for too long, but that this was not satisfactory and some might break.

Prior to beating, vessels are usually placed on an ash-covered floor and, as they are beaten, they are supported on *kantla*, the cut-off rims of *kareli* and *karela* (see below). The *goli*, however, has to be supported in depressions scooped out in a specially created platform of ash (Fig. 65). A first beating expanded a *dohni* from 14 cm to 19 cm maximum diameter, and by completion the vessel had reached 24 cm. A *kunda* was expanded in its first beating from 16 cm to 21 cm and by completion had reached 29 cm.

During the throwing on the wheel, the yellow clay with donkey dung tempering was used for all but seven vessels which are to be used on the hearth. These latter are thrown with the mixed clay, also using donkey dung tempering (see Table 14). After they have been thrown, they receive an additional treatment. The potter makes a disc of the black clay, prepared with a sand tempering, and as the

Fig. 65. *Goli* drying in ash-pit during beating

pot is taken with one hand from the wheel, this disc is applied to the base. Fig. 66 shows this treatment applied to the *dohni*. The two are pressed together by pushing the fist down on to the base when the pot is placed on the ground. The beating process will result in an effective bonding between these two clays and their inclusions, but with the black earth and sand tempering being concentrated on the base of the vessels. I have found references to this practice of throwing one combination of earth and inclusion for the top of cooking pots, and beating another for the base, from as far apart as west Bengal (Das and Ray 1966), Kashmir (Saraswati 1979: 4) and Gujerat (Fischer and Shah 1970: 154).

The method of beating is basically identical for all vessels. It is in most respects that which is described as the 'North-Western technique of beating' by Saraswati and Behura (1966: 55–8). A straw-filled, sack-covered, metal bowl (*tagari*) is used as a base. The potter squats, holding the stone anvil within the pot and a wooden paddle in his other hand (Fig. 67). The conventional term 'anvil' is a misnomer, since during the beating the stone held within the pot is hit against the wall with as much force as the paddle from without. In the first stage, the flat paddle is used to beat the walls out, each group of nine or ten strokes starting with the heaviest and gradually becoming lighter. In later stages, the more concave-surfaced paddles are used and beating eventually gives way to a virtual stroking motion, which smoothes the finished form. Water and ash are applied to retain the correct texture.

The beating strokes usually follow a sequence around the circumference of the vessel, approximating to a series of rings, starting from the base and working

Fig. 66. Adding basal disc of black earth to cooking vessel

upwards, although this is not strictly adhered to. Unlike throwing on the wheel, which takes 1.5 to 3 minutes for a container vessel, beating can be a laborious process. A *goli* was observed to require four main 'sessions' for the first beating, which took 755 strokes. The next beating, in eight sessions, took 1,405 strokes, while the third beating in thirteen sessions took 751 strokes. A more typical vessel, the *matka*, takes about 500 strokes in each of the first and second beatings and about 650 for the third. The time taken is from about 4.5 minutes for an early beating on a large pot to about 1.5 minutes for a later beating on a smaller pot. There are a few variations on these methods, the most pronounced being the *dhatri*, which tends first to have some excess clay scythed off from the bottom before being beaten flat against the ground with the anvil, once the base is fully closed.

This description of beating employs the term 'sessions', which are periods of continuous beating in a horizontal ring around the pot. It is this feature which is

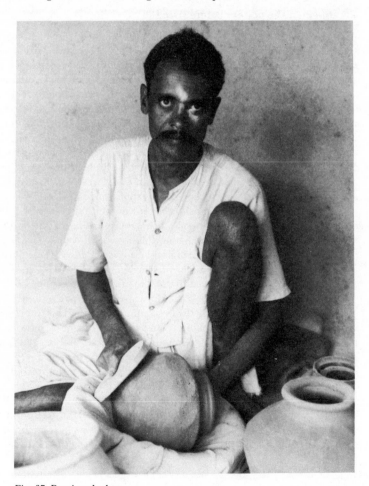

Fig. 67. Beating the base

exploited in the creation of difference. Some pots are simply beaten to as round a profile as possible: the name *goli* (which means round) indicates that this is one example. If the profiles in the reference list of pottery are inspected (pp. xi–xiii above), it will be apparent that some vessels have an angular shoulder. This angularity is produced as an effect of the beating process moving up from base to neck, as beating progresses. It is then removed, in making a round profile, but in other cases it is retained and accentuated by using a flat paddle on the shoulder. Such pots are said by the potters to have 'one *parti*'. A further extension is to create two points of angularity, with a flat facet between them, and such vessels, including the *divali matka* and the *batloi*, are said to have 'two *parti*'. The number of *parti* for each vessel is listed in Table 14. The same feature and a similar term are recorded by Saraswati and Behura for Gujerat and Madhya Pradesh (1966: 57, 163).

Treatment of the pottery before firing

All vessels, with the exception of some of the smallest, such as the *chhapa*, are treated with a self-slip formed by levigation in the clay pit. This is kept in the *pawanda* pot and applied immediately before painting or burnishing. One potter, at least, sometimes applied a separate slip for his black vessels, obtained from a site in the Ujjain region. The slip is rapidly applied with a piece of cloth. At this stage, distinctions are made between pots of the three basic wares. Those that will be red and buff have red ochre applied to their upper portion, and red ochre will also be used to cover entirely pots that are to be red or painted white. This ochre is obtained, through Ujjain, from a source called Satna, near Jabalpur, 550 km to the north-east. A white paint is also obtained through Ujjain from a source near Porbandar on the coast, 600 km to the west. A schist is occasionally applied as a final coating. Although the appearance of this is similar to that usually termed mica, the greenish tinge of the rock suggests that it is in fact a chlorite schist. A saddle quern has been set into one of the working areas especially for the purpose of crushing this rock with water. This *jalpa* is used merely for enhancement, but sparingly, since it is expensive. One potter applies it mainly to black vessels such as *dhakni*, two others mainly to water vessels, while a further three were not observed to use it at all.

Container forms of the third, black ware are first slipped and then burnished on the area above and including the maximum diameter. This, together with the slipping, is performed by the painter. Strings of either a nut[2] (see Fig. 56 above) or glass beads are placed over the mouth of the vessel and rotated from side to side with both hands, turning the pot occasionally to ensure an even polish over the whole vessel. Some of the black pots are then given impressed or incised decoration, which is never applied to vessels of the other two wares. The commonest form of decoration, applied after throwing, is a series of small triangles placed in groups of three or continuously, either around the neck or the top of the shoulder, or both. This is most often applied, with a broken sherd or cowrie shell (Fig. 68), to pots in the *dohni* group including the *chayra dohni* and the *jhawaliya*.

---

[2] *Caesalpinia bonduc* (L.) Roxb., a member of the Leguminosae. Identification courtesy of Kew Gardens.

Like the decoration applied on the wheel, which was described earlier, this does not appear to be used in a consistent fashion.

More elaborate decoration is rarely applied, but may include a series of fine curved lines, incised on the shoulder of the *jhawaliya*, or the use of plastic decorations, such as flower or *swastik* emblems, impressed as stamps with the paddle, four to six times around the body. Two instances of the use of a carved paddle were observed. One potter had the Hindi for 'Bombay' (Fig. 55 above) standing for 'made in Bombay', which he applied occasionally for fun. A use of this medium for marking was found when two potters shared the same pottery-making facilities in 1979, and each used a design to differentiate his pots, but these were no longer applied in 1981, when the two households had largely separated. Finally, there is the treatment of the *kareli* and *karela*, which is in no sense decorative. Both of these are scored with deep grooves when in the leather-hard state, the *kareli* a few millimetres about its point of maximum diameter, and the *karela* two or three centimetres above this point and then again one centimetre higher. This scoring will be used to separate the base from the top after firing. The *karela* is also pricked many times on the newly beaten base to produce a number of small holes to permit the passage of air. A description of the painting has been presented in Chapter 6.

Fig. 68. Adding impressed decoration with cowrie shell

Pottery firing

It is clear from Saraswati and Behura (1966: 103–29) that there are firing techniques of a great range of sophistication in India. Those found in the Ujjain area are amongst the simplest, based on an open firing. The regularity of firing depends upon the season. Usually, potters fire about every ten days, but before the festival of *divali* and *akhartij* there is a crescendo of activity, leading to firing every two days. The firing area is not fixed (only two of the six potters were using the same area in 1981 as in 1979), and the state of the underlying soil is often blamed for breakages. All but one potter used a shallow pit, an example being 212 cm in diameter and 45 cm deep at the centre.

Most of the fuel is collected on the day, or the day previous to the firing, although the potters will be on the lookout for suitable material for several days in advance. A wide range of fuel is acceptable, woods such as date palm, tamarind and *pipal*, various straws from the village crops, cow dung, and sawdust from the carpenters. The favourite fuel seemed to be the straw of wheat and chick-pea, while the large stalks of sorghum and maize were thought unsuitable. Wood was usually included only if thicker vessels such as *dhatri* were to be fired. A normal firing takes one to two donkey-loads of fuel. The leaves of the date palm, which burn quickly and fiercely, were used for starting and, to an extent, for controlling the fire. Potters would first try local supplies, including their *asami*, then local groves and river banks, and finally, if necessary, purchase fuel in nearby villages. In Ujjain town, by contrast, potters have to purchase all fuel at around 30 r for the 200 kg they require for a single firing, and in a number of parts of India, the shortage of fuel has become the major cause of a decline in potting (e.g. Bose 1980).

Firing tends to take place at around 6.30 to 7.00 p.m. The potters lay down fuel from around 4 to 5 p.m., or earlier if it needs drying in the midday sun. Over a layer of straw the largest pots, such as *kunda* or *goli*, are placed, with their mouths angled towards the centre and downwards, in approximate rows. Pots are then piled in layers of smaller circles, each being used to cover the gaps between the pots below, usually ending with the smallest forms, such as *divaniya* or *dhakni*. A further layer of fuel is then piled around the outside up to about half the height of the pile. Set within this, around the base, is a series of eight to ten broken pot mouths (Fig. 69). The potters then cover the pile (except these pot mouths) with broken sherds, first larger ones, covering any gaps between pots, and then smaller ones. An additional broken pot mouth is placed on the apex of the pile (Fig. 70). These pot mouths do not represent true fire channels, since they do not lead through to the centre of the fire, although such channels are found in this area, according to Saraswati and Behura (1966: 105–6). Finally the whole pile is covered by a layer of fuel. The pile is now about 1.5 to 3.0 m across and stands about 90 cm high.

The course of the firing may be described from three perspectives: the observations of the potters' activities, the statements of the potters, and the temperature of the fire. The potters first burn a small pile of straw and then take smouldering cinders and push them into each of the open pot mouths, blowing or adding date-palm leaves if they fail to catch. They then leave the fire for a period, often going to eat. As observed on a pyrometer placed in the centre and

Fig. 69. Pots for firing with fuel of straw

Fig. 70. Pots for firing covered with sherds

half-way to the edge of the fire (see Fig. 71a–d), the temperature rises slowly in the first hour to around 70°C. This may act as a 'pre-firing' driving off any remaining moisture. At this stage the painters and other women of the household start tossing in bundles of fuel through the holes as they walk around the fire. This is begun in a casual manner and often broken off, but gradually the activity assumes a greater intensity, when there may be several figures walking rapidly around the fire adding fuel, until five large baskets are used up.

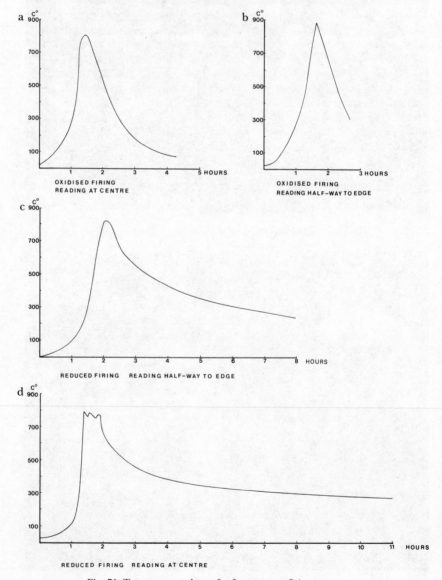

Fig. 71. Temperature charts for four pottery firings

At first the fire shows little response to this activity, with only an occasional burst of flame, but on the temperature charts, the curve, once it gains momentum, rises very rapidly to its maximum and is a close reflection of the crescendo of activity. The potters' own comments are various. It was agreed that the fire should not heat up too quickly. If they think this has happened they may remove some of the sherd cover to 'cool' the fire. They also use blankets to try to prevent too strong a wind from disturbing the firing. A variety of methods were described for ascertaining whether a sufficiently high temperature had been reached. Some looked at the pottery through the holes, others looked for flames shooting from the apical hole (Fischer and Shah (1970: 158) mention potters in Gujerat looking at the colour of the flame). The potters claimed that the temperature should be higher for a black firing; as one put it, 'If the red fire is 100 then the black fire should be 125', but the four examples measured did not show any obvious differences in the maximum temperatures reached, which tended to vary from 790°C to 880°C. It may be noted that one firing ended in a series of short peaks rather than a single climax (Fig. 71d); this reflected attempts to hold conversations while feeding the fire. An open firing of this kind is likely to result in highly variable maximum temperatures for different parts of the same firing (e.g. Rye 1981: 102–3).

Up to this stage the procedures for red and black firings have been identical. The potters' conception of firing pots black is of a smudging process, based on keeping smoke in. In practice, however, the process employed has the equal effect of keeping oxygen out, so as to produce a firing in reduced conditions. Once the temperature has reached its peak, the family first block the apical opening with a pot, and then throw in goat droppings, road tar or rubber to produce smoke. Prior to the firing, a large heap of wet ash is prepared beside the pottery, and this is now spread over the whole fire, in this case including the pot mouth holes. This is smoothed over and further wetted, until no wisps of smoke can be seen escaping through the cover. The effect of this operation is evident in the temperature charts, in that while the red firings plunge quite rapidly in temperature, losing most of their heat within two hours, the black firings retain a temperature of around 200°C when the fire is opened, which in both cases takes place at around 6 a.m. the next morning.

Once the fire is opened and the pots removed with sticks, they are tested in turn by a sharp rap with the knuckle, to discover, from the sound produced, any cracks which may not be visible, and underfired pots are also separated at this stage. In Table 15, the results of ten firings are given. It will be evident that refiring is more common with red pottery than black, although this may indicate merely that signs of underfiring are easier to locate in the case of the former. Pots will still be used if there is slight spalding, but may leak if these are serious. Cracks around the maximum diameter and base are common, and it is the largest forms which seem most susceptible to breakage. Pots may then be taken into the potter's house for storage or taken straight to market, and it is common for firings to be held on the evening before market day. The firings described are of the larger, more generalised variety. Small firings of specialised pots also occur, particularly for certain ritual events such as the *kundi* for a funeral, or the *warad* pots for a wedding. The fired pots range in weight from around 0.5 kg for a *chuklya* to over 3 kg for a large *goli*.

Table 15. *Results of ten firings*

	Oxidised firings
(1)	23 *goli*, 20 *matka*, 1 *batloi*, 3 *gagra*, 2 *brahman dohni*, 13 *kunda* Of these: Broken – 5 *goli* Needing refiring – 7 *matka*, 1 *batloi*, 2 *kunda*, 3 *gagra*
(2)	79 *divali matka*, 2 *dhakni*, 2 baskets *divaniya*, approximately 200 *kulhri* Of these: Broken – 15 *divali matka* Needing refiring – 10 *divali matka*
(3)	33 *goli*, 23 *matka*, 30 *kunda*, 22 *wariya*, 8 *dhakan*, 3 *bujhara* Of these: Broken – 1 *matka* Needing refiring – 1 *goli*
(4)	11 *goli*, 3 small *goli*, 18 *matka*, 4 *batloi*, 1 *kunda*, 4 *gagra* Of these: Broken – 2 *matka*, 1 *kunda*, 1 *gagra* Needing refiring – 6 *matka*
(5)	34 *divali matka*, 2 *kunda*, 4 *kalash*, 1 *brahman dohni*, 1 basket *divaniya/kulhri* Of these: Broken– 7 *divali matka*, 4 *kalash*

	Reduced firings
(1)	23 *batloi*, 18 *dohni*, 3 *tapeli*, 58 *kareli*, approximately 12 *karela*, 10 *wariya* Of these: Broken – 2 *batloi*, 1 *tapeli*
(2)	24 *goli*, 16 *dohni*, 5 *tapeli*, 14 *karela*, 11 *kareli* Of these: Broken – 2 *goli*, 1 *dohni*, 1 *tapeli*
(3)	19 *dhatri*, 1 basket *dhakni* Of these: Broken – 4 *dhatri*
(4)	16 *goli*, 12 *matka*, 10 *kunda* Of these: Broken – 2 *goli*, 6 *matka* Needing refiring – 3 *kunda*
(5)	8 *dhatri*, 9 *dohni*, 9 *chayra dohni*, 22 *tapeli*, 32 *karela*, 43 *kareli*, 6 *harawla*, 6 *wariya*, 30 *dhakni*, 4 mini *dhakni*, 2 *kundali* Breakages: not observed

BIBLIOGRAPHY

Adams, M. 1973. Structural aspects of a village art. *American Anthropologist* 75: 267–79

Allchin, F. 1959. Poor men's thalis. *Bulletin of the School of Oriental and African Studies* 22: 250–7

1978. The archaeological significance of a modern Indian potter's technique. In D. Chattipadhyaya (ed.), *History and Society: Essays in Honour of Prof. Niharranjan Ray*. Calcutta

Allen, W., and Richardson, J. 1971. The reconstruction of kinship from archaeological data: the concepts, the methods and the feasibility. *American Antiquity* 36: 41–53

Anand, M. 1957. *The Hindu View of Art*. Asia Publishing House, Bombay

Ansari, Z. D., and Dhavalikar, M. K. 1975. *Excavations at Kayatha*. Deccan College, Pune

Apte, V. 1978. *The Sacrament of Marriage in Hindu Society*. Ajanta Pub., Bombay

Arnold, D. 1971. Ethnomineralogy of Ticul, Yucatan potters: etics and emics. *American Antiquity* 36: 20–40

1975. Ceramic ecology of the Auycucho Basin, Peru: implications for prehistory. *Current Anthropology* 16: 183–205

1983. Design structure and community organisation in Quinua, Peru. In D. Washburn (ed.), *Structure and Cognition in Art*. Cambridge University Press

Audouze, F., and Jarrige, C. 1979. A third millennium pottery-firing structure at Mehrgarh and its economic implications. In M. Taddei (ed.), *South Asian Archaeology 1977*. Istituto Universitario Orientale, Naples

Babb, L. 1975. *The Divine Hierarchy: Popular Hinduism in Central India*. Columbia University Press, New York

Bandyopadhyay, S. 1973. *Foreign Accounts of Marriage in Ancient India*. Firma Mukhopadhyay, Calcutta

Bannister, D. (ed.). 1977. *New Perspectives in Personal Construct Theory*. Academic Press, London

Barthes, R. 1973. *Mythologies*. Paladin, London

1977. *Image–Music–Text*. Fontana, London

Basham, A. 1971. *The Wonder That was India*. Fontana, London

Basso, K. 1976. 'Wise words' of the Western Apache: metaphor and semantic theory. In K. Basso and H. Selby (eds.), *Meaning in Anthropology*. University of New Mexico Press, Albuquerque

233

Baudrillard, J. 1975. *The Mirror of Production*. Telos Press, St Louis
    1981. *For a Critique of the Political Economy of the Sign*. Telos Press, St Louis
Bayly, C. 1983. *Rulers, Townsmen and Bazaars*. Cambridge University Press
Beck, B. 1969. Colour and heat in South Indian ritual. *Man* 4: 553–73
Behura, N. 1978. *Peasant potters of Orissa*. Sterling Press, New Delhi
Beidelman, T. 1959. A comparative analysis of the Jajmani system. *Monographs for the Association of Asian Studies* 8. New York
Benton, T., and Benton, C. (eds.). 1975. *Form and Function*. Crosby Lockwood Staples, London
Bernstein, B. 1971. *Class Codes and Control*, vol. 2. Routledge and Kegan Paul, London
Beteille, A. 1969. *Castes Old and New*. Asia Publishing House, New Delhi
Bhaskar, R. 1978. *A Realist Theory of Science*. Harvester Press, Sussex
Biebuyck, D. 1973. *The Lega: Art Initiation and Moral Philosophy*. California University Press, Berkley
Binford, L. 1962. Archaeology as anthropology. *American Antiquity* 28: 217–25
    1973. Interassemblage variability – the Mousterian and the 'functional' argument. In C. Renfrew (ed.), *The Explanation of Culture Change*, Duckworth, London
    1978. *Nunamiut Ethnoarchaeology*. Academic Press, New York
    (ed.). 1979. *For Theory Building in Archaeology*. Academic Press, New York
Birmingham, J. 1975. Traditional potters of the Kathmandu valley: an ethno-archaeological study. *Man* 10: 370–86
Bloch, M. 1977. The past and the present in the present. *Man* 12: 278–92
Boas, F. 1955. *Primitive Art*. Dover, New York
Bobrow, D., and Winograd, T. 1977. An overview of KRL–O a knowledge representation language. *Cognitive Science* 1: 3–46
    1979. KRL: another perspective. *Cognitive Science* 3: 29–42
Boden, M. 1977. *Artificial Intelligence and Natural man*. Harvester Press, Sussex
Boner, A., and Sharma, S. 1972. *New Light on the Sun Temple Konarak*. Chowkhamba Sanskrit Series Office, Varanasi
Bonnichsen, R. 1973. Millie's camp: an experiment in archaeology. *World Archaeology* 4: 277–91
Bose, P. K. 1980. *Traditional Craft in a Changing Society*. Centre for Social Studies, Surat
Bourdieu, P. 1977. *Outline of a Theory of Practice*. Cambridge University Press
Braithwaite, M. 1982. Decoration as ritual symbol: a theoretical proposal and an ethnographic study in southern Sudan. In I. Hodder (ed.), *Symbolic and Structural Archaeology*. Cambridge University Press
Braun, D. 1983. Pots as tools. In A. Keene and J. Moore (eds.), *Archaeological Hammers and Theories*. Academic Press, New York
Braun, D., and Plog, F. 1982. Evolution of 'tribal' social networks: theory and prehistoric north American evidence. *American Antiquity* 47: 504–24
Census of India 1931, Volume XX. Central India Agency, Calcutta (1933)
Census of India 1971: Madhya Pradesh. Part X, Ujjain District. Bhopal (1974)
Chapman, R., Kinnes, I., and Randsborg, K. (eds.). 1981. *The Archaeology of Death*. Cambridge University Press

Chattopadhaya, K. 1975. *Handicrafts of India*. Indian Council for Cultural Relations, New Delhi

Chomsky, N. 1957. *Syntactic Structures*. Mouton, The Hague

Clarke, D. 1968. *Analytical Archaeology*. Methuen, London

1970. *Beaker Pottery of Great Britain and Ireland*. Cambridge University Press

Cohen, A. 1974. *Two-Dimensional Man*. Routledge and Kegan Paul, London

Collins, A., and Loftus, E. 1975. A spreading-association theory of semantic processing. *Psychology Review* 82: 407–28

Coomaraswamy, A. K. 1908. *Medieval Sinhalese Art*. Essex House Press, Broad Campden

1934. *The Transformation of Nature into Art*. Harvard University Press

Corton, J., and Klanzsky, R. 1978. *Semantic Factors in Cognition*. Lawrence Erlbaum, New Jersey

Coward, R., and Ellis, J. 1977. *Language and Materialism*. Routledge and Kegan Paul, London

Crooke, W. 1926. *Religion and Folklore of Northern India*. Oxford University Press

Das, R., and Ray, G. 1966. Potter's craft in a village in West Bengal. *Bulletin of the Cultural Research Institute (Govt. of West Bengal)* 5: 48–58

Das, V. 1977. *Structure and Cognition*. Oxford University Press, New Delhi

David, K. 1977. Hierarchy and equivalence in Jaffna, north Sri Lanka: normative codes as mediator. In K. David (ed.), *The New Wave*. Mouton, The Hague

David, N. 1971. The Fulani compound and the archaeologist. *World Archaeology* 3: 111–31

DeBoer, W., and Lathrap, D. 1979. The making and breaking of Shipibo–Conibo Ceramics. In C. Kramer (ed.), *Ethno-archaeology*. Columbia University Press

Deetz, J. 1967. *Invitation to Archaeology*. Natural History Press, New York

Dethlefsen, E., and Deetz, J. 1966. Death's head, cherub and willow trees: experimental archaeology in colonial cemeteries. *American Antiquity* 31: 502–10

Dhavalikar, M. 1979. Early farming cultures of the Deccan. In D. Agrawal and D. Chakrabarti (eds.), *Essays in Protohistory*. B.R. Publishers, Delhi

Dhavalikar, M., and Marathe, A. 1979. Jorwe pottery – a statistical study. *Bulletin of Deccan College Research Institute* 38: 17–22

Doran, J., and Hodson, F. 1975. *Mathematics and Computers in Archaeology*. Edinburgh University Press

Douglas, M. 1966. *Purity and Danger*. Routledge and Kegan Paul, London

1975. Deciphering a meal. In *Implicit Meanings*. Routledge and Kegan Paul, London

Douglas, M., and Isherwood, B. 1980. *The World of Goods*. Penguin Books, Harmondsworth

Dumont, L. 1952. A remarkable feature of South Indian pot-making. *Man* 52: 81–3

1972. *Homo Hierarchicus*. Paladin, London

Dunnell, R. 1972. *Systematics in Prehistory*. Macmillan, New York

1978. Style and function: a fundamental dichotomy. *American Antiquity* 43: 192–202

1980. Evolutionary theory and archaeology. In M. Schiffer (ed.), *Advances in Archaeological Method and Theory* 3: 38–101

Durkheim, E., and Mauss, M. 1963. *Primitive Classification*. Cohen and West, London

Ellen, R., and Reason, D. (eds.). 1979. *Classifications and their Social Context*. Academic Press, London

Ennew, J. 1976. Examining the facts in fieldwork. *Critique of Anthropology* 7: 43–66

Faris, J. 1972. *Nuba Personal Art*. Duckworth, London

 1983. From form to content in the structural study of ceramic systems. In D. Washburn (ed.), *Structure and Cognition in Art*. Cambridge University Press

Fernandez, J. 1974. The mission of metaphor in expressive culture. *Current Anthropology* 15: 119–45

Fischer, E., and Shah, H. 1970. *Rural Craftsmen and their Work*. National Institute of Design, Ahmedabad

Ford, J. 1954. The type concept revisited. *American Anthropologist* 56: 42–53

Forde, D. 1934. *Habitat, Economy and Society*. Methuen, London

Foucault, M. 1972. *The Archaeology of Knowledge*. Tavistock, London

Franken, R. 1974. *In Search of the Jericho Potters*. North Holland, Amsterdam

Fransella, F., and Bannister, D. 1977. *A Manual for Repertory Grid Technique*. Academic Press, London

Freed, R., and Freed, S. 1963. Utilitarian pottery manufacture in a North Indian village. *Anthropological Quarterly* 36: 34–42

 1980. Rites of passage in Shanti Nagar. *Anthropological Papers of the American Museum of Natural History* 56

Freed, S., and Freed, R. 1978. Shanti Nagar: the effects of urbanisation in a village in North India. *Anthropological Papers of the American Museum of Natural History* 55

Friedman, J., and Rowlands, M. 1977. Notes towards an epigenetic model of the evolution of civilisation. In J. Friedman and M. Rowlands (eds.), *The Evolution of Social Systems*. Duckworth, London

Friedrich, M. 1970. Design structure and social interaction: archaeological implications of an ethnographic analysis. *American Antiquity* 55: 332–43

Fuller, C. 1977. British India or traditional India? an anthropological problem. *Ethnos* 28: 95–121

Furth, H. 1969. *Piaget and Knowledge*. Prentice Hall, London

Gait, E. 1897. The manufacture of pottery in Assam. *Journal of Indian Art* 7: 5–8

Gardener, P. 1978. Phenomenal levels in the structure of Indian civilisation. In S. Vatuk (ed.), *American Studies in the Anthropology of India*. Manohar, New Delhi

Gardin, J.-C. 1965. On the possible uses of componential analysis in archaeology. In E. Hammel (ed.), *Formal Semantic Analysis*. American Anthropologist

Garfinkle, H. 1967. *Studies in Ethnomethodology*. Englewood Cliffs, New Jersey

Geertz, C. 1973. *The Interpretation of Cultures*. Basic Books, New York

Gell, A. 1975. *Metamorphosis of the Cassowaries*. Athlone Press, London

Gellner, E. 1982. What is structuralisme? In C. Renfrew, M. Rowlands and B. Segraves (eds.), *Theory and Explanation in Archaeology*. Academic Press, London

Ghurye, G. 1950. *Caste and Class in India*. Popular Book Depot, Bombay

Giddens, A. 1979. *Central Problems in Social Theory*. Macmillan, London

Gilsenan, M. 1976. Lying, honour and contradiction. In B. Kapferer (ed.), *Transaction and Meaning*. Institute for the Study of Human Issues, Philadelphia

1983. *Recognising Islam*. Croom Helm, London

Glassie, H. 1975. *Folk Housing in Middle Virginia: A Structural Analysis of Historical Artifacts*. University of Tennessee Press, Knoxville

Goffman, E. 1974. *Frame Analysis: An Essay on the Organisation of Experience*. Harper and Row, New York

Gold, MS. Worship of Pathwari Ma and Celebration of Ganga: Ritual of Departure and Return for Rajasthani Pilgrims

Gombrich, E. 1969. The use of art for the study of symbols. In J. Hogg (ed.), *Psychology and the Visual Arts*. Penguin Books, Harmondsworth

1979. *The Sense of Order*. Phaidon, London

Good, A. 1980. Only Siva is in the cemetery. *Working Papers in Social Anthropology*. University of Durham

1982. The actor and the act: categories of prestation in South India. *Man* 17: 23–41

1983. A symbolic type and its transformations: the case of South Indian Ponkal. *Contributions to South Asian Sociology* 17: 223–44

Gough, K. 1981. *Rural Society in South East India*. Cambridge University Press

Gould, H. 1967. Priest and contrapriest: a structural analysis of jajmani relationships in the Hindi plains and Nilgiri hills. *Contributions to Indian Sociology* 1: 26–55

Gould, R. (ed.). 1978. *Explorations in Ethnoarchaeology*. University of New Mexico, Albuquerque

1980. *Living Archaeology*. Cambridge University Press

Graves, M. 1981. Ethnoarchaeology of Kalinga Ceramic Design. University Microfilms, Ann Arbor

Gunn, J. 1975. An envirotechnological system for Hogup Cave. *American Antiquity* 40: 3–21

Gupta, G. 1974. *Marriage, Religion and Society*. Curzon Press, London

Habermas, J. 1982. Modern and post-modern architecture. *9H* 4: 9–14

Haggett, P. 1965. *Locational Analysis in Human Geography*. Arnold, London

Hammel, E. (ed.). 1965. Formal semantic analysis. *American Anthropologist* 67: part 2

Hardin, M. 1983. The structure of Tarascan pottery painting. In D. Washburn (ed.), *Structure and Cognition in Art*. Cambridge University Press

Harper, E. (ed.). 1964. *Religion in South Asia*. University of Washington Press, Seattle

Harre, R. 1979. *Social Being*. Basil Blackwell, Oxford

Harris, M. 1979. *Cultural Materialism*. Random House, New York

Havell, E. 1927. *Indian Architecture*. John Murray, London

Heider, E. 1972. Probabilities, sampling and ethnographic method: the case of the Dani color names. *Man* 7: 447–55

Hill, J. 1970. Broken K Pueblo: prehistoric social organisation in the American south-west. *Anthropological Papers of the University of Arizona* 18. Tucson

Hill, J., and Evans, R. 1972. A model for classification and typology. In D. Clarke (ed.), *Models in Archaeology*. Methuen, London

Hill, J., and Gunn, J. (eds.). 1977. *The Individual in Prehistory*. Academic Press, New York

Hobart, M. 1983. Meaning or moaning? some ethnographic notes on a little understood tribe. In D. Parkin (ed.), *Semantic Anthropology*. Academic Press, London

Hodder, I. 1977. The distribution of material culture items in the Baringo District, Western Kenya. *Man* 12: 239–70

(ed.). 1978. *The Spatial Organisation of Culture*. Duckworth, London

1979. Social and economic stress and material culture patterning. *American Antiquity* 44: 446–54

1982a. *Symbols in Action*. Cambridge University Press

1982b. *The Patterned Past*. Batsford, London

(ed.). 1982. *Symbolic and Structural Archaeology*. Cambridge University Press

1984. Burials, houses, women and men in the European Neolithic. In D. Miller and C. Tilley (eds.), *Ideology, Power and Prehistory*. Cambridge University Press

Hodder, I., and Orton, C. 1976. *Spatial Analysis in Archaeology*. Cambridge University Press

Holder, E. 1897. Madras pottery. *Journal of Indian Art* 7: 10

Hole, F. 1984. Analysis of structure and design in prehistoric ceramics. *World Archaeology* 15: 326–47

Hole, F., and Heizer, R. 1973. *Introduction to Prehistoric Archaeology*. Holt Rinehart and Winston, New York

Howard, H., and Morris, E. (eds.). 1981. *Production and Distribution: A Ceramic Viewpoint*. British Archaeological Reports 120. Oxford

Humphrey, C. 1971. Some ideas of Saussure applied to Buryat magical drawings. In E. Ardener (ed.), *Social Anthropology and Language*. Tavistock, London

Hunt, E. 1978. Imageful thought. In J. Corton and R. Klanzsky (eds.), *Semantic Factors in Cognition*. Lawrence Erlbaum, New Jersey

Hunter-Anderson, R. 1979. A theoretical approach to the study of house form. In L. Binford (ed.), *For Theory Building in Archaeology*. Academic Press, New York

Hymes, D. 1970. Linguistic models in archaeology. In J. Gardin (ed.), *Archaeologie et Calculateur*. C.N.R.S., Paris

Indian Council for Social Science Research. 19875. *Status of Women in India*. Allied Publishers, New Delhi

Jacobsen, D. 1973. *Hidden Faces: Hindu and Muslim Purdah in a Central Indian Village*. University Microfilms, Ann Arbor

1977. Flexibility in Central Indian kinship and residence. In K. David (ed.), *The New Wind*. Mouton, The Hague

Jain, K. 1972. *Malwa Through the Ages*. Banarsidass, New Delhi

Jones, R. 1978. Why did the Tasmanians stop eating fish? In *Exploration in Ethnoarchaeology*. University of New Mexico Press, Albuquerque

Kane, D. 1930–1962. *History of the Dharmasastra*. Bhandarkar Oriental Research Institute, Poona

Kant, I. 1934. *Critique of Pure Reason*. J. M. Dent, London

1953. *Prolegomena*. Manchester University Press

Kaplan, F., and Levine, D. 1981. Cognitive mapping of a folk taxonomy of Mexican pottery: a multivariate approach. *American Anthropologist* 83: 868–84

Keesing, R. 1972. The new ethnography and the new linguistics. *South-western Journal of Anthropology* 28: 219–32

Kempton, W. 1978. Category grading and taxonomic relations: a mug is a sort of a cup. *American Ethnologist* 5: 44–65
1981. *The Folk Classification of Ceramics.* Academic Press, New York
Khanna, M. 1979. *Yantra: The Tantric Symbol of Cosmic Unity.* Thames and Hudson, London
Khare, R. 1976a. *Culture and Reality.* Indian Institute for Advanced Study, Simla
1976b. *The Hindu Hearth and Home.* Vikas, Delhi
Kimball Romney, A., and D'Andrade, R. (eds.). 1964. Transcultural studies in cognition. *American Anthropologist* 66: part 2
Kolenda, P. 1968. Region, caste and family structure: a comparative study of the Indian joint family. In M. Singer and B. Cohn (eds.), *Structure and Change in Indian Society.* Aldine Publishing Company, Chicago
1978. *Caste in Contemporary India,* Benjamin/Cummings, Menlo Park, California
1983. Woman as tribute, woman as flower: images of women in North and South India. *American Ethnologist* 11: 98–117
Kramer, C. (ed.). 1979. *Ethnoarchaeology.* University of New Mexico Press, Albuquerque
Kramrisch, S. 1946. *The Hindu Temple.* University of Calcutta Press
Krause, R. 1978. Towards a formal account of Bantu ceramics. In R. Dunnell and E. Hall (eds.), *Archaeological Essays in Honour of Irving B. Rouse.* Mouton, The Hague
Kroeber, A. 1948. *Anthropology.* Harcourt Brace and Jovanovich, New York
Labov, W. 1972. *Sociolinguistic Patterns.* Basic Blackwell, Oxford
1973. The meaning of words and their boundaries. In C.-J. Bailey and R. Shuy (eds.), *New Ways of Analysing Variation in English.* Georgetown University Press, Washington
Lacan, J. 1979. *The Four Fundamental Concepts of Psychoanalysis.* Penguin Books, Harmondsworth
Lakoff, G. 1973. Hedges and meaning criteria. In R. McDavid and A. Druckert (eds.), *Lexicography in English.* Academy of Sciences, New York
Langer, S. 1960. *Philosophy in a New Key.* Harvard University Press
Larrain, J. 1979. *The Concept of Ideology.* Hutchinson, London
1982. On the character of ideology: Marx and the present debate in Britain. *Theory, Culture and Society* 1: 5–22
Lathrap, D. 1983. Recent Shipibo–Conibo ceramics and their implications for archaeological interpretation. In D. Washburn (ed.), *Structure and Cognition in Art.* Cambridge University Press
Lehrer, A. 1974. *Semantic Fields and Lexical Structures.* North Holland, Amsterdam
Leroi-Gourhan, A. 1968. The evolution of Paleolithic art. *Scientific American* 218: 58–70
Levinson, S. 1982. Caste rank and verbal interaction in western Tamilnadu. In D. McGilvray (ed.), *Caste Ideology and Interaction.* Cambridge University Press
1983. *Pragmatics.* Cambridge University Press
Lévi-Strauss, C. 1970. *The Raw and the Cooked.* Jonathan Cape, London
1977. *Structural Anthropology 2.* Allen Lane, London
1981. *The Naked Man.* Jonathan Cape, London
1982. *The Way of the Masks.* University of Washington Press, Seattle

Lewis, G. 1980. *Day of Shining Red*. Cambridge University Press
Lewis, O., and Barnouw, V. 1967. Caste and the jajmani system in a north Indian village. In J. Potter, J. Dias and M. Foster (eds.), *Peasant Society: A Reader*. Little Brown and Co., Boston
Libbee, M. 1980. Territorial endogamy and the spatial structure of marriage in rural India. In D. Sopher (ed.), *An Exploration of India*. Longman, London
London, G. 1981. Dung-tempered clay. *Journal of Field Archaeology* 8: 189–96
Longacre, W. 1970. Archaeology as anthropology. *Anthropological Papers of the University of Arizona* 17. Tucson
    1981. Kalinga pottery: an ethnoarchaeological study. In I. Hodder, G. Isaac and N. Hammond (eds.), *Patterns of the Past*. Cambridge University Press
Lyons, J. 1977. *Semantics*, vol. 1. Cambridge University Press
McGilvray, D. (ed.). 1982. *Caste Ideology and Interaction*. Cambridge University Press
McGregor, R. 1972. *Outline of Hindi Grammar*. Oxford University Press, New Delhi
Madan, T. *et al.* 1971. On the nature of caste in India: a review symposium on Louis Dumont's *Homo Hierarchicus*. *Contributions to Indian Sociology* 5: 1–82
Malone, C. 1974. *Peoples of South Asia*. Holt Rinehart and Winston, New York
Manchanda, O. 1972. *A Study of the Harappan Pottery*. Oriental Publishers, Delhi
Marquardt, W. 1978. Advances in archaeological seriation. In M. Schiffer (ed.), *Advances in Archaeological Method and Theory* 1. Academic Press, New York
Marriot, McKim. 1955. Little communities in an indigenous civilisation. In McKim Marriot (ed.), *Village India*. University of Chicago Press
    1968. Caste ranking and food transactions: a matrix analysis. In M. Singer and B. Cohn (eds.), *Structure and Change in Indian Society*. Aldine Publishing Company, Chicago
    1976. Hindu transactions: diversity without dualism. In B. Kapferer (ed.), *Transactions and Meaning: Directions in the Analysis of Exchange and Symbolic Behaviour*. I.S.H.I., Philadelphia
Marriot, McKim, and Inden, R. 1977. Towards an ethnosociology of South Asian caste systems. In K. David (ed.), *The New Wind: Changing Identities in South Asia*. Mouton, The Hague
Marx, K. 1974. *Capital*. Lawrence and Wishart, London
Marx, K., and Engels, F. 1970. *The German Ideology*, ed. C. Arthur. International Press, New York
Mateson, F. 1965. Ceramic ecology: an approach to the study of early cultures of the Near East. In F. Mateson (ed.), *Ceramics and Man*. Viking Fund Publications in Anthropology, New York
Mathur, K. 1964. *Caste and Ritual in a Malwa Village*. Asia Publishing House, Bombay
Mauss, M. 1970. *The Gift*. Cohen and West, London
Mayer, A. 1956. Some hierarchical aspects of caste. *South Western Journal of Anthropology* 12: 117–44
    1960. *Caste and Kinship in Central India*. University of California Press, Berkeley
Mead, S., Birks, L., and Shaw, L. 1973. The Lapita style of Fiji and its associations. *Journal of the Polynesian Society* 82: 1–98
Mepham, J. 1979. The theory of ideology in *Capital*. In *Issues in Marxist Philosophy*, vol. 3. Harvester Press, Sussex

Mervis, C., and Rosch, E. 1981. Categorisation of natural objects. *Annual Review of Psychology* 32: 89–115

Metcalf, P. 1981. Meaning and materialism: the ritual economy of death. *Man* 16: 563–78

Miller, D. 1976. MS. Preliminary report on archaeological fieldwork carried out in the Central Maluku, Eastern Indonesia. B.A. Dissertation. Haddon Library, Cambridge

1980a. Settlement and diversity in the Solomon Islands. *Man* 15: 451–66

1980b. Archaeology and development. *Current Anthropology* 21: 709–26

1982a. Explanation and social theory in archaeological practice. In C. Renfrew, M. Rowlands and B. Segraves (eds.), *Theory and Explanation in Archaeology*. Academic Press, New York

1982b. Structures and strategies: an aspect of the relationship between social hierarchy and cultural change. In I. Hodder (ed.), *Structural and Symbolic Archaeology*. Cambridge University Press

(ed.). 1983. Material culture studies: THINGS ain't what they used to be. *Royal Anthropological Institute Newsletter* 59

Forthcoming a. Ideology and the Harappan, *Journal of Anthropological Archaeology*

Forthcoming b. Alienation and exchange in the jajmani system

Miller, D., and Tilley, C. (eds.). 1984. *Ideology Power and Prehistory*. Cambridge University Press

Miller, G. 1978. Practical knowledge and lexical knowledge. In E. Rosch and B. Lloyd (eds.), *Cognition and Categorisation*. Lawrence Erlbaum, New Jersey

Miller, G., and Johnson-Laird, D. 1976. *Language and Perception*. Cambridge University Press

Minsky, M. 1977. Frame-system theory. In P. Johnson-Laird and P. Wason (eds.), *Thinking*. Cambridge University Press

Moffatt, M. 1979. *An Untouchable Community in South India*. Princeton University Press

Muller, J. 1977. Individual variation in art styles. In J. Hill and J. Gunn (eds.), *The Individual in Prehistory*. Academic Press, New York

Müller, M. (ed.). 1886. *Sacred books of the East*, vol. XXIX. Clarendon Press, Oxford

(ed.). 1892. *Sacred books of the East*, vol. XXX. Clarendon Press, Oxford

Munn, N. 1973. *Walibiri Iconography*. Cornell University Press, Ithaca

1977. Spatiotemporal transformations of Gawa canoes. *Journal de la Société des Océanistes* 33: 39–52

Neich, R. 1982. A semiological analysis of self-decoration in Mount Hagen, New Guinea. In I. Rossi (ed.), *The Logic of Culture*. Tavistock Press, London

Nicklin, K. 1971. Stability and innovation in pottery manufacture. *World Archaeology* 3: 13–48

Nie, N., *et al.* 1975. *Statistical Packages for the Social Scientist*. McGraw Hill, New York

O'Flaherty, W., and Derrett, J. 1978. *The Concept of Duty in South Asia*. Vikas, Delhi

Orenstein, H. 1962. Exploitation and function in the interpretation of the jajmani. *South Western Journal of Anthropology* 18: 302–15

Ortner, S. 1978. *Sherpas through their Rituals*. Cambridge University Press

Papernek, V. 1974. *Design for the Real World*. Paladin, London

Parry, J. 1979. *Caste and Kinship in Kangra*. Routledge and Kegan Paul, London

Peacock, D. (ed.). 1977. *Pottery and Early Commerce*. Academic Press, London
Peirce, C. 1931–1958. *Collected Papers*. Harvard University Press
Pettigrew, J. 1975. *Robber Noblemen*. Routledge and Kegan Paul, London
Piaget, J. 1962. *Plays, Dreams and Imitations in Childhood*. Routledge and Kegan Paul, London
     1972. *The Principles of Genetic Epistemology*. Routledge and Kegan Paul, London
Picton, J. (ed.). 1984. *Earthenware in Asia and Africa*. Percival David Foundation for the Study of Chinese Art, London
Pike, K. 1967. *Language in Relation to a Unified Theory of Human Behaviour*. Mouton, The Hague
Piper, J. 1980. The spatial structure of Suchindram. *Art and Archaeology Research papers* 17: 65–80
Plog, S. 1976. Measurement of prehistoric interaction between communities. In K. Flannery (ed.), *The early Mesoamerican Village*. Academic Press, New York
     1980. *Stylistic Variation in Prehistoric Ceramics*. Cambridge University Press
     1983. Analysis of style in artifacts. *Annual Review of Anthropology* 12: 125–42
Pocock, D. 1962. Notes on Jajmani relationships. *Contributions to Indian Sociology* 6: 79–85
     1972. *Kanbi and Patidar*. Clarendon Press, Oxford
Polanyi, K. Arensberg, C., and Pearson, H. (eds.). 1957. *Trade and Markets in the Early Empires*. Free Press, Glencoe, Illinois
Possehl, G. (ed.). 1983. *Harappan Civilisation*. Aris and Phillips, Warminster
Pradhan, M. 1967. *The Political System of the Jats of Northern India*. Oxford University Press
Ramamirtham, C. 1974. Clay. In A. Jussawalla (ed.), *New Writings in India*. Penguin Books, Harmondsworth
Redman, C. 1977. The 'analytical individual' and prehistoric style variability. In J. Hill and J. Gunn (eds.), *The Individual in Prehistory*. Academic Press, New York
     1978. Multivariate artifact analysis: a basis for multidimensional interpretations. In C. Redman *et al.* (eds.), *Social Archaeology*. Academic Press, London
Reina, R., and Hill, J. 1978. *The Traditional Pottery of Guatemala*. University of Texas Press, Austin
Renfrew, C. (ed.). 1974. *British Prehistory*. Duckworth, London
Rosch, E. 1976. Classification of real-world objects: origins and representations in cognition. In S. Ehrlich and E. Tulving (eds.), *La mémoire sémantique*. Bulletin de Psychologie, Paris
     1978. Principles of categorisation. In E. Rosch and B. Lloyd (eds.), *Cognition and Categorisation*. Lawrence Erlbaum, New Jersey
Rouse, I. 1960. The classification of artifacts in archaeology. *American Antiquity* 25: 313–23
Rowlands, M., and Gledhill, J. 1977. The relation between archaeology and anthropology. In M. Spriggs (ed.), *Archaeology and Anthropology*. British Archaeological Reports 19
Roy, B. S. 1969. Literary references to pottery. In B. Sinha (ed.), *Potteries in Ancient India*. Department of Ancient Indian History and Archaeology, University of Patna

Rubertone, P. 1979. Social Organisation of an Islamic Town: A Behavioural Explanation of Ceramic Variability. University Microfilms, Ann Arbor

Rye, O. 1976. Keeping your temper under control. *Archaeology and Physical Anthropology in Oceania* 11: 205–11

1981. *Pottery Technology*. Taraxacum Press, Washington

Rye, O., and Evans, C. 1976. Traditional pottery techniques of Pakistan. *Smithsonian Contributions to Anthropology* 21

Sackett, J. 1977. The meaning of style in archaeology: a general model. *American Antiquity* 42: 369–80

1982. Approaches to style in lithic archaeology. *Journal of Anthropological Archaeology* 1: 59–112

Sahi, J. 1980. *The Child and the Serpent*. Routledge and Kegan Paul, London

Sahlins, M. 1976. *Culture and Practical Reason*. University of Chicago Press

Saksena, J. 1979. *The Art of Rajasthan*. Sundeep Prakashan, Delhi

Sankalia, H. 1974. *The Prehistory and Protohistory of India and Pakistan*, Deccan College, Pune

1977. *Prehistory of India*. Munishiram Manoharlal, Bombay

Sankalia, H., and Deo, S. 1955. *Report on the Excavations at Nasik and Jorwe. 1950–51*. Deccan College, Pune

Sankalia, H., Deo, S., and Ansari, Z. 1969. *Excavations at Ahar*. Deccan College, Pune

1971. *Chalcolithic Navadatoli*. Deccan College, Pune

Sankalia, H., Deo, S., Ansari, Z., and Ehrhardt, S. 1960. *From History to Prehistory at Nevasa (1954–56)*. Deccan College, Pune

Saraswati, B. 1979. *Pottery-Making Cultures and Indian Civilisation*. Abhinav, New Delhi

Saraswati, B., and Behura, N. 1966. *Pottery Techniques in Peasant India*. Anthropological Survey of India, Calcutta

Saussure, F. de. 1959. *A Course in General Linguistics*. Philosophical Society, New York

Saxe, A. 1973. The Social Dimensions of Mortuary Practices. University Microfilms, Ann Arbor

Schiffer, M. 1976. *Behavioural Archaeology*. Academic Press, New York

Selwyn, T. 1979. An analysis of a Hindu marriage ceremony. *Man* 14: 684–98

Seneviratne, H. 1978. *Rituals of the Kandyan State*. Cambridge University Press

Shanks, M., and Tilley, C. 1982. Ideology, symbolic power and ritual communication: a reinterpretation of neolithic mortuary practices. In I. Hodder (ed.), *Symbolic and Structural Archaeology*. Cambridge University Press

Sharma, U. 1969. Hinduism in a Kangra Village. Ph.D. Thesis, London University

1970. The problem of village Hinduism: fragmentation and integration. *Contributions to Indian Sociology* 4

Shepard, A. 1956. *Ceramics for the archaeologist*. Carnegie Institute of Washington

1965. Rio-Grande glaze-paint pottery: a test of petrographic analysis. In F. Mateson (ed.), *Ceramics and Man*. Viking Fund Publications in Anthropology, New York

Silverstein, M. 1976. Shifters, linguistic categories, and cultural description. In K. Basso and H. Selby (eds.), *Meaning in Anthropology*. University of New Mexico, Albuquerque

Simmel, G. 1968. *The Conflict in Modern Culture and other Essays*, ed. K. Eyzkork. Teachers College Press, New York

Singh, R. Y. 1978. *The Malwa Region: Habitat, System, Structure and Change*. International Centre for Rural Habitat Studies, Varanasi

Singh, S. 1969. Vedic literature on pottery. In B. Sinha (ed.), *Pottery in Ancient India*. Dept. of Ancient Indian History and Archaeology, University of Patna

Skinner, B. 1972. *Beyond Freedom and Dignity*. Penguin Books, Harmondsworth

Smith, N. (ed.). 1982. *Mutual Knowledge*. Academic Press, London

Smith, N., and Wilson, D. 1979. *Modern Linguistics: The Results of Chomsky's Revolution*. Harvester Press, Sussex

Spaulding, A. 1953. Statistical techniques for the discovery of artifact types. *American Antiquity* 18: 305–13

1960. The dimensions of archaeology. In G. Dole and R. Carneiro (eds.), *Essays in the Science of Culture in Honour of Leslie A. White*. Thomas Y. Crowell Co., New York

1982. Structure in archaeological data: nominal variables. In R. Whallon and J. Brown (eds.), *Essays in Archaeological Typology*. Centre for American Archaeology Press, Evanston, Illinois

Sperber, D. 1974. *Rethinking symbolism*. Cambridge University Press

1980. Is symbolic thought pre-rational? M. Foster and S. Brandes (eds.), *Symbol as Sense*. Academic Press, New York

Sperber, D., and Wilson, D. 1982. Mutual knowledge and relevance in theories of comprehension. In N. Smith (ed.), *Mutual Knowledge*. Academic Press, London

Spriggs, M., and Miller, D. 1979. Ambon-Lease, a study of contemporary pottery manufacture and its archaeological relevance. In M. Millett (ed.), *Pottery and the Archaeologist*. Institute of Archaeology, London, Occasional Papers No. 4

Srinivas, M. 1966. *Social Change in Modern India*. Orient Longman, New Delhi

Srivastava, S. 1969. Rajasthan's post-Harappan pottery. In B. Sinha (ed.), *Potters in Ancient India*. Department of Ancient History and Archaeology, University of Patna.

Stanislawski, M. 1978. If pots were mortal. In R. Gould (ed.), *Explorations in Ethnoarchaeology*. University of New Mexico Press, Albuquerque

Steadman, P. 1979. *The Evolution of Designs*. Cambridge University Press

Stevenson, S. 1920. *The Rites of the Twice Born*. Oxford University Press

Strathern, A., and Strathern, M. 1971. *Self-Decoration in Mount Hagen*. Duckworth, London

Stutley, M., and Stutley, J. 1977. *A Dictionary of Hinduism*. Routledge and Kegan Paul, London

Taylor, C. 1971. Interpretation and the science of man. *Review of Metaphysics* 25: 1–45

Terrell, J. 1977. Geographical systems and human diversity in the North Solomons. *World Archaeology* 9: 62–81

Toll, H. 1981. Ceramic comparisons concerning redistribution in Chaco Canyon,

New Mexico. In H. Howard and E. Morris (eds.), *Production and Distribution: A Ceramic Viewpoint*. British Archaeological Reports 120

Toren, C. 1983. Thinking symbols; a critique of Sperber (1979). *Man* 18: 260–8

Tourangeau, R., and Sternberg, R. 1982. Understanding and appreciating metaphors. *Cognition* 11: 203–44

Turner, T. 1969. A central Brazilian tribe and its symbolic language of bodily adornment. *Natural History* 78: 1–8
    1973. Piaget's structuralism. *American Anthropologist* 75: 351–73

Turner, V. 1975. Symbolic studies. *Annual Review of Anthropology* 4: 145–61

Tyler, S. (ed.). 1969. *Cognitive Anthropology*. Holt Rinehart and Winston, New York
    1973. *India: An Anthropological Perspective*. Goodyear, California
    1978. *The Said and the Unsaid*. Academic Press, New York

Van der Leeuw, S. 1976. *Studies in the Technology of Ancient Pottery*. Amsterdam

Veblen, T. 1970. *The Theory of the Leisure Class*. Unwin Books, London

Vira, R. 1934. Implements and vessels used in Vedic sacrifice. *Journal of the Royal Asiatic Society* 283–305

Wakankar, V. S. 1982. Chalcolithic Malwa. In R. K. Sharma (ed.), *Indian Archaeology: New Perspectives*. Agam Kala Prakashan, Delhi

Washburn, D. 1978. A symmetry classification of Pueblo ceramic designs. In P. Grebinger (ed.), *Discovering Past Behaviour*. Academic Press, New York
    (ed.). 1983. *Structure and Cognition in Art*. Cambridge University Press

Whallon, R., and Brown, J. (eds.). 1982. *Essays in Archaeological Typology*. Centre for American Archaeology, Evanston, Illinois

Wheeler, M. 1968. *The Indus Civilisation*. Cambridge University Press

White, L. 1959. *The Evolution of Culture*. McGraw-Hill Book Co., New York

Wiessner, P. 1983. Style and social information in Kalahari San projectile points. *American Antiquity* 48: 253–76

Wiser, 1958. *The Hindu Jajmani System*. Lucknow Publishing House, Lucknow

Wishart, D. 1978. *CLUSTAN User Manual: 3rd Edition*. Edinburgh University Program Library Unit

Wittgenstein, L. 1958. *Philosophical Investigations*. Blackwell, Oxford

Wobst, H. M. 1977. Stylistic behaviour and information exchange. In C. Cleland (ed.), For the director: essays in honour of James B. Griffen. *University of Michigan Museum of Anthropology Anthropological Papers* 61: 317–42

Woods, A. Forthcoming. Quartz calcite and cooking pots. In A. Woods (ed.), *Ceramic Technology: Ethnography and Experiment*

Yellen, J. 1977. *Archaeological Approaches to the Present*. Academic Press, New York

Zadeh, L. 1965. Fuzzy sets. *Information and Control* 8: 338–53

INDEX